T0375783

Philosophies of Multiculturalism

This edited collection offers a comparative approach to the topic of multiculturalism, including different authors with contrasting arguments from different philosophical traditions and ideologies. It puts together perspectives that have been largely neglected as valid normative ways to address the political and moral questions that arise from the coexistence of different cultures in the same geographical space. The essays in this volume cover both historical perspectives, taking in the work of Hobbes, Tocqueville and Nietzsche among others, and contemporary Eastern and Western approaches, including Marxism, anarchism, Islam, Daoism, Indian and African philosophies.

Luís Cordeiro-Rodrigues is a postdoctoral fellow at CLEA, University of Fort Hare.

Marko Simendić is an assistant professor at the University of Belgrade – Faculty of Political Sciences (Serbia).

Studies for the International Society for Cultural History

Series Editors: Howard Chiang
Christopher E. Forth

Titles in this Series

1   Statistics, Public Debate and the State, 1800–1945
Jean-Guy Prévost and Jean-Pierre Beaud

2   A History of Emotions, 1200–1800
Jonas Liliequist (ed.)

3   A Cultural History of the Radical Sixties in the San Francisco Bay Area
Anthony Ashbolt

4   Breast Cancer in the Eighteenth Century
Marjo Kaartinen

5   Crime and the Fascist State, 1850–1940
Tiago Pires Marques

6   McLuhan's Global Village Today: Transatlantic Perspectives
Carmen Birkle, Angela Krewani and Martin Kuester (eds)

7   Cultural Histories of Sociabilities, Spaces and Mobilities
Colin Divall (ed.)

8   A Cultural Study of Mary and the Annunciation
Gary Waller

Forthcoming Titles

Philosophies of Multiculturalism: Beyond Liberalism
Luís Cordeiro-Rodrigues and Marko Simendić (eds)
www.pickeringchatto.com/isch

Philosophies of Multiculturalism
Beyond Liberalism

Edited by Luís Cordeiro-Rodrigues
and Marko Simendić

LONDON AND NEW YORK

First published 2017
by Routledge
2 Park Square, Milton Park, Abingdon, Oxon OX14 4RN

and by Routledge
711 Third Avenue, New York, NY 10017

Routledge is an imprint of the Taylor & Francis Group, an informa business

© 2017 Editors and Contributors

The right of Luís Cordeiro-Rodrigues and Marko Simendić to be identified as the authors of the editorial material, and of the authors for their individual chapters, has been asserted in accordance with sections 77 and 78 of the Copyright, Designs and Patents Act 1988.

All rights reserved. No part of this book may be reprinted or reproduced or utilised in any form or by any electronic, mechanical, or other means, now known or hereafter invented, including photocopying and recording, or in any information storage or retrieval system, without permission in writing from the publishers.

Trademark notice: Product or corporate names may be trademarks or registered trademarks, and are used only for identification and explanation without intent to infringe.

British Library Cataloguing in Publication Data
A catalogue record for this book is available from the British Library.

Library of Congress Cataloging-in-Publication Data
Names: Cordeiro-Rodrigues, Luís, editor. | Simendic, Marko, editor.
Title: Philosophies of multiculturalism : beyond liberalism / edited by
    Luís Cordeiro-Rodrigues and Marko Simendic.
Description: Abingdon, Oxon ; New York, NY : Routledge, 2017. |
    Series: Studies for the international society for cultural history ; 9 |
    Includes bibliographical references and index.
Identifiers: LCCN 2016019177 (print) | LCCN 2016031089 (ebook) |
    ISBN 9781848936065 (hbk) | ISBN 9781315516370 ()
Subjects: LCSH: Multiculturalism—Philosophy. | Multiculturalism—
    Political aspects.
Classification: LCC HM1271 .P488 2017 (print) | LCC HM1271
    (ebook) | DDC 305.8001—dc23
LC record available at https://lccn.loc.gov/2016019177

ISBN: 978-1-8489-3606-5 (hbk)
ISBN: 978-1-315-51637-0 (ebk)

Typeset in Sabon
by Apex CoVantage, LLC

Contents

Acknowledgments	vii
Introduction	1
LUÍS CORDEIRO-RODRIGUES AND MARKO SIMENDIĆ	

SECTION 1
Cultural diversity in the history of political thought   13

1 **Cultural diversity for the sake of political freedom: Tocqueville's perspective on multiculturalism**   15
DEMIN DUAN

2 **Unity and diversity in a Hobbesian commonwealth**   29
MARKO SIMENDIĆ

3 **Nietzschean perspectives on multiculturalism**   43
REBECCA BAMFORD

SECTION 2
Multiculturalism and Western contemporary political theory   61

4 **Anarchism and multiculturalism**   63
URI GORDON

5 **Multiculturalism and oppression: The Marxist perspectives of Fraser, Lenin, and Fanon**   80
ANDREW RYDER

6 **Associative democracy, heterosexism and sexual orientation**   97
LUÍS CORDEIRO-RODRIGUES

vi *Contents*

7 Utilitarianism, religious diversity and progressive pluralism 115
ERIC RUSSERT KRAEMER

SECTION 3
Eastern philosophy approaches to multiculturalism 131

8 Multiculturalism, Indian philosophy, and conflicts over cuisine 133
LISA KEMMERER

9 A Daoist stance on multiculturalism?: The case of Zhang Taiyan 153
LIN MA

10 Islamic multiculturalism: Coexistence overcoming "Kufr"
in Tayeb Saleh's *Season of Migration to the North* and
Hanan El-Sheik's *Beirut Blues* 170
GEORGE SADAKA

SECTION 4
Multiculturalism, African and African heritage 187

11 Toward an African recognition theory of civil rights 189
CHRISTOPHER ALLSOBROOK

12 The Pan-African philosophy and movement: Social and
educational praxis of multiculturalism 209
KERSUZE SIMEON-JONES

Contributors 225
Index 229

Acknowledgments

We would like to thank our families: Wenwen Shi, Catarina Cordeiro, Ricardo Rodrigues, Baoling Shi, Meiqin Zhang, Shilei Shi, Paco and Simone. We would also would like to thank our colleagues at the University of Fort Hare and the University of Belgrade – Faculty of Political Sciences for their support. Some academics that were extremely helpful at various levels and for whom we are deeply thankful are Chris Allsobrook, Rianna Oelofsen, Abraham Olivier, Filip Maj, Sampie Terreblanche, Matthew Festenstein, Monica Mookherjee and Mihaela Mihai. Additionally, we would like to thank the various editors who worked with us on this project: Janka Romero, Max Novick and Jennifer Morrow. Finally, we would also like to thank the *Internet Encyclopedia of Philosophy* for letting us republish an entry previously written there as part of the introduction to this volume.

Introduction

Luís Cordeiro-Rodrigues and Marko Simendić

This volume, *Philosophies of Multiculturalism: Beyond Liberalism*, offers a group of innovative approaches to the topic of multiculturalism. In particular, it puts together perspectives that have been largely neglected as valid normative ways to address the political and moral questions that arise from the coexistence of different cultures in the same geographical space. In this initial introduction, we intend to contextualise the debate of multiculturalism in contemporary political theory and locate this volume within the debate. With this purpose in mind, this chapter is divided into three sections. In the first, we outline our definition of multiculturalism. In section 2, we summarise the debates on multiculturalism within political theory and explain how such debates have centred on a liberal perspective. In the third section, we outline the chapters in this volume.

1 – What is multiculturalism?

Cultural diversity has been present in societies for a very long time. In Ancient Greece, there were various small regions with different costumes, traditions, dialects and identities; for example, those in Aetolia, Locris, Doris and Epirus. In the Ottoman Empire, Muslims were in the majority, but there were also Christians, Jews, pagan Arabs and other religious groups. In the 21st century, societies remain culturally diverse, with most countries having a mixture of individuals from different races, linguistic backgrounds, religious affiliations and so forth. Contemporary political theorists have labeled the phenomenon of different cultures existing in the same geographical space, 'multiculturalism'. That is, one of the meanings of multiculturalism is the coexistence of different cultures. In particular, this is the meaning that is used for the term 'multiculturalism' in this book.[1]

When the term 'multiculturalism' is used in this sense, i.e., to describe a condition of society where a variety of different cultures coexist, it can mean many things. That is, there are a variety of ways whereby societies can be diverse, for example, culture can come in many different forms (Gurr 1993: 3). Perhaps the chief ways in which a country can be culturally diverse is through different religious groups, different linguistic groups,

2 Luís Cordeiro-Rodrigues and Marko Simendić

groups that define themselves by their territorial identity and variant racial groups.

Religious diversity is a widespread phenomenon in many countries. India can be given as an example of a country which is religiously diverse, with its citizens identifying as Sikhs, Hindus, Buddhists and as members of other religious groups. The United States is also another religiously diverse nation, including Mormons, Amish, Hutterites, Catholics, Jews and so forth. These groups can be differentiated from each other due to a variety of factors. Some of these are the type of Gods worshipped, the public holidays and religious festivals celebrated and the variant dress codes embraced by each group.

Linguistic diversity is also widespread. In the 21st century, there are more than 200 countries in the world and around 6000 spoken languages (Laitin 2007). Linguistic diversity usually results from two kinds of groups. First, it results from immigrants who move to a country where the language spoken is not their native language (Kymlicka 1995). This is the case for those Cubans and Puerto Ricans who immigrated to the United States; it is also the case for Ukrainian immigrants who moved to Portugal. The second kind of group that causes linguistic diversity is made up of national minorities. National minorities are groups that have settled in a country for a long time, but do not share the same language as the majority. Some examples include Quebecois in Canada, Catalans and Basques in Spain and the Uyghur in China. Usually, these linguistic groups are territorially concentrated; furthermore, minority groups that fall into this category usually demand a high degree of autonomy. In particular, minority groups usually demand that they have the regional power to self-govern, that is, to run their territory as if it was an independent country or to secede and become a different country.

A third kind of group diversity can result from a distinct territory location. This territory location does not necessarily mean that members of distinct cultures are, in fact, different. That is, it is not necessarily the case that habits, traditions, customs and so forth are significantly different. However, these distinct groups identify themselves as different from others because of the specific geographical area in which they are located. In the United Kingdom, this is possibly what distinguishes the Scots from the English. Even though there are historical differences between the two, if one assumes that they actually have little to distinguish themselves from each other, other than geographical location, they would fit this third kind of group diversity. As mentioned above, these differences are conceptual; in practice, cultural groups are characterised by a variety of features and not just one.

The fourth kind of group diversity is race. Races are groups whose physical characteristics are imbued with social significance. In other words, race is a socially constructed concept in the sense that it is the result of individuals giving social significance to a set of physical characteristics they consider as standing out; this may include skin colour, eye colour, hair colour, bone/jaw structure and so forth. However, the mere existence of different physical characteristics does not mean that there is automatically a multicultural environment/society. For instance, it cannot be affirmed that Sweden is multicultural just because there are Swedes with blue eyes and others with green. Physical characteristics create a multicultural environment only when these physical characteristics mean that groups strongly identify with their physical characteristics and where these physical characteristics are socially perceived as strongly differentiating them from other groups. That is, racial cultural diversity is not simply the existence of different physical characteristics. Rather, these different physical characteristics must entail a sense of common identity, which, in turn, is socially perceived as differentiating the members of that group from others. However, this idea of common identity is regularly exaggerated. For instance, even though there is the idea that a black culture exists in the United States, Kwame Appiah (1996) denies that it does, since there is no common identity among blacks in the United States. An example of a physical difference that is considered socially significant and, therefore, constitutive of a multicultural society/environment, can be seen in the Tutsis and Hutus of Rwanda. In general terms, Tutsis and Hutus are very similar, due to the fact that they speak the same language, share the same territory and follow the same traditions. Nevertheless, Tutsis are usually taller and thinner than Hutus. The social significance given to these physical differences is sufficient for members of both groups to, broadly speaking, identify as members of one group or the other, and subsequently oppose each other.

Obviously, groups are not, most of the time, identified *only* by being linguistically different, territorially concentrated or religiously distinct. In fact, most groups have more than one of these characteristics. For instance, in India, Sikhs, besides being religiously different, are also characterised, in general terms, by their geographical location. Namely, they are localised in the Punjab region of India. The Uyghur, from China, have a different language, are usually Muslims and are usually located in Xinjiang. Thus, while the classification is helpful for understanding the characteristics of each group, it does not mean that these groups are simply defined by that characteristic.

2 – Multiculturalism in political theory

Normatively speaking, the issues that arise from the coexistence of cultures has been, in general terms, discussed only from the perspective of liberal political philosophy. In this context there have been two waves of writings on multiculturalism (Kymlicka 1999). In Kymlicka's view (1999: 112), the first wave focused on "assessing the justice of claims by ethnic groups for the accommodation of their cultural differences". In this first wave of writings, contemporary liberal political philosophers discussed what kinds of inequalities exist between majorities and minorities and how these should be addressed. Put differently, the topic of discussion of this first wave of

4 Luís Cordeiro-Rodrigues and Marko Simendić

writings was mainly about the role of the state in dealing with inequalities between groups. In general terms, philosophers of contemporary liberal politics who have written about this topic have taken two different stands. On the one hand, some defend that state institutions should be blind to difference and that individuals should be given a uniform set of rights and liberties. In these authors' views, cultural diversity, religious freedom and so forth are sufficiently protected by those sets of rights and liberties, especially freedom of association and conscience. Therefore, those who stand for a uniform set of rights and liberties contend that ascribing rights on the basis of membership to a particular group is a discriminatory and immoral policy that creates citizenship hierarchies that are undesirable and unjust (Kymlicka 1999: 112–113). Thus, from the point of view of these contemporary liberal philosophers, the state is duty bound to not participate or be involved in the cultural character of society.

On the other hand, some philosophers have taken the opposite view on this matter. For example, there are those contemporary liberal political philosophers who are more sympathetic with the idea of ascribing rights to groups and who have defended difference-sensitive policies. As Kymlicka (1999: 112) points out, these contemporary liberal political philosophers have tried "to show that deviations from difference-blind rules which are adopted in order to accommodate ethnocultural differences are not inherently unjust". In general terms, these contemporary political philosophers argue that a regime of difference-sensitive policies does not necessarily entail a hierarchisation of citizenship and unfair privileges for some groups. Rather, they argue that difference-sensitive policies aim at correcting intergroup inequalities and disadvantages in the cultural market. Moreover, some of these philosophers contend that difference-blind policies actually favour the needs, interests and identities of the majority (Kymlicka 1999: 112–114). Finally, some philosophers, like Kymlicka and Taylor, have defended that difference-sensitive policies are not only compatible with liberalism but, in some cases, can in fact promote liberalism.

To sum up, in this first wave of writings on multiculturalism, the debate has centred on discussing the justice of difference-sensitive policies in the liberal context. On the whole, there are two different positions taken by contemporary liberal political philosophers who have written on multiculturalism: some defend that difference-sensitive policies are justified, whereas others argue that they are a deviation from the core values of liberalism. In general terms, there are eight distinct categories of difference-sensitive policies that are discussed in this debate: namely, exemptions, assistance rights, symbolic claims, recognition, special representation, self-government, external rules and internal rules.

More recently, a second wave of writings on multiculturalism has appeared. In this, contemporary liberal political philosophers have not focused so much on debates about justice between different groups, but rather have focused on justice within groups. Thus, the debate has changed to the analysis of the potentially perverse effects of policies for protecting minority cultural groups with regard to the group members. Contemporary liberal political philosophers have now switched to discussing the practical implications that those that aimed at correcting intergroup equality could have for the members of those groups that the policies are directed to. In particular, the worry is that the policies for enabling members of minority groups to pursue their culture could favour some members of minority groups over others. That is, this new debate is about the risks that those policies for protecting cultural groups could have in terms of undermining the status of the weaker members of these groups.

The reason why philosophers worry about this is because multicultural policies may give the leaders of cultural groups power for decision-making and institutionalising practices that facilitate the persecution of internal minorities. In other words, such policies may give group leaders all kinds of power that reinforce or facilitate cruelty and discrimination within the group (Shachar 2001: 3, 4, 15–16; Reich 2005: 209–210; Phillips 2007: 13–14). In short, as Shachar (2001: 3) points out, the most vulnerable members of minority cultures may be "injured by the very reforms that are designed to promote their status as group members in the accommodating, multicultural state".

This discussion about the practical implications of cultural policies for the most vulnerable individuals within minorities is the result of the acknowledgement of two important ideas. First, the idea that minority groups are internally diverse or heterogeneous. That is to say, that within cultural minorities there are other minorities with different interests and characteristics (Mahajan 2005: 94). For example, the Scots are a minority in the UK but Gaelic-speaking individuals are a minority among Scots. The Amish are a minority in the United States, and gay Amish are a minority within the Amish community. As Mahajan (2005: 94) points out, this means that "communities are neither homogeneous entities nor self-evidently given wholes".

The second idea that has been acknowledged is that many groups have illiberal beliefs, norms and practices that can interfere with the interests of some of the members of these groups. That is, many groups reject the values of liberty, equality, neutrality and other liberal values, and this rejection can be damaging for some vulnerable individuals within minority groups. In practice, this means that groups have practices and beliefs that are discouraging or forbidding of some group members' interests, liberties and rights; these include sexual freedom, religious freedom, freedom of conscience, freedom of association, freedom of expression, freedom from torture, bodily and psychological integrity, safety and other interests. Indeed, some cultural practices are violent, discriminatory and cruel to the extent that some of them can only be coercively enforced. This happens to a variety of vulnerable individuals within minorities: women, children, dissenters and sexual minorities are some examples (Levy 2000: 41, 51–52, 62; Reich 2005: 210–211; Swaine 2005: 44–45; Phillips 2007: 12).

6   Luís Cordeiro-Rodrigues and Marko Simendić

What can be concluded from the summary of current debates in political theory is that multiculturalism has been debated mostly from the liberal philosophical perspective. This is problematic for at least three reasons. Firstly, it creates a hegemonic philosophical culture where liberal moral dilemmas and solutions appear to be the only valid ones. Secondly, the focus on only one epistemological paradigm is correlated with a history of racism and oppression (Parris 2015). In the work of philosophers such as David Hume, Thomas Jefferson and Immanuel Kant, racist and degrading passages regarding non-whites and their intellectual skills can be found. This casts a dark shadow over philosophy, which, in order to be avoided, requires a de-colonial attitude of openness towards different views (Parris 2015) Thirdly, and related to the previous points, this narrow debate framed by liberal-ism is unphilosophical. As Ward Jones (Jones 2006) contends, philosophy seeks to deliver an improved understanding of the questions it addresses. If debates on multiculturalism are only discussed from a liberal perspective, then the understanding of the phenomenon of multiculturalism and its moral and political dilemmas is substantially neglected. For multicul-turalism is not a liberal western reality only; it is a historical phenomenon that is present across various countries. In fact, very often, multicultural-ism is described as a contemporary western phenomenon, when, in fact, as explained in the first section, it is a phenomenon that has been present in various societies across time. As diachronic continuity and the territorial extension of the phenomenon of multiculturalism demands examination that falls outside the liberal perspective, this study aims to thus reach out historically and conceptually in an effort to offer various alternatives to the dominant paradigm.

3 – Relevance and outline of this book

A narrow conceptual framework considerably limits academic discussion and often contributes to the same major philosophical traditions. A great number of edited volumes have contributed to making multiculturalism one of the most important topics of contemporary political philosophy in the last decade, but none have approached multiculturalism in a comparative way and none have discussed the topic by taking into consideration distinct conceptual frameworks.

Even though much of the literature on multiculturalism, in particular edited volumes, have been quite well organised, making an important con-tribution to knowledge, they have not been very innovative, instead offering quite a limited conceptual approach. Firstly, these volumes are usually not very multicultural in themselves, that is, in the sense that they usually only include authors from North America and the UK, leaving aside contribu-tors from other countries. Given the nature of the topic, and since multi-culturalism has a gained significant international presence, both as a set of policies and a rich body of thought, it is important to include insights from all over the world in order to offer a wider perspective on the topic. This volume, in contrast to present scholarship, includes authors from North America, the UK, Lebanon, Portugal, Israel, China, South Africa and Serbia. Secondly, as explained, current scholarship has approached multiculturalism from a liberal point of view, i.e., the topics discussed and the solutions offered are mostly those that liberals would provide. Therefore, they offer a very thin and limited conceptual framework for discussing multiculturalism, always raising the same problems and giving similar normative solutions. Contrastingly, in this volume, different perspectives are considered, and, therefore, a richer perspective on multiculturalism is offered. Hence, this volume, contrary to the existing literature, is multicultural in the sense that it gives credit to, and highlights, different traditions of philosophy and ideologies, stretching from west to east and also Africa, both synchronically and diachronically.

This edited volume offers the first comparative approach to multiculturalism, including different authors with contrasting arguments from different philosophical traditions and ideologies. And even though there is considerable literature on multiculturalism, there is no comparable work that deals with multiculturalism by using different concepts and ideologies. The chapters in this volume are innovative insofar as they provide new insights and approaches which are not usually employed in dealing with such a widely debated topic. In particular, the volume is divided into four sections: i) historical perspectives of multiculturalism, ii) western philosophy, iii) eastern philosophy and iv) African philosophy.

The section on the historical perspectives of multiculturalism presents three distinct historical approaches to the question of cultural diversity and two opposing ways of thinking about it. At one end stands Thomas Hobbes, with an insistence on peace brought about by the absolute authority of the sovereign, as well as the stability and unity of the state. At the opposite end of the spectrum we can place Friedrich Nietzsche, a proponent of struggle and different and dynamically changing human identities, an author for whom diversity is not merely a fact to be dealt with pragmatically, but the very basis of freedom and human flourishing. Alexis de Tocqueville's ideas stand in the middle of this spectrum. Unlike Hobbes, Tocqueville insists on freedom and asserts cultural diversity to be instrumentally valuable for its realization, while, in contrast to Nietzsche, the context of freedom is the modern democratic society. The three historical perspectives offered in this section are very distinct, with both the intentions and argumentations of the three authors vastly different. None of these three authors are commonly referenced in scholarly arguments about multiculturalism, but all of them, in their own ways, discuss the same social fact regarding the diversity of groups. This section reminds us that diversity is not only a problem of our times, but shows that at least some alternatives to contemporary modes of thinking about multiculturalism can be found in unlikely historical places.

8 Luís Cordeiro-Rodrigues and Marko Simendić

Hobbes is most certainly not the first author that comes to mind as a philosopher who has something to say about cultural diversity and multiculturalism. However, even within the wider framework of the notorious proponent of absolute authority, one can find a degree of tolerance towards the diversity of various groups, some of which are related through a shared identity and tied by religion, territory or a shared goal. Marko Simendić's chapter shows Hobbes as a pragmatic thinker who leaves some space for various associations that may enjoy a certain degree of autonomy within his otherwise absolutist conception of the state. Tocqueville's focus on freedom and democracy places his account in stark contrast to Hobbes's. However, as Demin Duan's reading of Tocqueville shows, the French aristocrat also views diversity as instrumentally valuable. Cultural and religious diversity is not simply a state of affairs that marks life in America or the French colonies, but also a useful resource that is to be nurtured and set against both the prospects of classical despotic rule and the increasing similarity of people that plagues freedom in a modern democracy. Nietzsche shares Tocqueville's highly critical stance towards the sameness of modern man but, for him, neither democracy nor liberalism is conducive to freedom. Rebecca Bamford shows that, in Nietzsche's view, the pluralism of identities is a prerequisite for health and flourishing. If uniformity and stability indeed defy life, Nietzsche's commitment to pluralism becomes particularly important for affirming the value of different and mixed identities within multicultural contexts. The multicultural locus of mixed identities thus becomes the context of freedom, as thinking about oneself in fluid, dynamic and open-ended terms helps us overcome the self-imposed limitations of an ossified self.

Mainstream multiculturalism is located within liberalism as a dominant form of western political thought. However, one should not forget that there are contemporary alternatives to this worldview that also stem from the broad spectrum of western political ideas. The second section of this book thus concerns four diverse western contemporary schools of thought that provide alternatives to liberal multiculturalism: utilitarianism, anarchism, Marxism and associative democracy. Eric Kraemer's account of progressive utilitarianism draws from his reading of John Stuart Mill and focuses on the diversity of cultures and religions within a single society. Not unlike Tocqueville, Mill opposes uniformity, but multicultural diversity is seen as not valuable only as an opposition to sameness. More importantly, Mill suggests that co-existing cultures with varied ways of life are beneficial to us as a pool of resources from which we can draw optimal responses for facing our society's challenges. Cultures can learn from each other's practices and this helps them devise optimal strategies for avoiding harm and maximising utility. Similar to the tensions that exist between the principle of aggregation and the cultural diversity inherent to utilitarianism, the eclectic body of anarchist thought carries within itself both universalist and particularistic stances towards cultural and ethnic diversities. Uri Gordon's chapter moves away from the universal humanist beginnings of anarchism

Introduction 9

to emphasise its newer post-colonial aspects. Multiculturalist policies are seen as the state's effort to mask deep structural injustices that can only be remedied by revolutionary change. The anarchist alternative proposed focuses on the decolonial approach, which is sensitive to the colonial and structurally oppressive underpinnings of contemporary social and ethnic diversity. Diversity is therefore more than a mere fact of the contemporary world. It is a segment of reality that often carries with it marks of racism, coercion, hegemony and domination, and this is something that, in the author's view, should not be ignored by today's radical left. Another leftist alternative to liberal multiculturalism comes from the Marxist tradition. Andrew Ryder draws from Nancy Fraser's egalitarian criticism of liberal multiculturalism and builds on the ideas of V. I. Lenin and Frantz Fanon. This reading employs oppression as the key element of a politically relevant concept of cultural diversity. Oppression of a certain group can take many forms, and while national self-determination remains a viable emancipatory resource, Fanon's ideas complement Lenin's account with a more nuanced reading of racism and domination in a colonial context. Cultural and class oppression are interlinked, so resisting the dominant culture and combating national oppression serves a revolutionary purpose. Oppression, however, is not only a relation between two groups. Intra-cultural relations can also be oppressive, and this is the problem to which Luís Cordeiro-Rodrigues presents associative democracy as a solution. Associative democracy is seen as particularly valuable for multicultural societies because it embraces the plurality of associations within a society by giving them the means by which to influence state policies and the autonomy by which to create their own institutions. There are limits to the autonomy of associations, as they need to remain democratic, with the basic rights of their members protected by the state. The fine balance between autonomy and the abuse of power within minority groups is achieved by opening up political and economic possibilities through which individuals can freely associate and devise their own institutions, while protecting their basic rights within associations.

The third section presents three approaches from outside the dominant western paradigm: Indian, Chinese and Islamic. The alternatives presented in this section are found in three very different eastern schools of thought. Lisa Kemmerer draws ideas from Indian philosophical and religious thought and offers an account that seeks to enrich the western practices of multiculturalism. This chapter discusses various dietary conventions in the United States and argues in favour of a vegan diet and the ethical treatment of animals. Such an approach is based on *Ahimsa* (non-injury), an idea shared across major world religions. It thus helps establish a common ground for cooperation, acceptance and toleration between different cultures. Another way of thinking about multiculturalism comes from Daoism, with Lin Ma discussing Zhang Taiyan's (1869–1936) complex argument. Zhang is a prominent political thinker and activist whose Daoist approach sees equality in diversity as a basic world fact. The normative consequence of this idea is that cultural and other differences should never be suppressed. Zhang's political ideas, however, are also marked by his sinocentrism and support for a single-nationality Chinese state. However, although he is clearly not a proponent of multicultural China, Zhang does describe the state as an empty vessel, advocating for a limited central government that is careful not to interfere with the autonomy of its democratic provinces. The third non-western perspective is put forward by George Sadaka. The author discusses cultural and religious diversity and coexistence in societies that are divided by religion and the residues of colonial times. The two aspects of the argument are elucidated by a reading of two popular novels, Tayeb Saleh's *Season of Migration to the North* and Hanan El-Sheikh's *Beirut Blues*. Sadaka discusses cross-cultural and intra-cultural encounters presented in the two literary works and offers an Islamic model of a "non-libidinal form of love" as a means of overcoming the major divisions between cultures and religions.

The final section of the book seeks to go beyond the north-south ideological and cultural divide and instead looks for alternatives to liberal multiculturalism from African and pan-African standpoints. Kersuze Simeon-Jones draws on the classical works of W. E. B. Du Bois, Edward Blyden, Marcus Garvey and other prominent authors in forming an argument which connects to contemporary multiculturalism in two related ways. First, it focuses on the protection and recognition of different cultures. Second, it points to education as both a way of reaffirming and strengthening African identity and a foundation for cooperation and dialogue between cultures. These two aspects mirror two important and intrinsic multicultural features of pan-Africanism: the recognition of differences between various African identities combined with efforts at achieving the political unity needed for achieving liberty for all members. The second account approaches civil rights from an African perspective. Chris Allsobrook argues against the application of an ahistorical and essentialist western conception of rights in favour of a recognition theory of rights based on Kwame Gyekye's soft communitarianism. By putting aside purely western conceptions of ethics, justice and personhood, this account paves the way towards reconciling the two separate spheres that regulate postcolonial social life in Africa: western constitutionalism and customary law and authority.

As this outline of the volume suggests, the chapters in this book differ substantially in their methodology and the topics discussed. That is, the essays in this volume differ in assessing the value of cultural diversity, in the considerations and conceptual framework that they view as central to resolving the conflicts that result from cultural diversity as well as the main values they use as tools to resolve these conflicts. Hence, the following question may arise: what unites the chapters of this book and what makes combining them particularly relevant? The answer is that the essays in this volume share at least three aspects. First, all of them share in the discussion of the topic of cultural diversity and multiculturalism as defined in the first section

Introduction   11

of this volume. Second, all the essays acknowledge the normative problems that arise from the existence of cultural diversity and the need for these to be urgently addressed. There is also the recognition that a real normative problem exists. Third, all these essays try to offer a normative solution to these problems from their own theoretical perspective. Put differently, all chapters contribute a normative solution from their own particular school of thought in relation to the normative problem that they identify.

Conclusion

To conclude, there are four important points to keep in mind here. Firstly, in this volume, multiculturalism is understood as the coexistence of different cultures within the same geographical space. Secondly, normative debates on multiculturalism have been carried out mainly from a liberal point of view. Thirdly, the focus on the liberal perspective has monopolised multicultural debates in ways that neglect other schools of thought that can provide insightful and normatively relevant philosophical resources for addressing multiculturalism. Fourthly, this volume aims at filling this gap in the literature by including various schools of thought that can provide insightful and relevant normative contributions to issues related to multiculturalism.

The relevance of studies such as this lies in overcoming the liberal hegemonic discourse that is currently prevalent in philosophy. In current political philosophy, that is, in general terms, the only normative questions that count are those corresponding to liberal moral and political dilemmas. By including a wide range of philosophical perspectives, this volume identifies that there are more moral and political dilemmas and more solutions beyond the strictly liberal paradigm. That is, the relevance and objective of putting these chapters together is to demonstrate that there is moral and political philosophy beyond liberalism, and that the philosophy that goes beyond liberalism can offer insightful solutions to real life dilemmas. This is a diverse contribution to a diverse and omnipresent set of issues. Not all the responses offered in this volume will be equally valuable all the time, but their variety is a resource that alone carries importance. If we are to understand the dynamics and challenges of contemporary multicultural coexistence, we need to resort to using some untainted pools of philosophical resources. This book is such an attempt.

Note

1   The term 'multiculturalism' can also be used to refer to a kind of policy. This kind of policy has two main characteristics. First, it aims to address the different demands of cultural groups. In other words, it is a kind of policy that refers to the different normative challenges (ethnic conflict, internal illiberalism, federal autonomy and so forth) that arise as a result of cultural diversity. Second, multicultural policies are policies that aim at providing groups with the means by which individuals can pursue their cultural differences.

12 *Luís Cordeiro-Rodrigues and Marko Simendić*

Bibliography

Appiah, K. (1996) *Colour Conscious: The Political Morality of Race*, Princeton: Princeton University Press.

Gurr, T. R. (1993) *Minorities at Risk: A Global View of Ethnopolitical Conflicts*, Washington, DC: United States Institute of Peace Press.

Jones, W. E. (2006) 'Philosophers, Their Context, and Their Responsibilities', *Metaphilosophy* 37: 623–645. doi:10.1111/j.1467–9973.2006.00462.x

Kymlicka, W. (1995) *Multicultural Citizenship: A Liberal Theory of Minority Rights*, Oxford: Oxford University Press.

Kymlicka, W. (1999) 'Comments on Shachar and Spinner-Halev: An Update from the Multiculturalism Wars', in C. Joppke and S. Lukes (eds.) *Multicultural Questions*, Oxford and New York: Oxford University Press.

Laitin, D. (2007) *Nations, States and Violence*, Oxford: Oxford University Press.

Levy, J. T. (2000) *The Multiculturalism of Fear*, Oxford: Oxford University Press.

Levy, J. T. (2005) 'Sexual Orientation, Exit and Refugee', in A. Eisenberg and J. Spinner-Halev (eds.) *Minorities within Minorities: Equality, Rights and Diversity*, Cambridge: Cambridge University Press.

Mahajan, G. (2005) 'Can Intra-Group Equality Co-exist with Cultural Diversity? Re-Examining Multicultural Frameworks of Accommodation', in A. Eisenberg and J. Spinner-Halev (eds.) *Minorities within Minorities: Equality, Rights and Diversity*, Cambridge: Cambridge University Press.

Parris, L. T. (2015) *Being Apart: Theoretical and Existential Resistance in Africana Literature*, Charlottesville: University of Virginia Press.

Phillips, A. (2007) *Multiculturalism without Culture*, Princeton: Princeton University Press.

Reich, R. (2005) 'Minors within Minorities: A Problem for Liberal Multiculturalists', in A. Eisenberg and J. Spinner-Halev (eds.) *Minorities within Minorities: Equality, Rights and Diversity*, Cambridge: Cambridge University Press.

Shachar, A. (2001) *Multicultural Jurisdictions: Cultural Differences and Women's Rights, Contemporary Political Theory*, Cambridge: Cambridge University Press.

Swaine, L. (2005) 'A Liberalism of Conscience', in A. Eisenberg and J. Spinner-Halev (eds.) *Minorities within Minorities: Equality, Rights and Diversity*, Cambridge: Cambridge University Press.

Section 1

Cultural diversity in the history of political thought

1 Cultural diversity for the sake of political freedom

Tocqueville's perspective on multiculturalism

Demin Duan

Alexis de Tocqueville is famous for his defence of freedom in the age of democracy, advocating self-government and decentralisation, which he considers the basis for any hope of political freedom in modern society. Given this line, it is only logical that he endorses the value of cultural diversity within society, for people can only meaningfully participate in politics when they are free to live in their own culture and according to their own beliefs. This emphasis on cultural diversity is also corroborated by his thesis on race and colonial governance, as will be elaborated on in this chapter. People's independence in their own culture is considered by Tocqueville as instrumentally useful in preparing them for political freedom. This chapter will discuss these issues in order to understand Tocqueville's standpoint on multiculturalism, considered as the coexistence of diverse cultures within a certain political community (Kymlicka 2002: 327–376). First, we will consider Tocqueville's position on cultural diversity in correlation with his idea of freedom. Second, his writings on race and colonial rule, which are the most directly 'multicultural' part of his oeuvre, will be discussed. Third, the issue of religion will be brought up in order to gain a deeper understanding of his 'relationship' with contemporary multiculturalism.

Cultural diversity in the age of equality

One of Tocqueville's greatest fears regarding democracy is that it could tend a society towards uniformity, since people are universally 'equal'. Equality of conditions is "the generative fact" for Tocqueville's analysis, which he claims to be the "central point at which all my observations came to an end" (Tocqueville 2000: 3). This equality means that people are less and less 'different' from each other, with the same desires, the same tastes, the same emotions, the same intellectual habits, and more importantly, the same political tendencies. This sameness shocks Tocqueville, for it leads to things that are mediocre, petty, unholy, tedious, and above all despotic. Mainly for this reason, Tocqueville puts tremendous emphasis on things that could 'stand out', things with particularity: for instance, good taste, individuality, religious faith, and so on.[1]

16 Demin Duan

The diversity of cultures is often connected with people's customs, traditions and religious beliefs, as well as sometimes, prejudices. But modern society, where people are equal to each other, is not so friendly to these things. Tocqueville noticed this when he discussed the 'philosophic method of the Americans', commenting that "America is therefore the one country in the world where the precepts of Descartes are least studied and best followed" (Tocqueville 2000: 403). Tocqueville illustrated this Descartian method in practice as follows:

> To escape from the spirit of system, from the yoke of habits, from family maxims, from class opinions, and up to a certain point, from national prejudices; to take tradition only as information, and current facts only as a useful study for doing otherwise and better; to seek the reason for things by themselves and in themselves alone, to strive for a result without letting themselves be chained to the means, and to see through the form to the foundation.
>
> (Tocqueville 2000: 403)

This 'democratic' method is followed when "conditions had finally become nearly the same and men almost alike" (Tocqueville 2000: 405). It gives rise to so-called 'general ideas', ideas that are about what is true for every human being. If men are equal and alike, then it is necessary to see the world through the lens of different cultures and customs in order to understand the universal nature of people. But as Tocqueville says, "God does not ponder the human race in general", and "general ideas do not attest to the strength of human intelligence, but rather to its insufficiency, because there are no beings in nature exactly alike: no identical facts, no rules indiscriminately applicable in the same manner to several objects at once" (Tocqueville 2000: 411).

The equality and sameness of individuals may lead to despotism if there is nothing stopping it. For the most universal need of human beings is their material need. Tocqueville sees that there is a great danger in this tendency, namely whereby "men are no longer bound except by interests". In his thinking, despotism is the ultimate dystopia for modern democracy, as it rules out difference and free will, both of which are central to his idea of freedom. In modern democratic societies, as Tocqueville asserts, despotism would take on a unique style when compared with the ancient kind of tyranny. He depicts it as follows:

> Above these an immense tutelary power is elevated, which alone takes charge of assuring their enjoyments and watching over their fate. It is absolute, detailed, regular, far-seeing, and mild. It would resemble paternal power if, like that, it had for its objects to prepare men for manhood; but on the contrary, it seeks only to keep them fixed irrevocably in childhood; it likes citizens to enjoy themselves provided that they

Cultural diversity for political freedom 17

think only of enjoying themselves. . . . So it is that every day it renders the employment of free will less useful and more rare; it confines the action of the will in a smaller space and little by little steals the very use of free will from each citizen.

(Tocqueville 2000: 663)

Tocqueville calls this kind of despotism "new despotism" or "democratic despotism" in order to differentiate it from the older type (Tocqueville 2000: 662). In ancient times, a tyrant may not have acted according to law, and he was usually unable or even unwilling to rule out any kind of difference in his realm. Being tyrannical is the opposite of the rule of law. But modern despotism as described by Tocqueville means that the state would not only regulate people's lives in detail, but also encourage them to stay isolated from each other, turning to the 'tutelary power' for guidance in their lives. Here, 'reason' may still be the foundation for this kind of political life, as centralization necessarily requires the calculation and distribution of people's responsibilities, although it would still largely be based on material needs and instruments for their satisfaction. As Tocqueville sees it, the strongest penchant of modern individuals is material enjoyment (Tocqueville 2000: 506–507), which is perhaps the only thing that is truly universal and effective in uniting individuals.

Tocqueville pictured the contrast between uniformity and diversity, but his picture is at the same time a reflection of double contrasts between the past and the present, or between the New World and old Europe. We find the following paragraphs in the notebook he kept when he was travelling in the United States in 1831:

I had noticed in Europe that the more or less withdrawn position in which a province or town is placed, its wealth or its poverty, its smallness or its extent, exercised an immense influence on the ideas, the morals, the whole civilization of its inhabitants, and often caused a **difference** of several centuries between the various parts of the same area.

. . . Nothing is true in this picture. . . . In America, even more than in Europe, there is one society only. It may be rich or poor, humble or brilliant, trading or agricultural, but it is made up everywhere of the **same** elements; it has been leveled out by an egalitarian civilization. The man you left behind in the streets of New York, you will find him again in the midst of almost impenetrable solitude: same dress, same spirit, same language, same habits and the same pleasures.

(Tocqueville 1959: 332–333) [emphasis in bold mine]

Perhaps for Tocqueville, the truest kind of cultural diversity only exists in the past and in aristocratic societies. Inequality of conditions creates diversity, or rather impassable boundaries, among people. The gap between the

18 *Demin Duan*

two 'classes" – the aristocracy and the commons – almost indicates two different kinds of civilization: different dress, different spirit, different languages, different habits, and different pleasures. Indeed, "When conditions are very unequal and the inequalities are permanent, individuals little by little become so unalike that one would say there are as many distinct humanities as there are classes" (Tocqueville 2000: 412).

However, as much as he may love the past, Tocqueville is very aware that the democratic tendency with its equality of conditions is irreversible, although he does make it very clear that equality does not necessarily equate to freedom. Equality of conditions creates individuals with no great differences between them, but these are individuals craving equality even if it would mean the negation of freedom. Tocqueville says, "Men cannot enjoy political freedom unless they purchase it with some sacrifice. . . . But the pleasures brought by equality offer themselves" (Tocqueville 2000: 481). Furthermore, "They want equality in freedom, and if they cannot get it, they still want it in slavery" (Tocqueville 2000: 482).

However, we should keep in mind that for Tocqueville, America represents the hope for freedom in modern democracy, and not the opposite. For him, what was left of French society following the 1789 Revolution offers the real proof of equality in terms of slavery (Tocqueville 1988: 131). What Tocqueville sees in America has thus intrigued many scholars of social and political study ever since.[2] What is certain is that he is against the social phenomenon that he calls "individualism" (Wolin 2001: 482–484), which makes him an unorthodox liberal, if he is 'liberal' at all. Roger Boesche emphasises his 'illiberal side' and bluntly calls his thought a "strange liberalism" (Boesche 1987). Some others highlight the communitarian, conservative, or republican sides of his thinking and contrast them with orthodox liberalism (Kahn 1992; Nelson 2002). Tocqueville says that "individualism is a reflective and peaceable sentiment that disposes each citizen to isolate himself from the mass of those like him and to withdraw to one side with his family and his friends. . . . He willingly abandons society at large to itself". In individualistic societies, "the bond of human affections is extended and loosened" (Tocqueville 2000: 182–483). In questioning this tendency, Tocqueville obviously highlights the value of community and the values that link people together in modern society.

In Tocqueville's illustration of America, we can find many clues to his peculiar idea of 'freedom'. In his famous book, *Tocqueville Between Two Worlds*, Sheldon Wolin points out that, apart from an America of equality, there exists for Tocqueville, a 'feudal America'. A big discovery Tocqueville made in America is that, despite it being a society in which the principle of equality of conditions has been practiced to its limit, it is a much 'older' kind of society than most Europeans would think. By 'old' Tocqueville means that its equality of conditions has not yet led to a despotic government with a highly centralised administrative system. Put differently, although individuals are equal and alike, the society itself is not mired in mediocre sameness.

As a matter of fact, America is characterised by significant inner differences and thus diversity.

First and foremost, in Tocqueville's eyes, the political system in America in some ways resembles the feudal society of old Europe. In his later book, *The Old Regime and the Revolution*, Tocqueville goes to great length to prove that France had already become a 'democratic' society before the Revolution and its political system had been based upon this new social condition. In the hundreds of years of what Tocqueville calls *ancien régime*, the nobility had been gradually losing power, with people becoming more and more equal and monarchical power becoming ever stronger. One of Tocqueville's most incisive discoveries was that France had actually lost its feudal past before the Revolution took place (Tocqueville 1988: 118–123).

In America, however, he saw the feudal past still in existence, albeit under the cloak of democratic social conditions. While local self-government in France became replaced by centralised state administration (Tocqueville 1988: 104–105), it still existed in a very good way in the United States. Local townships and states held genuine power that was to a large extent independent of the Federal government. More importantly, in local townships, the most active public life was thriving. As Tocqueville states, townships have two great merits that unite people: independence and power (Tocqueville 2000: 63). Indeed, townships greatly resemble aristocratic local political entities, except for the fact that they have been built upon a new principle of equality. What Tocqueville values most in America is that there exist points and mechanisms that are able to check the equalising and centralising tendency of modern democracy; local self-government and diversity of power are crucial in this regard. Sheldon Wolin comments that, for Tocqueville, "[the] aristocracy is represented as the instinctive opposition to any form of massed power, monarchical or popular" (Wolin 2001: 233).

In order to avoid a kind of democratic despotism and have a chance of preserving freedom, it is important to have something that has characters of difference, independence, and diversity of values. In this regard, it is worthwhile to mention Tocqueville's analysis of the "tyranny of the majority" (Tocqueville 2000: 239–240). In describing this kind of tyranny, he compares it with the "absolute government of one alone": "despotism struck the body crudely, so as to reach the soul; and the soul, escaping from those blows, rose gloriously above it; but in democratic republics, tyranny does not proceed in this way; it leaves the body and goes straight for the soul" (Tocqueville 2000: 244). Tocqueville also calls it the "moral empire of the majority", which is a "theory of equality applied to intellects" (Tocqueville 2000: 236). The number of men should not be able to exert authority as to what is right and what is wrong, otherwise the cultural minority would have no legitimate standing in any society at all. This should function as a necessary precondition for the preservation of the diversified existence of cultures.

20   *Demin Duan*

Along this line, Tocqueville gives high value to what he calls the "associations" of modern democracy (Tocqueville 2000: 489–490). In *Democracy in America*, he interestingly compares the voluntary associations of modern times with aristocratic social bodies, which were once headed by lords (Tocqueville 2000: 490). But the difference is that "in aristocratic societies men have no need to unite to act because they are kept very much together" (Tocqueville 2000: 490), while in modern societies they have to voluntarily unite over a certain value or aim. This association is so important that "in order that men remain civilized or become so, the art of associating must be developed and perfected among them in the same ratio as equality of conditions increases" (Tocqueville 2000: 492). We can infer from this that, since cultural existence is necessarily based on individuals associating with each other under a particular belief or doctrine, Tocqueville is leaving plenty of room for advocating cultural diversity in modern society. Without it, individuals would easily fall prey to the power of the state.

Race, colonial rule, and cultural boundaries

It would be a significant anachronistic mistake if we tried to place Tocqueville's thinking on a par with contemporary multiculturalism. His writing has little to do directly with today's so-called 'politics of difference', 'identity politics', or 'politics of recognition'. However, that said, Tocqueville did reflect on the intriguing fact that American society had been entangled with cultural/racial differences from its inception. On the other hand, we can also notice that Tocqueville's writings covered similar topics in France, although not in metropolitan France, but in French overseas colonies, especially Algeria. Through these materials, we may find more specific answers to Tocqueville's position on cultural diversity.

(1) Cultural boundaries in racial relationships

Tocqueville's thinking in the first volume of *Democracy* is focused on equality of conditions and its impact on American society. But there was something else on his mind, which apparently had nothing to do with 'democracy' itself. As a matter of fact, it relates to the opposite of equality: inequality among peoples. At the beginning of chapter 10, where he opens the topic, he suggests that "the principal task that I imposed on myself is now fulfilled", but that "one encounters in America something more than an immense and complete democracy; the peoples who inhabit the New World can be envisaged from more than one point of view" (Tocqueville 2000: 302). The new topic is about "the three races that inhabit the territory of the United States".

Apparently, in the United States, the equality of conditions did have its limits. It only applied to the European settlers, among whom there was no

Cultural diversity for political freedom   21

such social hierarchy as we find in aristocratic societies. But there did exist slavery. Tocqueville took great effort to document the conditions of black slaves in America and their relationship with the whites. It is not surprising then that he took a solid stance against slavery, as an anti-slavery position had become more and more popular among intellectuals after the 1789 Revolution. But he also incisively analysed the 'practical' deficiencies of slavery, using the comparison between those southern states holding onto slavery and those northern states rejecting it. As he commented, "On the left bank of the Ohio work is blended with the idea of slavery" and is thus "degraded, while on the right bank, it is blended with that of well-being and progress" (Tocqueville 2000: 332). Therefore, as Tocqueville succinctly said, "in reality, the slave has cost more than the free man and his work has been less productive" (Tocqueville 2000: 333).

What should really interest us here is another very important idea from Tocqueville. That is, even though slavery has been abolished, racial discrimination not only persists, but also seems to grow stronger. The reason is that, as Tocqueville notes, white people turn out to be more repulsive when seeing that their former slaves have become their equals (Tocqueville 2000: 329), thus, although former slaves were nominally granted freedom and rights, they were nevertheless no more free than before. Tocqueville said, "You can make the Negro free, but cannot do it so that he is not in the position of a stranger vis-à-vis the European" (Tocqueville 2000: 327). Few liberal thinkers in Tocqueville's time dug so deep into the relationship between different peoples, and Tocqueville's insight in this regard almost reaches the height of modern recognition theory.[3]

The same holds true for the Indians in America. Tocqueville appears amazed by the English settlers' absolute legal, pacific, and even gentle means for seizing the Indians' land, with the settlers' government usually sending a solemn embassy to the Indians and asking them to trade their land for wool clothes, barrels of brandy, glass necklaces, tin bracelets, earrings, and mirrors produced by the white people, "half-convinced, half-compelled, the Indians move out; they go to inhabit new wilderness, where the whites will hardly leave them in peace for ten years" (Tocqueville 2000: 312). However, living beside the white people brings them misery too, for they have neither the knowledge nor the material force to elevate themselves to the equal of the white settlers. If they have strength, Tocqueville says, "They would be in a state, if not to maintain their independence, at least to have their rights to the soil recognized and to incorporate with the vanquishers" (Tocqueville 2000: 317). This is not a choice because the Europeans had already gained a much superior force, but when they decide they do want to live peacefully among the white settlers, they are immediately reduced to a lower class because they do not have time to acquire the skills that the latter has accumulated over thousands of years: "The one makes great harvests grow without trouble, the other extracts fruit from the land

22　*Demin Duan*

only with a thousand-fold effort" (Tocqueville 2000: 318). In viewing this, Tocqueville comments:

> Living within the freedom of the woods, the Indian of North America was miserable, but he did not feel himself inferior to anyone; from the moment that he wants to enter into the social hierarchy of the whites, he can occupy only the lowest rank in it; for he enters ignorant and poor into a society where science and wealth reign.
>
> (Tocqueville 2000: 317)

During the eighteenth and nineteenth centuries, many people in the west believed that their 'advanced culture' would bring civilization to those they considered 'inferior' simply through contact with it. Tocqueville was among the first important intellectuals who pointed out the opposite; that those 'inferior' people were actually powerless and miserable as a result of such contact. Largely because of this, he states in *Democracy* that "the most dreadful of all the evils that threaten the future of the United States arises from the presence of blacks on its soil" (Tocqueville 2000: 326).

(2) Cultural boundaries in colonial rule

Although in metropolitan France there were no such complex racial relationship/conflicts, France had already become a large colonial empire by the time Tocqueville was writing. It is worth noting that Tocqueville was actually an enthusiastic advocate of French expansion projects overseas (Tocqueville 2001). Moreover, he personally visited North Africa twice – mostly the area of Algeria – to witness French undertakings there (France had been a colonial power in Algeria since the early 1830s). Tocqueville insisted that France should not back down from being a colonial power in this region, largely because otherwise its position there would be quickly replaced by other European powers. If this happened, France would be forced into a secondary place in Europe (Tocqueville 2001: 60–61); however, at the same time, French statesmen still had to face the task of governing a multi-race and multi-culture empire.

After reviewing the French administration in Algeria, Tocqueville said that the French have "made Muslim society much more miserable, more disordered, more ignorant, and more barbarous than it had been before knowing us" (Tocqueville 2001: 141). In his writings on colonial Algeria, he shows the same disgust with administrative centralisation as he does in *Democracy in America*, asserting, "I am convinced that taken as a whole the most oppressive and injurious power in Algiers is the civil power. It is not that it permits itself great acts of tyranny. But it shows itself everywhere and always, ruling, directing, modifying, touching and retouching everything" (Tocqueville 2001: 99). Moreover, "The indigenous towns were invaded, turned upside down, and sacked by our administration even more than by

Cultural diversity for political freedom   23

our arms" (Tocqueville 2001: 140). Actually, a large number of his essays on Algeria are dedicated to thinking through how to govern the land without directly administrating its people, which is also a major subject in his _Democracy in America_.

However, it should be said that, in confronting non-European peoples, Tocqueville retains a great deal of cultural pride. He constantly refers to indigenous people in North America and Algeria as 'uncivilized' and 'barbarous'. He even expresses his feeling that European – or perhaps French – civilization is somehow superior to other civilizations. This is visible in a letter he wrote to his friend, Henry Reeve, in 1840, where he says:

> So at last the mobility of Europe has come to grips with Chinese immobility! It is a great event, especially if one thinks that it is only the continuation, the last in a multitude of events of the same nature all of which are pushing the European race out of its home and are successively submitting all the other races to its empire or its influence. Something more vast, more extraordinary than the establishment of the Roman Empire is growing out of our times, without anyone noticing it.
> (Tocqueville 2001: 141)

Nevertheless, this cultural pride, so common among intellectuals in the nineteenth century, does not translate into the justification that Europeans are entitled to rule over other peoples on the basis of their superior culture, a popular ideology known as _mission civilisatrice_.[4] Early Enlightenment thinkers like Condorcet believed that non-European peoples were culturally inferior to Europeans, with Europeans thus bearing a kind of 'duty' to help them progress on the road of civilization (Condorcet 1988: 269). In this sense, contact between Europeans and other peoples, imperial rule, and even violent means are all conducive to the process.

This tenet was later developed by French statesman, Jules Ferry, and became the guiding principle of colonial relationships until the First World War. In his "Speech before the French Chamber of Deputies" of 1884, he stated that, "It is our right vis-à-vis inferior races (to colonize), it is also an exercise of duty. [. . .] If we have the right to go with the barbarians, then we have the obligation to civilize them" (Ferry 1897: 156). As mentioned above, this discourse has a resonance in the work of the British philosopher, John Stuart Mill, who similarly envisaged that British colonialism was beneficial for local people as it lifted them towards a "more advanced civilization" (Mill 1946: 314). This, however, completely veers away from the path that Tocqueville's overall thinking can be said to follow. If Tocqueville displays a certain degree of cultural pride in seeing European nations' power and prestige around the world, he definitely does not concur that European civilization is the future of all human races.

On the one hand, Tocqueville does not have any illusion that the contact between a so-called 'superior' civilization and a 'backward' civilization

24   *Demin Duan*

would necessarily lead to the latter's advancement. On the other, Tocqueville explicitly opposes absolute universalism as being against human nature. When addressing his *Essai sur l'Inégalité des Races Humaines* in a letter to his former secretary, Arthur de Gobineau,[5] Tocqueville directly rejects the latter's view as "very probably wrong and very certainly pernicious" (Tocqueville 1985: 298). This refers to a stringent theory of race that puts one race – the 'Aryan' – over others. For Tocqueville, this theory of predestination would undoubtedly lead to "a great contraction, if not a complete abolition, of human liberty" (Tocqueville 1985: 298). Perhaps the strongest opposition against absolute universalism comes from a comment that he makes in view of 'absolute systems' in general. In his *Recollections*, he says that:

> For my part I hate all those absolute systems that make all the events of history depend on great first causes linked together by the chain of fate and thus succeed, so to speak, in banishing men from the history of the human race. Their boasted breadth seems to me narrow, and their mathematical exactness false.
>
> (Tocqueville 1971: 78)

Therefore, we can see that Tocqueville holds a very understanding view towards cultural and racial differences. His standpoint is more in tune with a kind of contemporary multiculturalism than with early modern rationalistic universalism. This could also be counted as part of his 'strangeness' when compared with other liberal thinkers, such as J. S. Mill.

Religion and freedom in democracy

For Tocqueville, the Pascalian emphasis on mores is clearly set in opposition to the then popular Descartesian rationalist discourse (Kessler 1994: 24–26, 71). It is safe to say that this position makes him much more receptive to things that seem old and thus in a way pre-modern. If culture is by definition 'old', then religion can be considered as 'pre-modern', especially if we take into account the anti-religious atmosphere that prevailed following the Revolution. However, Tocqueville is one of the few thinkers during that period who dared say that modern men need religion in order to live freely.

Tocqueville observes that religion plays a very important role in American political society. In a letter to his childhood friend, Eugène Stoffels, soon after arriving in America, he says, "Mores here are very pure. [. . .] Respect for religion is pushed to the point of scrupulousness. No one, for example, would be permitted to go on a hunt, to dance, or even to play an instrument on Sunday. Even a foreigner is not free on this point" (Tocqueville 1985: 44). Trivial and ordinary as it appears, this observation is actually a new fact about America for Tocqueville. During the Revolution, religion had been considered by many an enemy of freedom. Catholicism, in particular, had

Cultural diversity for political freedom 25

been seen as one of the biggest – if not the biggest – hindrance to the realisation of a modern and free republic. In many of the political discussions that took place around the time of the Revolution, a liberal society would be one free of religion's influence, and instead based solely on the force of rationality (Tocqueville 1988: 96–98). However, what Tocqueville witnessed in America directly contradicts this assumption: for he saw America as a modern and free society, while at the same time one based on highly religious principles.

What Tocqueville sees in religion is more its instrumental function in uniting modern individuals for some greater good than its immediate material well-being. This is considered by Tocqueville as perhaps one of few options modern men have for avoiding despotism. Individuals in modern times may be equal and independent, but they are equally weak. They are vulnerable to any kind of power that can offer them basic equality and material welfare, be it the majority of the people or the despotic state. For Tocqueville, it is thus hugely important to 'prepare' individuals for this kind of situation and avoid the downside of democratic social conditions. In believing in a religious doctrine, individuals can be certain about what is right and what is wrong; they are not easily swayed by what is fed to them by the society or the state, and they are supported by their belief in some higher values. Conversely, the restless minds of equal individuals are the perfect material for despotism, and for whatever religion is the best cure (Lawler 1993). As Tocqueville acutely puts it, "Despotism can do without faith, but freedom cannot" (Tocqueville 2000: 282). He even goes so far as to say that "citizens risk brutalizing themselves less by thinking that their soul is going to pass into the body of a pig than in believing it is nothing" (Tocqueville 2000: 520). Religion prepares individuals to become self-respecting persons who aim higher than immediate material well-being, which is an important way of preventing despotism.

However, there is one condition that religion needs to fulfill in order to function in the modern world. That is, religion has to be separated from political power. Tocqueville says that the French people did not oppose religion before or during the Revolution because of what it teaches, but because religion was so deeply entangled with political institutions, stating, "The priests were not hated because they claimed to regulate the affairs of the other world, but because they were landowners, lords, tithe collectors, and administrators in this one" (Tocqueville 1988: 97). Religion was seen as losing its authentic appeal if it was somehow mixed with political power. For "when a religion seeks to found its empire only on the desire for immortality that torments the hearts of all men equally, it can aim at universality; but when it comes to be united with a government, it must adopt maxims that are applicable only to certain peoples" (Tocqueville 2000: 284). This is especially so in modern democracies, because governmental power changes hands much faster than before.

Therefore, in order for religions to touch human souls, they have to stay separated from power. On observing this fact in America, Tocqueville

26   *Demin Duan*

further comments that different Christian sects can coexist with each other in a harmonious way and all contribute to the good of people's mores, stating that, "what is most important [. . .] is not so much that all citizens profess the true religion but that they profess a religion. Besides, all the sects in the United States are within the great Christian unity, and the morality of Christianity is everywhere the same" (Tocqueville 2000: 278). Thus, we could say that, for Tocqueville, religious minorities should be at least tolerated, while religious diversity should also be respected. At least to a certain extent, he advocates religious freedom and the plurality of religions.

That said, however, we should also note that Tocqueville did make a particular comment that may irritate modern multiculturalism supporters, for in *Democracy in America* he stated that "there are religions that are very false and very absurd" (Tocqueville 2000: 418). It is clear from his texts that examples of what he means by 'false' or 'absurd'come from Islam. He states the following:

> Mohammed had not only religious doctrines descend from Heaven and placed in the Koran, but political maxims, civil and criminal laws, and scientific theories. The Gospels, in contrast, speak only of the general relations of men to God and among themselves. Outside of that they teach nothing and oblige nothing to be believed. That alone, among a thousand other reasons, is enough to show that the first of these two religions cannot dominate for long in enlightened and democratic times, whereas the second is destined to reign in these centuries as in all the others.
>
> (Tocqueville 2000: 419–420)

We can see that what Tocqueville is mainly worried about regarding Islam is that its doctrines are so embedded within political and legal establishments. Only in this respect, he thinks Islam is somehow 'inferior' to Christianity. We should also keep in mind that Tocqueville discussed this issue with a particular agenda in mind, namely that he was trying to determine the most favourable conditions for political freedom.

Conclusion

Tocqueville was not faced with a 'multicultural society' in the modern sense. But as we can see from the above, his comments support the idea of cultural diversity and spontaneous value attachment. He may not think that this diversity itself offers any kind of 'intrinsic' value, just as he seldom talks about 'natural' human rights, but he definitely opposes the idea that there should be only one value system and one culture in any given society. Unlike many contemporary thinkers who believe in the goodness of cultural diversity itself, Tocqueville mainly sees it in terms of the critical instrumental

Cultural diversity for political freedom   27

value necessary for preserving the prospect of (political) freedom in modern society. In any other case, despotism would take over and reign in places of cultural monism or cultural desolation.

Tocqueville incisively points out that modern individuals tend to be 'alike' when they are equal. The equality of conditions allows individuals to be free from different classes embedded in hierarchies, although the sameness of them could lock such individuals into a new kind of despotism. Tocqueville sees that only when people are able to freely participate in their own culture and be united in such a way can there be a true moderation of political power and freedom in modern society. He has the typical cultural pride common for his time, but is also sensitive enough to the emotional and cultural side of human existence to robustly reject any kind of political system based on either racism or cultural universalism.

The 'instrumental' nature of Tocqueville's support for cultural diversity also relates to another important aspect of his thinking. He does not see it as possible that people can really 'implement' cultural diversity in any given society. Surely certain institutions like separation between politics and religion can help with it, but, as we can see from the case of African Americans, meaningful cultural diversity can only 'grow' within a historical process in which people learn how to live with each other. Indeed, different peoples live together peacefully and harmoniously in their own diversified ways. If this is the ideal and challenge for most contemporary supporters of multiculturalism, it is the same for Tocqueville.

Notes

1   At first look, this abhorring of uniformity may have its source in Tocqueville's aristocratic background, since the comparison between the aristocratic and the democratic is all too obvious in his text. In fact, he deliberately spells out this dramatic contradiction in order to illustrate the peculiarity of modern democracy. Some may interpret this as a kind of conservative thinking, with the past being somehow better than the present. But actually, Tocqueville himself evidently says that, although he is emotionally attached to the aristocratic past, his sense of reason dictates him to stand with "what is living", the democratic. His comparison between the past and the present rises up above time to become a constant theme, in which diversity stands at the core. Tocqueville's biggest worry for democracy is that this diversity – with regard to value, culture, or political power – would likely die out in the face of universal equality.

2   For instance, Sheldon Wolin has made an incisive analysis of this (Wolin 2001: 229–240).

3   See, for instance, Fraser (1989) and Honneth (1995).

4   *Mission civilisatrice* is a mode of justification for intervention or colonisation on the basis of spreading civilization. It was the driving principle of the French and Portuguese colonization project in the late nineteenth century and early twentieth centuries.

5   Arthur de Gobineau is credited as the father of modern racial demography. His representative work is *Essai sur l'Inégalité des Races Humaines* (The Inequality of Human Races). His racial theory was later borrowed by Hitler and Nazism.

References

Boesche, R. (1987) *The Strange Liberalism of Alexis de Tocqueville*, Ithaca: Cornell University Press.

Condorcet, M. D. (1988) *Esquisse d'un Tableau Historique des Progrès Historique de l'Esprit Humain*, Paris: GF Flammarion.

Ferry, J. F. C. (1897) *Discours et Opinions de Jules Ferry*, Tome 5, P. Robiquet (ed.), Paris: Armand Colin & Cie.

Fraser, N. (1989) *Unruly Practices: Power, Discourse, and Gender in Contemporary Social Theory*, Minneapolis: University of Minnesota Press.

Frohnen, B. (2002) *Virtue and the Promise of Conservatism: The Legacy of Burke and Tocqueville*, Lawrence: University Press of Kansas.

Honneth, A. (1995) *The Struggle for Recognition: The Moral Grammar of Social Conflicts*, Cambridge: Polity Press.

Kahn, A. S. (1992) *Aristocratic Liberalism: The Social and Political Thought of Jacob Burckhardt, John Stuart Mill, and Alexis de Tocqueville*, Oxford: Oxford University Press.

Kessler, S. (1994) *Tocqueville's Civil Religion: American Christianity and the Prospects for Freedom*, Albany: State University of New York Press.

Kymlicka, W. (2002) *Contemporary Political Philosophy: An Introduction*, Oxford: Oxford University Press.

Lawler, P. A. (1993) *Restless Mind: Alexis de Tocqueville on the Origin and Perpetuation of Human Liberty*, Lanham: Rowman and Littlefield Publishers.

Mill, J. S. (1946) *On Liberty and Considerations on Representative Government*, R. B. McCallum (ed.), Oxford: Basil Backwell.

Nelson, E. (2002) *The Greek Tradition in Republican Thought*, Cambridge: Cambridge University press.

Tocqueville, A. D. (1959) *Journey to America*, J. P. Mayer (ed.), trans. George Lawrence, New Haven and London: Yale University Press.

Tocqueville, A. D. (1971) *Recollections*, J. P. Mayer and A. P. Kerr (eds.), trans. George Lawrence, Garden City, NY: Doubleday & Company, Inc.

Tocqueville, A. D. (1985) *Selected Letters on Politics and Society*, Roger Boesche (ed.), trans. J. Toupin and R. Boesche, Berkeley: University of California Press.

Tocqueville, A. D. (1988) *The Old Regime and the Revolution*, F. Furet and F. Mélonio (eds.), trans. A. S. Kahan, Chicago: University of Chicago Press.

Tocqueville, A. D. (2000) *Democracy in America*, trans. H. C. Mansfield and D. Winthrop, Chicago: University of Chicago Press.

Tocqueville, A. D. (2001) *Writings on Empire and Slavery*, trans. J. Pitts, Baltimore and London: Johns Hopkins University Press.

Wolin, S. (2001) *Tocqueville between Two Worlds: The Making of a Political and Theoretical Life*, Princeton and Oxford: Princeton University Press.

2 Unity and diversity in a Hobbesian commonwealth

Marko Simendić

Introduction

Thomas Hobbes is notorious for his arguments in favour of the sovereign's absolute authority. Throughout various reiterations of his argument, from *Elements of Law* to *Leviathan*, Hobbes's central contention remains the same: in order to be effective at keeping peace and, thus, at securing the foundations for the wellbeing of its subjects, the sovereign should be the only person (be it a group or an individual) that is endowed with absolute authority over everything except the bare lives of his subjects. The sovereign's will is the law and, thus, it becomes the will of his every subject. In fact, the very essence of the state is in the sovereign endowed with absolute authority; he is commonwealth's *condition sine qua non*. His will is the glue that keeps the disjointed individuals together and unites them in a single state. This "reall Unitie of them all" (Hobbes 1651: 87) comes from the subjects submitting their particular, different and conflicting wills to the singular will of the sovereign. Hobbes's remedy for the dangerous state of (naturally) conflicting individual wills is in the commonwealth, which rests on their externally enforced uniformity.

The Hobbesian commonwealth therefore seems to stand in stark contrast with contemporary liberal democracies that embrace multiculturalism. While the contemporary Western states generally encourage and protect the diversity and autonomy of their citizens, the Hobbesian state is designed to impede non-conformity. There are, however, limits to multicultural policies. Cultural practices that are harmful to the individual (genital mutilation, for example) are disallowed, and they cannot be justified by being a part of a certain group's tradition. Multiculturalism, therefore, stands on delicate foundations stretched between liberty and security, and contemporary political philosophers are engaged in discovering the sweet spot – the right balance between the two ends. The same is true for Hobbes. In the dedication of *Leviathan*, Hobbes (1651: 3–4) situates his writing between the opinions of "those that contend, on one side for too great Liberty, and on the other side for too much Authority". On one side there is a plethora of different and conflicting wills, and on the other we find absolute authority under the singular will of the sovereign. Of course, neither in Hobbes's time, nor in ours, the reality of political and social life has never perfectly corresponded

30 *Marko Simendić*

to either of the two extremes – unlimited authority and unrestrained licence. Actual societies are and have been much less fragmented to fit the first ideal type and much more diverse to fit the second one.

In this chapter, I aim to explore the balance between unity and diversity vis-à-vis the state and various kinds of social groups in Hobbes's theory. Since groups and identities that were of importance for Hobbes are just a subsection of groups that contemporary multicultural societies are comprised of, I will first address his account of groups in general terms and then, more concretely, turn to examining the position of religious groups. Not only were diversity of religious worship and its political consequences very important for Hobbes, but also religious communities are a significant part of contemporary multicultural societies. The parallel extends only that far, as it would certainly be anachronous to write about multiculturalism in seventeenth-century English political thought.

The term "multiculturalism" itself could not be usefully applied to Hobbes as he, for one, defines culture in two ways, and neither of them corresponds to the contemporary meaning of the term. The first meaning is the classical one: "that labour which a man bestowes on any thing, with a purpose to make benefit by it" and, in this sense, "labour bestowed on the Earth, is called *Culture*" (Hobbes 1651: 188–189). The second is synonymous to education. For example, "education of Children a [is] *Culture* of their mindes" (Hobbes 1651: 189). A similar meaning to this, Hobbes (1651: 189) argues, is "where mens wills are to be wrought to our purpose, not by Force, but by Compleasance", which he calls "courting" or "worship". However, although "multiculturalism" is far from Hobbes's vocabulary, he does address a seemingly perennial problem of weighing between diversity and unity or liberty and authority, to which multiculturalism is one of the possible contemporary solutions.

I will here consider Hobbes's ideas regarding social groups that share a politically relevant identity and/or strive towards a shared political goal. In Hobbes's (1651: 115) terms, those are kinds of "systemes" or "any numbers of men joyned in one Interest, or one Businesse". Also, as religion was the basis of another shared and politically relevant identity that was very important for Hobbes, I will devote special attention to discussing the ways in which Hobbes envisioned (co)existence of various religions. But before we discuss the relationship between the Hobbesian commonwealth and diverse social groups, let us sketch Hobbes's argument in favour of unity and absolute authority.

Hobbes's state, unity and absolute authority

Two main planks of Hobbes's account of state authority were already in place before *Leviathan*. The first is Hobbes's argument in favour of the superiority of the state over other forms of group personality. The second is his point about the state resting on the unity of the rulers with their subjects. Hobbes's argument from *Leviathan* reinforced both of these positions. This especially applies to the "unity argument". This argument was based in its turn on two supporting arguments: the first stressed the organic connection between the body politic and the sovereign as its head while the second conceptualised this unity within a (legal) notion of a singular person. In *Leviathan*, Hobbes significantly enriched these two supporting arguments by introducing the idea of representation and a much more sophisticated account of a person. This particular development of Hobbes's thought has received the most thorough scholarly attention by Quentin Skinner (1999, 2004, 2005, 2007), David Runciman (1997, 2000) and, more recently, Monica Brito Vieira (2009). Let us now briefly discuss the two main points that were established before and expanded in *Leviathan*.

First, Hobbes insisted on both the conceptual priority and the political superiority of the state to other forms of group personality. In *The Elements of Law*, Hobbes (1889: 172) views the charters in which the "subordinate corporations" are proclaimed to be one person in law as a model for the personality of the state. Here we can see that, although Hobbes borrows the model from the theory of corporations, he insists on those corporations being subordinate to the state. Somewhat clearer evidence of such an effort may be read in his accounts in *De Cive* and *Leviathan*. In both accounts Hobbes avoids using the vocabulary of personation and representation, and instead of "corporations", in *De Cive* he subsumes states and corporations under "civil persons", while in *Leviathan* he categorises them as "systems". The result is that states and corporations are subsumed under a more neutral category, so that one cannot consistently argue that corporations as forms of human association are conceptually prior to states. Finally, the move from "civil persons" to "systems", as we could see from his definition of the state, enabled Hobbes to argue that there was more to "systems" than personhood.

Second, Hobbes believed that it is the unity of all under one that makes a multitude and not simply its members. He expressed this thought in different ways. In *The Elements of Law* this unity is identified with the organic unity of the head with the body; *De Cive* offers a similar account of the soul and the body, while in *Leviathan* Hobbes introduces representation as a key feature of such unity. In all of these accounts Hobbes argues that the unity in question is the unity of a multitude of wills under the will of the sovereign. The difference, however, is in Hobbes's account of how the original contract creates this unity of will. While in all three accounts the parties to the contract relinquish their absolute rights, in *Leviathan* they also authorise their sovereign to represent them.

To summarise, the structure of Hobbes's argument involves the following elements:

1   A "superiority" argument (the state is superior to other groups);
2   A "unity" argument (the state is defined by the unity of the sovereign and the subjects);

    a   the unity is of organic nature (the sovereign head is inseparable from the body politic);
    b   the unity is in the sovereign (in *Leviathan* the sovereign is the representative who personates its subjects and, thus, unites them).

32   *Marko Simendić*

Hobbes developed his "unity" argument in two complementary directions. The first aspect of Hobbes's "unity" argument portrayed the state in organic terms and presented the relationship between the sovereign and its subjects as analogous to the relationship between the head and the body. The second is centred on the idea of group personality. The first aspect was extended into a very detailed organicist account of the state as an artificial man, while the second leads us from the state as a "person in law" or a "civil person" towards the notion of the person of the state (*persona civitatis*). With his bi-directional argument, fully expanded in *Leviathan*, Hobbes offered us two ways of thinking about the unity of the state.

The first way of thinking about the unity of the state, as the organic connection between the sovereign and the subjects, goes back to Plato and is reaffirmed in his own way by Robert Filmer. On this view, in order for the state to function, every part needs to play the role assigned to it by God or nature – roughly speaking, the sovereign needs to rule and the subjects need to follow the orders. Like organs in the human body, the various elements of the state are related through their interdependence and their shared purpose in sustaining the organism.

The outlines of the argument that the unity of the state rests in the sovereign had already been sketched in *The Elements of Law*, where Hobbes (1889: 109) discussed the "involvement" of the multiple wills of particular subjects in the single will of the sovereign. This thought is significantly expanded in Hobbes's account from *Leviathan*, where he demonstrates how representation can be seen as sustaining the unity of a commonwealth through the interdependence of the subjects and the sovereign. It is not just that the people without their sovereign would be left without guidance or protection. For Hobbes, without unity through representation there simply are no people, just a multitude of disjointed individuals. In *Leviathan* Hobbes applied this idea of representation to his existing account of a "civil person". In the process, Hobbes turned to the classical theatrical and legal notion of *persona* as a mask or a role, and representation became equated with personation (Simendić 2012a). In other words, to represent the state is to "bear" its person and, at the same time, that person unites the multitude of individuals as a people.

Opposition to diversity as a purpose of Hobbes's argument

Hobbes's entire argument in favour of absolute authority is conjured around the opposition to different kinds of diversity of wills. The first kind is found in the state of nature. Embodied in the heterogeneity of the individuals' particular wills, such a diversity is made a dangerous threat to peace due to individuals having unlimited natural liberty. Paradoxically, although individuals' particular wills differ, the primary causes of war come from them being alike and wanting the same things. Those causes are: "First, Competition; Secondly, Diffidence; Thirdly, Glory. The first, maketh men invade for

Unity and diversity 33

Gain; the second, for Safety; and the third, for Reputation" (Hobbes 1651: 61–62). Individuals equally seek safety, they are also generally intolerant to other people's opinions, they "hardly believe there be many so wise as themselves" and, more often than not, their desire for things that other people want or already have results in conflict (Hobbes 1651: 61–62). The solution is to create "a common Power to keep them all in awe" (Hobbes 1651: 61–62). Famously, Hobbes (1651: 87) requires the natural individuals to "conferre all their power and strength upon one Man, or upon one Assembly of men, that may reduce all their Wills, by plurality of voices, unto one Will [. . .] and therein to submit their Wills, every one to his Will, and their Judgements, to his Judgment".

The problem of different and conflicting individual wills persists in the civil society. And, as Hobbes's state of nature is only hypothetical, such dissenting voices that can be heard from inside the commonwealth are the problem that Hobbes is trying to resolve. Although they seek similar things (and, again similarly, quarrel about them), the people are different and their "diversity of Nature, rising from their diversity of Affections" leads to conflict and causes them to behave unsociably (Hobbes 1651: 76). In response, Hobbes formulates his fifth natural law as "COMPLEASANCE; that is to say, *That every man strive to accommodate himselfe to the rest*" (Hobbes 1651: 76). And the sovereign, by promulgating laws and exercising its will, enforces this and other natural laws: "The Law of Nature therefore is a part of the Civill Law in all Common-wealths of the world. Reciprocally also, the Civill Law is a part of the Dictates of Nature" (Hobbes 1651: 138). Hobbes's insistence on unity of individual wills, achieved through their submission to the absolute authority, is a part of his wider "unity" argument: there can be no state without the subjects being united through their submission to the absolute sovereign power.

The dangers coming from the second kind of diversity of wills are ameliorated by Hobbes's "superiority" argument. This kind of diversity is the diversity of various groups or, to phrase it as Hobbes did, "systems". And before we move on to examining the compatibility of Hobbes's account of groups with the contemporary idea of a self-governing minority group, let us turn to examining the potential dangers that Hobbes saw in groups. When discussing one of the "infirmities" of the commonwealth, Hobbes (1651: 174) famously compares groups to "the little Wormes, which Physicians call *Ascarides*". These metaphorical parasites hurt the body of the commonwealth both by growing in size and by growing in number:

> Another infirmity of a Common-wealth, is the immoderate greatnesse of a Town, when it is able to furnish out of its own Circuit, the number, and expence of a great Army: As also the great number of Corporations; which are as it were many lesser Common-wealths in the bowels of a greater, like wormes in the entrayles of a naturall man.
>
> (Hobbes 1651: 174)

Hobbes's point is that groups should never be allowed to develop into political agents that might contest the sovereign's seat and endanger his rule. Furthermore, Hobbes sees no value in the diversity of groups. On the contrary, he believes that their number alone might cause problems for the stability of a commonwealth. Consequently, the number of groups should be limited and their multiplication restrained.

Another danger to a commonwealth arises from the belief that a church has spiritual authority over its congregation. Hobbes (1651: 174) pejoratively calls this a "ghostly" kingdom or "a Kingdome of Fayries", recognition of which leads to having two sovereigns and, in turn, two competing commonwealths: "where one is Soveraign, another Supreme; where one can make Lawes, and another make Canons; there must needs be two Commonwealths, of one & the same Subjects; which is a Kingdome divided in it selfe, and cannot stand". Again, Hobbes (1651: 174) underlines his "superiority" argument and implies that a prudent sovereign should never let religious groups have the "Right to declare what is Sinne", nor influence his subjects in any other politically relevant way. As we will see in the final part of this chapter, removing such powers from the church leads Hobbes to supporting an account that, at least in part, entails religious toleration.

The purpose of Hobbes's argument is clear. Hobbes argues in favour of the absolute authority of the sovereign and believes that only the sovereign entrusted with absolute power can successfully maintain peace. In contrast to the absolute liberty of individuals in the state of nature and their power-hungry counterparts in the civil society stands the absolute authority of the sovereign. Against various groups, eager to grow in power and inclined to grow in numbers, stands the unifying, singular and absolute power of the sovereign. From its very foundations, Hobbes's state is set to react to diversity by containing, if not eradicating, it. But, between containment and utter unification there is a lot of space for the sovereign to manoeuvre. With this in mind, the next section will bring Hobbes's account a bit closer to contemporary multicultural practice by examining the potential for the existence of self-governing minority groups in Hobbes's theory. After that, in the final section, we will turn to examining the ways in which the Hobbesian state would deal with the diversity of religious groups – a topic that Hobbes was very concerned about.

The potential for self-governing minority groups in Hobbes's theory

Hobbes's (1651: 115) definition of a group (a "system") is very broad, as this is "any numbers of men joyned in one Interest, or one Businesse". Hobbes offers an extensive typology of such groups in *Leviathan* and formulates the state's response to them accordingly. Systems can be regular or irregular, lawful or unlawful. Regular systems can be represented by a single person or an assembly, while irregular systems have no representatives. Regular systems are thus more permanent than irregular systems, which are formed *ad hoc* and "consist only in concourse of People" (Hobbes 1651: 115). The commonwealth is a regular, absolute and independent system. On the other hand, groups that function within the state are, in Hobbes's terminology, subordinate/dependent systems. And, within this class, Hobbes distinguishes between political ("Bodies Politique") and private systems. Political systems are founded by the sovereign authority, and the private systems "are constituted by Subjects amongst themselves, or by authoritie from a stranger" (Hobbes 1651: 115).

In *Leviathan*, political systems are very broadly defined, and Hobbes (1651: 117–118) writes:

> The variety of Bodies Politique, is almost infinite: for they are not onely distinguished by the severall affaires, for which they are constituted, wherein there is an unspeakable diversitie; but also by the times, places, and numbers, subject to many limitations.

Some of these "bodies politique" "are ordained for Government", and they include provinces, colonies, towns and even universities and churches (Hobbes 1651: 118). Again, provinces are defined broadly as "those Countries where the Soveraign is not resident, but governs by Commission" (Hobbes 1651: 118). Hobbes's language is obviously not the contemporary language of *recognition* of groups, their rights and autonomy. Instead, his emphasis is on the sovereign "ordaining", "committing" or "making" such systems. Similarly, provinces are governed by "publique ministers", representatives of the state who are appointed by the sovereign and who "have no other right, but what depends on the Soveraigns Will" (Hobbes 1651: 124). Hobbes indeed seldom fails to emphasise that their authority is only derivative and that there can be no authority higher than the sovereign's (Simendić 2012b: 26). But, although the sovereign's authority is absolute, and even though most of Hobbes's examples relate to administrative delegation of the sovereign's authority in colonies or others "farre distant in place", Hobbes does not negate the possibility of the sovereign accommodating cultural specificities of a certain province by giving it a special status within the commonwealth.

In this sense, Hobbes's provinces might resemble today's autonomous regions, in which special status and self-government serve to accommodate the cultural specificities of their inhabitants. Although Hobbes never discusses such communities *per se*, they are certainly not prohibited within his commonwealth – he neither denies this possibility, nor believes that territorial autonomy is unfeasible or dangerous to the commonwealth. In fact, Hobbes (1651: 118) explicitly writes that "in one Common-wealth there be divers Countries, that have their Lawes distinct one from another". There is, therefore, a possibility for the sovereign to enforce different legislation in different provinces of his commonwealth. This, in turn, opens up the

36   *Marko Simendić*

possibility of having autonomous regions, even within the Hobbesian commonwealth. Hobbes is not too concerned with the reasons why a certain sovereign would grant a special status to some of his subjects, but if the sovereign judges that such an arrangement is conducive to the preservation of his commonwealth, giving a special status to certain minority groups remains a possibility.

The second argument in favour of such a possibility arises from Hobbes's discussion of groups' autonomy in pecuniary matters. Hobbes (1651: 117–118) certainly presupposes such autonomy, as he discusses in great detail the group representative's responsibility for borrowing money from a creditor. This discussion illustrates another important element of Hobbes's account of groups. The representative is not necessarily a single person – a group can also be represented by an assembly (Hobbes 1651: 116). Hobbes (1651: 118) is explicit about this: "As first, the Government of a Province may be committed to an Assembly of men, wherein all resolutions shall depend on the Votes of the major part; and then this Assembly is a Body Politique, and their power limited by Commission". Although I am not arguing in favour of Hobbes's theory of representation as proto-democratic (cf. Runciman 2010), this remains a very important point, as Hobbes implicitly acknowledges a possibility that a group can be represented democratically. Furthermore, if a province is governed by an assembly, it is not governed by a single person. And since "publique ministers" are individual persons, a group that is already being represented by an assembly cannot be represented by the sovereign's minister. The exclusion of appointed "publique ministers" from representing certain groups loosens up the province's ties to the central government and opens up a window of opportunity for its members to be represented democratically and to enjoy certain autonomy, even within the Hobbesian commonwealth. Hobbes (1651: 118) is aware of this, and he, in prose that is untypically mild in tone, recommends against appointing an assembly to govern a province:

> where [men] cannot be present, they are by Nature also enclined, to commit the Government of their common Interest rather to a Monarchicall, then a Popular form of Government: which is also evident in those men that have great private estates; who when they are unwilling to take the paines of administring the businesse that belongs to them, choose rather to trust one Servant, then an Assembly either of their friends or servants.

Hobbes is not strongly against provinces being governed by assemblies; he only believes that the sovereign's interests might be served better if a province would be represented by an individual.

So far we have established that Hobbes's theory allows (or that it at least does not explicitly disallow) the existence of political groups (provinces) that are 1) not under the sovereign's direct authority; 2) functioning under legislature that is specific to them and different from the other parts of the commonwealth; 3) governed by an assembly. Such groups may roughly correspond to contemporary cultural groups, which have their group rights recognized in liberal democracies and which exercise a certain level of self-government. Of course, this is not to say that Hobbes is a proto-multiculturalist. He is in no way interested in the validity of argumentation behind political claims that could be put forward by various minority groups, and he does not ascribe any political value to their culture, identity or autonomy. However, although Hobbes does not anticipate contemporary multiculturalist policies, his account of groups does not make it impossible for the sovereign to accommodate such claims.

Finally, there is another interesting Hobbesian argument that contemporary multiculturalists could find appealing. When he discusses the decision-making process within the assemblies that represent groups, he argues that: "whatsoever debt is by that Assembly contracted; or whatsoever unlawfull Act is decreed, is the Act onely of those that assented, and not of any that dissented, or were absent, for the reasons before alledged" (Hobbes 1651: 118). Hobbes is making two related points here. First, if the group's assembly borrows money from somebody, those who voted against such a decision and those who were absent from the vote do not owe any money to the lender. Second, if the majority votes in favour of acting illegally, its absent members and members who were against the illegal proposal are both absolved from prosecution. Unlike the majority in the sovereign assembly, the majority in the subordinate assembly cannot force a dissenting individual to take responsibility for the assembly's decision. Hobbes (1651: 117) argues that: "in Bodies Politique subordinate, and subject to a Soveraign Power, it is sometimes not onely lawfull, but expedient, for a particular man to make open protestation against the decrees of the Representative Assembly, and cause their dissent to be Registred, or to take witnesse of it". Regardless of the legality of the group assembly's decision, a dissenting voter cannot be made responsible for it. This principle is reminiscent to a "right to exit" (Spiecker et al. 2006): if a member of a group chooses not to align himself with certain practices that are enforced by other members, he is free to leave the group. Similarly, a dissenting voter in Hobbes's "Bodies Politique subordinate" does not share the effects of the majority's decision that he opposed. It is important to note that rule is valid only for decision-making within a group, whereas in the commonwealth every subject is considered responsible for their sovereign's every decision.

Hobbes and diversity of religious groups

Religion is one sphere of social life in seventeenth-century Western Europe where belonging to one of the groups was more politically important than it is in today's West. From the Thirty Years' War to the English Civil War and the Glorious Revolution, religious differences played a pivotal role

38   *Marko Simendić*

in seventeenth-century politics and conflicts, both in England and on the continent. Hobbes not only devotes a large portion of *Leviathan* to politically salient religious matters, but he also discusses such problems in *Behemoth*, *Historical Narration Concerning Heresy* and *Historia Ecclesiastica*. Diversity of religious belief and political demands coming from people who shared religious identity were both a reality of Hobbes's times and a topic of his writing. How does a Hobbesian commonwealth, then, deal with religious diversity and its political aspects?

Hobbes has a secular account of the state. The church is not only considered as separate from the state, it is subordinated to it (Curley 2007: 309). Hobbes sees great danger in the church engaging in political matters; it challenging the sovereign's authority and, ultimately, paves the road for a civil war (Martinich 1992: 15). For this, the Holy See is a particular target of Hobbes's (1651: 316) critique: "the Pope [. . .] wanteth three things that our Saviour hath not given him, to *Command*, and to *Judge*, and to *Punish*, otherwise than (by Excommunication) to run from those that will not Learn of him". Finally, Hobbes (1651: 198) is also very sceptical about the people claiming to have been divinely inspired: "seeing therefore Miracles now cease, we have no sign left, whereby to acknowledge the pretended Revelations, or Inspirations of any private man".

Simply separating the church from the state and retaining its autonomy in religious matters does not guarantee a stable political order. Even seemingly purely religious questions, such as the definition of a sin, can lead to sedition by influencing believers' actions and lead them to oppose the civil government or fight each other (Curley 2007: 310). For Hobbes (1651: 171), with "Sinne being nothing but the transgression of the Law", to decide what constitutes a sin is to decide the content of the law, and such a power should exclusively belongs to the sovereign. Moreover, it is the sovereign who has the final say on religious matters. As Edwin Curley (2007: 310) summarises, "The sovereign's many rights include the right to determine which books of Scripture are canonical [. . .], the right to decide how we should interpret passages in those books [. . .], and the right to give legal force to the teachings of Scripture". Such a doctrine was fiercely opposed by many of Hobbes's contemporaries. They believed that, if Britain was to remain Christian, only the clergy should decide on doctrinal matters and that the sovereign ought to enforce their decisions (Ryan 2009: 54).

In the Hobbesian commonwealth, religious groups do not have any influence on the civil authority, and in this sense his theory is secular. The converse is not true, however, as the sovereign has the right to interfere in religious matters. If he judges that such an action is conducive to maintaining peace, the sovereign should impose his will and determine the church's organisation or doctrine. But what is the scope of the sovereign's interference? The sovereign has every right to interfere in the matters of any religious group as much as he deems appropriate, but will this absolute right turn into *de facto* absolute control? It may seem plausible, in the interest of

Unity and diversity 39

the unity of the state and its preservation, that the sovereign should impose one unifying (civil) religion, make all of his subjects practice it, ban every other religion. Or, on the other hand, he might ban religion altogether and "pull down all the churches" (Curley 2007: 321). Neither is true.

Hobbes was a pragmatist in religious matters and he believed that forcing uniformity of religious belief or suppressing it altogether was counterproductive. As Curley (2007: 311) points out, in *Behemoth* (1682: 103) Hobbes writes that:

> A State can constrain obedience, but convince no error, nor alter the mind of them that believe they have the better reason. Suppression of Doctrines does but unite and exasperate; that is, increase both the malice and power of them that have already believed them.

Religious groups, therefore, would not find their beliefs systematically supressed in a Hobbesian commonwealth just for the sake of unity. Since repression has negative effects on the stability of the state, certain kinds of religious learning would be deemed illegal only if the benefits outweigh the costs, i.e., only if the sovereign truly believes that they present danger to peace and stability. Here we can see that religious communities would be, for the most part, "left alone" in the Hobbesian commonwealth. The possibility of a relative autonomy of groups that we established in the previous section of this essay is now made explicit with regards to religious groups.

The other relationship that remains to be explored is the one between various religious groups in Hobbes's state. Two points should be made here. First, Hobbes's cautious stance towards suppressing religious doctrines implies that he believed that the state would, at least to an extent, tolerate religious diversity. Second, him not recognising the supreme authority of clergy on religious (or any other) matters in the state suggests that, in his view, the state should not favour any particular church. Now, if Hobbes allows religious diversity, at least until the number of different religious groups makes them resemble "little Wormes", how would he regulate their mutual relations?

A famous passage from the *Leviathan* might shed some light on this question. Hobbes (1651: 385; Curley 2007: 325–336; Ryan 2009: 41) writes:

> And so we are reduced to the Independency of the Primitive Christians to follow Paul, or Cephas, or Apollos, *every man as he liketh best*: Which, if it be without contention [. . .] is *perhaps the best*: First, because there ought to be no Power over the Consciences of men, but of the Word it selfe, working Faith in every one [. . .] and secondly, because it is *unreasonable* [. . .] to require of a man endued with Reason of his own, *to follow the Reason of any other man*, or of the most voices of many other men; Which is little better, then to venture his Salvation at crosse and pile.
> (emphasis mine)

40 *Marko Simendić*

In this passage Hobbes underlines the idea that religious beliefs should not be imposed. Instead of the state or the clergy, it is God who should be "working Faith in every one". Also, everybody should search for his or her own path to salvation, and external pressure can only be counterproductive. Making somebody follow another man's reason might very well lead him to eternal damnation. Finally, there is a cautious claim in favour of religious pluralism: "independency to follow Paul, or Cephas, or Apollos [. . .] is perhaps the best". If religious diversity is not something that necessarily leads to sedition, and if the suppression of religious belief could prove very costly, it is very likely that the Hobbesian commonwealth would allow religious diversity and protect the members of various religious groups from harming each other.

In this important passage from *Leviathan*, Hobbes offers some typical arguments in favour of religious toleration, not unlike those put forward by John Locke (2003) in his *Letter Concerning Toleration*. However, although being charged for heresy certainly made Hobbes an enemy of intolerance (Curley 2007: 312–313), the idea that Hobbes was an advocate of religious toleration is an object of contestation in contemporary scholarship. For example, this thought is strongly put forward by Richard Tuck and, in a more reserved manner, supported by Curley (2007) and Alan Ryan (2009), but opposed by Glen Newey (2008). However, such a discussion is outside the scope of this chapter. My goals here are more modest, and it will suffice to say that, in today's terms, Hobbes's overall argument allows a certain level of cultural diversity and autonomy. This is implied by his account of groups, where he leaves room for groups' autonomy, and underlined by him allowing and cautiously supporting diversity of religious beliefs.

Conclusion

In Hobbes's theory, diversity is a state of affairs, a situation to be taken into consideration, rather than a value. But although there is nothing particularly good about diversity, and even though there are some great merits to unity, Hobbes's theory is not focused on simply choosing one over the other. Instead of mutually exclusive alternatives, they are the two far ends of a spectrum from which a pragmatic sovereign should choose the policy that is in the interest of peace and the stability of his commonwealth. The Hobbesian sovereign weighs liberty and diversity against security and uniformity, not unlike contemporary governments. And with regards to Hobbes's position on social groups, their diversity and uniformity, we can make at least two points. First, although this is outside the focus of his main argument, we may argue that Hobbes is not explicitly against the autonomy of social groups, including some form of self-government. This includes some interesting points on the responsibility of members of such groups. When a group is democratically self-governed, those who oppose the majority vote are not responsible for the consequences of the majority's decision.

Therefore, similarly to the contemporary idea of a "right to exit", a dissenting member of a Hobbesian group can choose to leave the group and suffer no consequences for doing so.

Second, Hobbes's state is a secular state that supports religious diversity, prohibits intolerance and discourages strife between religious groups. This is a concrete example that shows that the reading of Hobbes's theory as being open to diversity and limited autonomy of social groups is not too optimistic. And although Hobbes is a pragmatist and not a multiculturalist, his theory can be read as being broad enough to accommodate at least some of the basic requirements of multiculturalist policies. This might not seem too generous of an allowance, but one cannot ask more from an early modern proponent of the sovereign's absolute authority, especially from the author who proudly writes that in his magnum opus he "hath *framed* the minds of a thousand gentlemen to a conscientious obedience to present government" (Hobbes 1656: 335–336; emphasis mine).

Works cited

Brito Vieira, M. (2009) *The Elements of Representation in Hobbes: Aesthetics, Theatre, Law, and Theology in the Construction of Hobbes's Theory of the State*, Leiden: Brill.

Curley, E. (2007) 'Hobbes and the Cause of Religious Toleration', in P. Springborg (ed.) *The Cambridge Companion to Hobbes's Leviathan*, Cambridge: Cambridge University Press.

Hobbes, T. (1682) 'Behemoth, the History of the Causes of the Civil Wars of England, from 1640 to 1660', in *Tracts of Mr. Thomas Hobbs of Malmsbury*, London.

Hobbes, T. (1889) *Elements of Law*, F. Tönnies (ed.), London: Simpkin, Marshall.

Locke, J. (2003) *Two Treatises of Government and a Letter Concerning Toleration*, vol. I, I. Shapiro (ed.), New Haven: Yale University Press.

Martinich, A. P. (1992) *The Two Gods of Leviathan: Thomas Hobbes on Religion and Politics*, Cambridge: Cambridge University Press.

Newey, G. (2008) *Routledge Philosophy Guidebook to Hobbes and Leviathan*, London: Routledge.

Runciman, D. (1997) *Pluralism and the Personality of the State*, Cambridge: Cambridge University Press.

Runciman, D. (2000) 'What Kind of Person is Hobbes's State? A Reply to Skinner', *The Journal of Political Philosophy* 8(2): 268–278.

Runciman, D. (2010) 'Hobbes's Theory of Representation: Anti-Democratic or Proto-Democratic?' in I. Shapiro et al. (eds.) *Political Representation*, Cambridge: Cambridge University Press.

Ryan, A. (2009) 'A More Tolerant Hobbes?' in S. Mendus (ed.) *Justifying Toleration: Conceptual and Historical Perspectives*, Cambridge: Cambridge University Press.

Simendić, M. (2012a) 'Thomas Hobbes's Person as Persona and "Intelligent Substance"', *Intellectual History Review* 22(2): 147–162.

Simendić, M. (2012b) 'Hobbes and Coke on Corporations : Parallels and Dissonances', in M. A. Jovanović and B. Spaić (eds.) *Jurisprudence and Political*

42   *Marko Simendić*

Philosophy in the 21st Century – Reassessing Legacies, Frankfurt am Main: Peter Lang.

Skinner, Q. (1999) 'Hobbes and the Purely Artificial Person of the State', *The Journal of Political Philosophy* 7(1): 1–29.

Skinner, Q. (2004) 'Hobbes and the Purely Artificial Person of the State', in *Visions of Politics Vol. 3: Hobbes and Civil Science*, Cambridge: Cambridge University Press.

Skinner, Q. (2005) 'Hobbes on Representation', *European Journal of Philosophy* 13(2): 155–184.

Skinner, Q. (2007) 'Hobbes on Persons, Authors and Representatives', in P. Springborg (ed.) *The Cambridge Companion to Hobbes's Leviathan*, Cambridge: Cambridge University Press.

Spiecker, B., Ruyter, D. D. and Steutel, J. (2006) 'Taking the Right to Exit Seriously', *Theory and Research in Education* 4(3): 313–327.

Tuck, R. (1990) 'Hobbes and Locke on Toleration', in M. G. Dietz (ed.) *Thomas Hobbes and Political Theory*, Lawrence: University Press of Kansas.

3 Nietzschean perspectives on multiculturalism

Rebecca Bamford

A culture is "a human community larger than a few families that is associated with ongoing ways of seeing, doing, and thinking about things" (Gutmann 1993: 171). Following the definition adopted by this volume, multiculturalism involves the coexistence of two or more cultures in the same geographical space. When people of different cultures inhabit the same space, a challenge arises: those who claim membership in one, or more, of the relevant cultural communities must learn to navigate, and sometimes to incorporate, ways of seeing, doing, and thinking about things that may be quite different from their original ways. Injustice may arise as a result of failures of this process. Examples of relevant forms of injustice include racism, xenophobia, and religious discrimination. These injustices may be further complicated by intersecting forms of oppression, such as sexism, classism, homophobia, transphobia, and ableism.

Liberalism has been proposed as a way of grounding a commitment to pluralism of cultural values, which has been proposed as a way to ground justice within multicultural contexts. The need to address injustice has led to an increasing concern with developing and sustaining what is often referred to as 'respect for diversity'. The call to respect diversity has formed part of international debate on multiculturalism since at least the early 1990s; for example, at a European Union summit meeting in Maastricht in 1992, the EU reaffirmed its commitment to "respect the interests and diversity of member states"; this was to be accomplished through a range of interventions, which included making the EU more open as a community, promoting respect for national traditions, and promoting democracy (Schmidt 1992).

However, the strategy of appealing to liberalism has been called into question on the basis that liberalism is sufficient neither to tackle structural forms of injustice, such as marginalization or cultural imperialism (Young 2011), nor to address injustices that are tied to the lived experiences of people with mixed identities who have strong commitments to several cultures or races (Alcoff 2000). These accounts show that framing an approach to multicultural justice in terms of respecting, or appreciating, diversity is too simplistic. First, respect and appreciation do not go far enough to effect the kind of change required for full justice. Second, if respect and appreciation

44   Rebecca Bamford

are presented to us as a sufficient strategy, this may actually inhibit further movement towards justice, for instance, by encouraging complacency, or by making it more challenging to engage in the kinds of difficult and often uncomfortable conversations that combatting injustice requires.

In light of these concerns with the strategy of appealing to liberalism, it seems that what is required to promote justice is a more substantive commitment to pluralism. In particular, a pluralism that encompasses a more inclusive account of knowing, and a more flexible and dynamic conception of cultural identity, not simply of cultural values within multicultural societies, is needed. In this essay, I aim to show how such a form of pluralism might be successfully affirmed through Nietzschean conceptual resources. Nietzschean pluralism, I suggest, facilitates a diverse ways of knowing as well as a more flexible concept of identity, adoption of which would help to avoid or reduce some of the injustices affecting people in multicultural societies. My discussion in this essay thus contributes to the tradition of scholarship that engages with the value of Nietzsche's thinking on pluralism, and deploys it within a range of wider political contexts and debates, such as freedom and postcolonialism (Schutte 1984, 1993, 2000, 2004), the futurity of politicized identities (Brown 1995), democracy, pluralism, and agonistic respect (Connolly 2002), and most recently, melodrama as a political discourse that shapes the contemporary politics of freedom (Anker 2014).

I begin by laying out the main reasons why Nietzsche adopts a critical stance towards liberalism and its capacity to sustain human freedom. In light of this, I consider some of the ways in which Nietzsche's perspectivism and his thinking on subjectivity incorporate not only pluralism of perspectives but also a dynamic pluralism with respect to each person's subjective sense of themselves, internally and in relation to others (Gooding-Williams 1998; Alcoff 2000). In the final part of the essay, I discuss some of the consequences of this Nietzschean pluralism for the project of sustaining justice within multiculturalist contexts.

Nietzsche's critical engagement with liberalism

As well as identifying ways in which early bourgeois liberalism excluded people who were perceived to be insufficiently rational or independent, Iris Marion Young has pointed out that liberalism may be insufficient as a means to counter oppression (2011: 54). Young shows that oppression may not always involve a "tyrannical power" that directly aims to subjugate people; rather, as she suggests, "the everyday practices of a well-intentioned liberal society" give rise to a world in which injustice arises structurally, through institutional practices and through the "unconscious assumptions and reactions of well-meaning people" (2011: 41). As she puts it, "liberally-minded" people who intend "to treat everyone with equal respect" may still give "aversive or anxious reactions to the bodily presence of others" that generate or promote forms of oppression such as marginalization; moreover, dependent persons remain problematically marginalized and excluded from equal citizenship rights in ways "barely hidden beneath the surface", such as through the workings of social welfare institutions that control access to resources (Young 2011: 11, 54).

Nietzsche offers a critique of liberalism that chimes with Young's concerns about the institutional basis of systemic forms of oppression. However, as I will discuss, Nietzsche's reasons are not – unlike those of Young – grounded in a personal commitment on his part to democratic theory. Nietzsche bases his criticism of liberalism, or "herd-animalization" as he calls it in *Twilight of the Idols*, on the damaging effects that he suggests liberal institutions have upon human freedom:

> The value of a thing sometimes lies not in what one attains with it, but in what one pays for it – what it *costs* us. Let me give an example. Liberal institutions stop being liberal as soon as they have been set up: afterward there is no one more inveterate or thorough in damaging freedom than liberal institutions.
>
> (1998b "Expeditions" §38)

So long as we are engaged in struggle for liberal institutions, then according to Nietzsche's claim here, such institutions can be understood as strong promoters of freedom. However, liberal institutions are no longer truly liberal once this struggle ceases – even though we might continue to think and talk of these institutions as such. Liberal institutions are truly liberal during the process of struggle, Nietzsche claims, because engaging in such struggle enables the contest of "illiberal instincts", such as the delight in war and victory, to persist and gain mastery over our other instincts (1998b "Expeditions" §38). However, the *illiberalism* of liberal institutions arises once a struggle concludes and our illiberal instincts no longer hold sway over us. Nietzsche continues this line of argument by suggesting that the highest type of free human beings is to be found wherever the highest resistance is constantly being overcome, which according to him, is "a short step away from tyranny, right on the threshold of the danger of servitude" (1998b "Expeditions" §38). The particular "tyrants" to which Nietzsche refers are the instincts that require maximum psychological discipline and authority from us in order to make our freedom possible; Nietzsche's example is Julius Caesar, who according to him, was an exemplar of a type of human in possession of the necessary kind of psychological command and control.

These well-known remarks from *Twilight of the Idols*, while illustrative of Nietzsche's critical engagement with liberalism, are not the first iteration of Nietzsche's concern with the *illiberality* of liberal institutions. His emphasis upon the importance of understanding freedom as something attained in and through a process of struggle had already been explored in an earlier text, *Beyond Good and Evil*. In that text, Nietzsche draws an important

46   *Rebecca Bamford*

distinction between two types of free spirit, on which his thinking about freedom and liberalism in that text is based.

Nietzsche begins by discussing the "philosophers of the future", who, he says, will be "*very* free spirits" – not merely free spirits, but something "more, higher, greater, and fundamentally different" (1998a: §44). In contrast to this first type, Nietzsche then describes a second type of free spirit that is characterized by what he calls "democratic taste", and which he claims is present in Europe and America of that time period (1998a: §44). Nietzsche refers to this second type of free spirit as "*levellers*", as being "unfree and superficial", and as problematically concerned with efforts to promote "equal rights" and "compassion for all suffering" (1998a: §44). A little later on, he characterizes this 'leveller' type as a 'free spirit' commensurate with " 'libre-penseurs', 'liberi pensatori', 'freethinkers' ", and more generally with "honourable advocates of 'modern ideas' " – of all of whom he is critical (1998a: §44).

This leads us to the issue of why Nietzsche affirms the former (nonliberal) type, and why he adopts a highly critical attitude towards the latter (liberal) type. His reasons, similarly to his remarks in *Twilight of the Idols*, are based on his concern with the harmful effects of liberalism upon human growth and development. Nietzsche contrasts the type of society that is envisaged by a 'leveller' with the conditions under which, according to him, the "plant 'human being' has most vigorously grown tall" (1998a: §44). He criticizes the leveller's ideal society as a society based on a "common green pasture of happiness", which fails to promote human growth and development. In contrast, the conditions that have always promoted the most substantial human growth and development are, Nietzsche claims, the *opposite* ones to those that the leveller endorses:

> the precariousness of the plant's situation had first to increase enormously; that its power of invention and disguise (its 'spirit' –) had to become subtle and daring through long periods of pressure and discipline; that its life-will had to be intensified into an unconditional power-will.
>
> (1998a: §44)

Nietzsche suggests we might do better to affirm conditions of precariousness in which we need to struggle. His purpose in contrasting the two types of human in *Beyond Good and Evil* is to illustrate that the first, 'very free', spirit type – the philosopher of the future – has greater potential for growth and development than the democratic 'leveller' type. Like a plant, he considers, a human being becomes most powerful and inventive under challenging conditions such as those of pressure and discipline (1998a: §44). So, Nietzsche is critical of the liberal type, and of adopting a commitment to liberalism, because he argues that establishing institutions which do not help us to engage in struggle via precariousness – and which inhibit risk-taking

Nietzschean perspectives   47

(including intellectual risk-taking) – actually *inhibit* human development and flourishing.

In response to this analysis of the reasoning behind Nietzsche's anti-liberalism, someone might immediately raise the worry that the leveller's ideal 'green pasture' society does not seem particularly problematic, especially when it is compared with Nietzsche's quasi-Spartan alternative proposal in which struggle, pressure, and challenge will form the basis of our lives. Such a life of struggle does not seem intuitively attractive: we have no strong incentive to accept Nietzsche's proposal in preference to the leveller's ideal, other than Nietzsche's assurance that struggle is better for our health and development. In the context of multicultural justice, we can raise the more specific worry that adopting Nietzsche's approach seems merely to promise to add to the burden of injustice that oppressed people already face. Thus adopting a Nietzschean perspective here may seem to do no more than *increase* oppression.

It is important to emphasize that Nietzsche's remarks on health, development, and flourishing are grounded in his understanding of all human beings as biological organisms, in order to provide the basis for an effective counter to these concerns. Nietzsche makes this more apparent when he underlines the connection between human political development and human biological situatedness (1998a: §259). He admits that "[m]utually refraining from wounding each other, from violence, and from exploitation, and setting one's will on the same level as others – these can in a certain crude sense become good habits among individuals, if conditions exist for that (namely, a real similarity in the quality of their power and their estimates of value, as well as their belonging together within a single body)" (1998a: §259). However, as he points out,

> as soon as people wanted to take this principle further and, where possible, establish it as the *basic principle of society*, it would immediately show itself for what it is, as the willed *denial* of life, as the principle of disintegration and decay. Here we must think through to the fundamentals and push away all sentimental weakness: living itself is *essentially* appropriation from and wounding and overpowering strangers and weaker people, oppression, hardness, imposing one's own forms, annexing, and at the very least, in its mildest actions, exploitation – but why should we always use these precise words, which have from ancient times carried the stamp of a slanderous purpose? Even that body in which, as previously mentioned, individuals deal with each other as equals – and that happens in every healthy aristocracy – must itself, if it is a living body and not dying out, do to other bodies all those things which the individuals in it refrain from doing to each other: it will have to be the living will to power, it will seek to grow, grab things around it, pull to itself, and acquire predominance – not because of some morality or immorality, but because it is *alive* and because living *is* simply

48 *Rebecca Bamford*

the will to power. But in no point is the common consciousness of the European more reluctant to be instructed than here. Nowadays people everywhere, even those in scientific disguises, are raving about the coming conditions of society from which "the exploitative character" is to have disappeared: – to my ears that sounds as if people had promised to invent a life which abstained from all organic functions. The "exploitation" is not part of a depraved or incomplete and primitive society: it belongs to the *essential nature* of what is living, as a basic organic function; it is a consequence of the real will to power, which is simply the will to life – Assuming that this is something new as a theory – it is, nonetheless, in reality the *fundamental fact* of all history: we should at least be honest with ourselves to this extent!

(1998a: §259)

One main point to notice in this set of remarks is that organisms that express power, or that engage in contest and struggle, are not fundamentally *immoral* for so doing: Nietzsche thinks that such a claim would be merely sentimental. He focuses on the point that living organisms exploit one another in various ways *because* they are living organisms, and because this is in the nature of living organisms. Nietzsche's particular concern is not with the practices of avoiding exploitation, violence, or wounding one another *per se*, but with establishing such avoidance as "*the basic principle of society*" (1998a: §259). Doing so involves our failing to affirm life, and thus inhibiting the ongoing development and flourishing of living organisms. Thus affirming life requires that we affirm all facets of life, including the exploitative and conflict-oriented ones, as ways of pursuing growth and development via struggle.

Continuing to consider concerns with Nietzsche's critique of liberalism, someone may propose the objection that Nietzsche's approach in *Beyond Good and Evil* §259 is immoral: it is not defensible to exploit anyone. Although Young (2006) shares Nietzsche's concerns with the effects of appealing to liberalism, her account would still remain commensurate with this kind of ethical objection. To counter the objection, Nietzsche's suggestion that exploitation should be counted as a part of the essential nature of living organisms needs to be framed within the context of his broader critical engagement with customary morality, as well as in terms of his broad concern to reconnect the ethical with the value of life. Nietzsche's critical engagement with customary morality in *Dawn*, another important text of the free spirit writings, provides an especially instructive example here.

One of Nietzsche's main critical concerns with customary morality in *Dawn* is the distinctive mood of superstitious fear that it fosters and supports amongst us, both socially and individually. Nietzsche argues that what he characterizes as "inexplicable, indeterminate power" (2011: §9) results in a social mood – of fear – that underpins our obedience to custom and tradition for the sake of others as well as oneself (Bamford 2014b: 62–63).

Nietzschean perspectives 49

To counter the chilling effect that our mood-enforced, fear-based obedience has upon the possibility of critical engagement with the ethical (and indeed with the liberal ethos enmeshed with a commitment to customary morality), Nietzsche encourages exploration of diverse affective responses that may prompt us to explore setting up new customs or traditions; in so doing, this promotes an alternative and more positive mood, which opens up space for new or divergent questions and a broader possible range for human development (2011: §§ 9, 28, 146, 283, 473; Bamford 2014b). And as Nietzsche also acknowledges, experimentation – especially when conducted with attention to the ethical and the affective – may be provisional, and may incorporate errors on our part (2011: §501; Bamford 2015b).

In another of his free spirit writings, *The Gay Science*, Nietzsche follows up on this line of reasoning concerning the ethos of experimentation by developing the claim that pursuing experimentation in ethos is virtuous (Bamford 2015b). This claim follows because pursuing experimentation, especially in a provisional sense, requires of us a particular commitment to honesty in scrutinizing "our experiences as severely as a scientific experiment – hour after hour, day after day" and through our wishing to be our own "experiments and guinea pigs" (1974: §319; Bamford 2015b). In the light of Nietzsche's critical engagement with customary morality, on which the immorality objection is based, we cannot simply deny Nietzsche's claims on the basis that they do not conform to customary morality. At the least, to sustain the immorality concern, an argument would need to be provided concerning why Nietzsche's critical engagement with customary morality is unconvincing or incomplete: simply dismissing Nietzsche's work on this score is not a sufficient response.

To summarize my argument thus far: Nietzsche's critique of liberalism and his affirmation of life allows us to claim: (i) that liberal institutions become a means of entrenchment of illiberalism; (ii) that suspicion of challenging a liberal ethos is connected with a broader problem, namely commitment to customary morality governed by fear – a form of morality that may, along with its conclusions and effects, be subjected to critical challenge; (iii) that on the basis of (i) and (ii), appealing to a liberal ethos or to liberal institutions as effective ways of supporting pluralism in multicultural contexts is not sufficient to ground justice. We need an alternative way to think about what pluralism might mean.

Pluralism as perspectival and dynamic

Previous scholarship has shown that Nietzsche's thinking on social and political matters may be put to work as a resource for democratic theory, even though his own political commitments were not democratic, and he is, as we have seen, suspicious of maintaining a firm commitment to liberalism (Schutte 1993; Hatab 1995; Schrift 2000). Relatedly, Nietzsche's philosophy has been claimed as an important source of support for the project of

50   *Rebecca Bamford*

overcoming the legacy of colonial oppression (Schutte 1995, 2003, 2004; Pugliese 1996). Ofelia Schutte has affirmed that even while Nietzsche's philosophy may not be sufficient in itself to sustain liberation projects, for instance in the context of Latin America or in the context of feminist liberation, she would "not want to take the journey without Nietzsche"; moreover, she claims that Nietzsche's thinking can be necessary in liberatory contexts (2004: 183; see also Bamford 2014a).

Schutte's key claim in this respect is that Nietzsche's thought can work as an important corrective to dualistic or binary thinking (2004: 184). She contends that binary or dualistic thinking puts our reasoning capacities on "automatic pilot", which in turn works to obstruct our reasoning about the politics of liberation; as she points out, historically it is clear that sectors of liberation movements run the risk of turning into self-righteous moral and political forces and that what is needed at such a point is a Nietzschean undermining of absolutes (2004: 183). Hence Schutte claims that Nietzsche's non-binary thinking can help us to work against forms of reasoning that are unhelpful to (and unhealthy for) liberation politics (2004: 184). As Schutte acknowledges, this includes Nietzsche's resistance to conceptualizing knowing along absolute lines, and his replacement of absolute knowing with perspectival knowing.

One of the best known examples of Nietzsche's critical engagement with an absolute approach to truth and knowledge as part of his perspectivism occurs in *On the Genealogy of Morals*. In section 12 of the Third Essay, Nietzsche provides a critical discussion of the "pure will-less, painless, timeless knowing subject", and of the corollary of such a subject, namely the absolute perspective that would be adopted by such a subject with respect to knowing and understanding itself and the world. Here, Nietzsche provides a warning against what he calls the "dangerous old conceptual fable" of the knowing subject who does not experience will, pain, or time (1996b: III, §12). He suggests that our belief in pure reason and absolute knowledge is problematic, because such belief always asks us to do something that we cannot do:

> to imagine an eye which is impossible to imagine, an eye which supposedly looks out in no particular direction, an eye which supposedly either restrains or altogether lacks the active powers of interpretation which first make seeing into seeing something.
>
> (1996b: III, §12)

For Nietzsche, our being asked to imagine such an eye involves that "a nonsense and non-concept is demanded of the eye" (1996b: III, §12); because the perspective in question is not open to an embodied human subject, Nietzsche thinks that it makes no sense to assume that truth and knowledge are timeless, disembodied, and universal (Bamford 2005). Instead of this, we should explore ways in which truth and knowledge are situated and embodied.

In some of his earlier free spirit writings, *Human, All Too Human* and *The Gay Science*, Nietzsche makes some further claims suggesting that knowledge and understanding are tied to human bodies and physical locations. For example, he writes that "we behold all things through the human head and cannot cut off this head" (1996a: §27), and he suggests that "the human intellect cannot avoid seeing itself in its own perspectives, and *only* in these" (1974: §374). While we human beings "cannot look around our own corner", we are, Nietzsche contends, at least "far from the ridiculous immodesty that would be involved in decreeing from our corner that perspectives are only permitted from this corner" (1996a: §374). The shift to an account of truth and knowledge that takes these concepts to be grounded in embodied perspectives involves that the world "*may include infinite interpretations*"; as such, if we value perspectival knowing, then Nietzsche suggests the world becomes "*infinite* for us once again" (1974: §374). This suggests that Nietzsche is committed not only (i) to the physiological or physical constitution of the interpreting perspective, but also (ii) to its relative, ecological, position in the world or the cosmos (Babich 1994: 84).

Katrina Mitcheson has further clarified Nietzsche's perspectival thinking on truth and knowledge by pointing out that for Nietzsche, the incorporation of truth – for instance by one of Nietzsche's very free spirits – is an open-ended practice, in which the truth that is to be incorporated has no fixed presuppositions, and where such free spirits learn about the limits that they create for themselves such that these limits cease to be absolute and eternal (Mitcheson 2015: 139, 153). Nietzsche suggests that there is no "one and only" *scientific method* that by itself leads to knowledge, and that therefore, we can work "experimentally" to pursue knowledge and understanding (2011: §432). As Mitcheson notes, he does not consider forms of inquiry that involve fixed and single methods, or which are so strictly marked out as to inhibit the pursuit of seeing, knowing, and understanding, to be appropriate (2015: 139). This account of perspectival knowing and of truth acquisition as distinctively open-ended provides a helpful framework within which to articulate two main reasons as to why Nietzsche's perspectivism can support a non-liberal form of pluralism.

First, Nietzsche's perspectivism opens up methodological space in which to experimentally pursue and incorporate new knowledge and understanding of oneself and the world, specifically including diverse cultures and associated values. Western philosophy has labored under the assumption that a commitment to knowing must incorporate a commitment to universalism. As Tamba Ndlandu has pointed out, affirming the universality of fundamental questions of human experience does not automatically entail affirming a universalist approach to human attempts to answer such questions; we can affirm the former while replacing the latter with acknowledgement of pluralism and fallibilism in such attempts (2001: 91). This grounds the necessary space for open-ended, experimental pursuit of knowledge and

52   Rebecca Bamford

understanding that is commensurate with incorporation and integration of multicultural perspectives.

Second, the account of incorporation of truth as open-ended helps us to clarify how Nietzsche's thinking on identity, in combination with his emphasis on experimentation, facilitates productive self-development. To follow up on this claim, we may begin by noting that Linda Martín Alcoff (2000) has pointed out an important concern with liberalism in multicultural contexts, namely that liberalism does not clearly address injustices that are tied to mixed identities. This includes cases in which a person's attachments to two or more races or cultures may involve far stronger attachments than those the person may have to, say, her national origin/s. Alcoff provides a particularly eloquent and powerful example of what it means for someone to experience living a mixed identity:

> I never wholly occupy the Angla or the Latina identity. Paradoxically, in white society I feel my Latinness, in Latin society I feel my whiteness, as that which is left out, an invisible present, sometimes as intrusive as an elephant in the room and sometimes more as a pulled thread that alters the design of my fabricated self.
>
> (2000: 160)

As Alcoff points out, while an ambiguous or mixed self should, for justice reasons, never be understood as intrinsically problematic, it remains the case that such a self may be perceived as pathological precisely because of its ambiguity. Moreover, Alcoff shows that the liberal focus on respecting and appreciating diversity may lead us, however unwittingly, into more problematic behaviors, such as commodifying, fetishizing, and fossilizing indigenous cultures and peoples (2000). In contrast to this pathological understanding of a *mestizo* or mixed identity, Alcoff explores the possibility of a positive account of mixed identity that may enable us to pursue what she terms "transformative" notions of identity and of multiculturalism.

Alcoff's concern with identity pluralism and her efforts to pursue transformative identities incorporate some limited attention to Nietzsche (Alcoff 2004); however, she does not make use of Nietzsche's thought as a significant resource. Yet Alcoff's work on identity might, I think, be fruitfully combined with Nietzsche's thinking on subjectivity to address the issue of how transformation of our notion of identity may take place. It is important to note that Alcoff herself adopts a highly skeptical approach with regard to the question of Nietzsche's utility as a resource for liberation politics (Alcoff 2004). For instance, responding to Schutte's affirmation of Nietzsche's utility for such purposes, Alcoff has expressed concern as to whether liberation could plausibly be achieved through the use of decontextualized tools such as Nietzschean thinking, and with regard to whether or not Nietzsche's taboo breaking and his anti-binary thinking is indeed always liberatory (Alcoff 2004: 151).

Following Schutte, and as I have suggested elsewhere, Nietzsche's advantage in response to Alcoff's concerns lies in the pragmatic dimension of his thinking on freedom: Alcoff's concern incorporates the kind of binary value hierarchy (for example: good/bad, liberatory/anti-liberatory) that Nietzsche's own thinking aims to resist (Schutte 2004; Bamford 2014a). This resistance is also true for Nietzsche's thinking on subjectivity. Open-ended experimentation, which Nietzsche explores and affirms in *Dawn*, for example, emphasizes development through self-cultivation: Nietzsche proposes that human instincts can be cultivated and developed in ways that promote health and virtue (2011: §248) in the same way that we cultivate healthy gardens (Bamford 2015a). Nietzsche contends that thinking of the subject as developmental helps us imagine one way in which free spirits might continuially develop towards a new or 'great health' that, he thinks, one "does not merely have but acquires continually" (1974: §382). One particularly relevant aspect of Nietzsche's thinking on subjectivity in *Dawn* (2011) occurs in aphorism §560. There, Nietzsche identifies our mistaken belief that our characters are complete, fully developed, and unchangeable 'facts'. He suggests that our mistaken belief in character fixity has been further reinforced by the work of presumptuous philosophers. If we believe our characters are fixed, then we remain unaware of our needs, of problems that may be blighting our lives, or even that there is a possibility of our pursuing meaningful change and development (Bamford 2015a).

As an alternative to the view that characters or selves are fixed entities, Nietzsche proposes that subjects are both dynamic (by virtue of change and development) and plural (by virtue of dependence on diverse experiences for development). For example, in a well-known aphorism in *Dawn*, Nietzsche uses the example of the polyp (a hydra) to ground a detailed analysis of how our self-knowledge is necessarily incomplete because of our partial knowledge of drives (2011: §119). As he claims, the "polyp-arms" of our being flourish or wither "depending on the nourishment that the moment does or does not supply" (2011: §119). Our experiences are all types of nourishment for the Nietzschean subject: however, as Nietzsche also points out, experiences are "seeds" sown without attention to existing hunger or abundance for nutrition (2011: §119).

Owing to what Nietzsche calls "contingent alimentation of the parts", the Nietzschean subject is contingent (2011: §119). Christine Daigle clarifies this subject's contingency when she discusses how Nietzschean subjects constitute themselves through their encounters with the world and as intentional consciousnesses, are constituted by that world (2015: 37). For Daigle, the Nietzschean subject is a "worldly being" because the world is filled with objects, and subjective consciousness of such objects enables consciousness to become what it is (2015: 37). The becoming of a Nietzschean subject is continuous, and at the same time the self-knowledge of the Nietzschean subject is continuously partial and incomplete because of the role that is played by psychophysical drives in producing the subject as a worldly being.

54 Rebecca Bamford

One further relevant dimension should be added to this account, following work by Carl B. Sachs: Nietzschean subjects are never *merely* a bundle of drives and affects, but should rather be understood as interpreted and interpreting drives and affects (2008: 94–95). Sachs differentiates between heteronomous subjectivity, where the subject is organized through procedures and techniques such as authority and tradition that are external to it, and autonomous subjectivity, which he defines as a continual work in progress (2008: 94–95). Rather than think of Nietzsche presenting us with a choice of accounts of the self in *Dawn* – either a 'self'-less composite of multiple drives or self as a unity of consciousness – it may be more useful to think of the self in both senses (Bamford 2015a). In other words, we can think of selves as plural by virtue of their ongoing development, as well as what Daigle (2015) accounts for as their worldliness. If we did so, we could commit to cultivating drives through nourishment and experience of thought and feeling, while acknowledging that the self can also be produced by structural, social, or material conditions without necessarily always being aware of this (2011: §120). Even when we acknowledge the worldliness of selves, Nietzschean subjects remain dynamic products-in-motion – albeit sometimes slow motion (2011: §148; Bamford 2015a).

Advantages of a Nietzschean approach for multiculturalism

Attending to work on the politics of recognition may help us to see why Nietzsche's thinking on the subject, in combination with his perspectivism, can sustain the kind of pluralism needed to sustain justice in multicultural contexts. In an analysis of the politics of recognition, Robert Gooding-Williams has directed our attention to the importance of self-recognition, which he defines as "seeing one's cultural identity in connection to the cultural identities of other members of one's community", in understanding cultural identity (1998: 36). If we pursue socially mediated self-recognition, as Gooding-Williams advocates, then there is a heightened possibility of bringing culturally hybrid or mixed selves, and others, into closer understanding with one another. As Gooding-Williams argues, this process of recognition may involve changing our own views of ourselves as well as coming to understand that our view may be closer to those of others than perhaps we initially imagined (1998: 36). Nietzsche's perspectival approach to truth and knowledge shifts our way of knowing from an absolute approach that fossilizes and fetishizes a universal approach to a plural way of knowing that incorporates diverse and sometimes conflicting perspectives (Hatab 1995; Nlandu 2001). At the same time, Nietzschean subjectivity provides the necessary cognitive framework for the developmental aspect of the process of recognition that Gooding-Williams explores. Because when taken in combination with his perspectivism, Nietzsche's thinking on subjectivity can be understood as dynamically plural, Nietzsche's thinking allows us to understand how Gooding-Williams's proposal might work in practice. Selves may understand through and learn from the incorporation of perspectival truth and knowledge, while remaining capable of ongoing development by virtue of their dynamic and changing natures.

To support this, we can note that Nietzsche's dance metaphor allows us to gain a better grasp of a conception of political identity that is opened up by this Nietzschean account (Bamford 2007). It is important to keep in mind that for Nietzsche, a metaphor is a practical tool that can be used to open up intellectual space in which to reconsider our commonly held notions and values both externally to oneself and with respect to one's own commitments: broadly, in his writing Nietzsche uses dance as a metaphor for positive cultural change and development, as well as for flexibility in intellectual and philosophical matters (Bamford 2007). For instance, he discusses how "*dancing* is not the same thing as staggering wearily back and forth between different impulses" and claims that a truly high culture – which is something for which we strive – will resemble a "daring dance" that requires strength and flexibility (*HA*, §278). Nietzsche's dance metaphor makes it possible for us to cultivate our "own earth" by affirming life and by creating one's own values (Madelon-Wienand 1998). For example, Nietzsche's Zarathustra is described as a dancer by virtue of Zarathustra's persistence in finding no objection to existence (2007, 'Thus Spoke Zarathustra', §6; Bamford 2007).

Nietzsche's concept of constitutional flexibility can further illuminate the health-promoting dimension of Nietzsche's thinking on illiberal pluralism, and can be usefully combined with his dance metaphor to mitigate against some of the injustices faced by mixed identities in multicultural contexts (Bamford 2007). As mentioned above, Nietzsche's critical engagement with liberalism in *Twilight of the Idols* means that for him, freedom should be measured – both for individuals and nations – by "the resistance which must be overcome, the effort it costs to stay *on top*" (1998b: IX, §38). This is because the highest type of free individual is found in places where the greatest resistance is constantly being overcome and where great danger forces recognition of virtues and strengths (1998b: IX, §38). Pessimistic strength is the strength that characterizes this kind of freedom, and the strength which Nietzsche deems worthy of respect. Such pessimistic strength is a sign of tremendous constitutional flexibility.

Nietzsche's concept of great health is tied directly to his idea of constitutional flexibility: as he describes it in *The Gay Science*, this is "the ideal of a human, superhuman well-being and benevolence that will often appear *inhuman*" (1974: §382). Great health involves playing "naively" and from a position of "overflowing power and abundance" with everything that we formerly used to call "holy, good, untouchable, divine" (1974: §382; Bamford 2007). A constitutionally flexible individual can engage in a process of value-creation, as well as in a process of drawing on and engaging with their attachments to cultures, races and ethnicities, and languages in positive and life-affirming ways. Constitutional flexibility, then, is a useful way to describe how political identities can understand themselves and their

56   *Rebecca Bamford*

attachments to particular values or cultures as positive and coherent, while also doing justice to the diverse and sometimes conflicting components of themselves, as well as to their sense of themselves as subjects of change.

Nietzsche's constitutionally flexible account of self, and the constitutionally flexible self's own subjective sense of itself, may be likened to the figure of a dancer (Bamford 2007). Nietzsche explicitly ties his dance metaphor to the exercise of critical reflection, including by philosophers. For instance, Nietzsche indicates that a good dancer desires "the greatest possible suppleness and strength" and claims he does not know "what the spirit of a philosopher might wish more to be than a good dancer" (1974: §381). As he contends, for a free-spirited philosopher, dancing is an ideal, the highest form of art, and the philosopher's only "piety" (1974: §381). Nietzsche argues that thinking needs to be learned "*as* a kind of dancing . . . you cannot subtract every form of *dancing* from *noble education*, the ability to dance with the feet, with concepts, with words" (1998b: VIII, §7). If thinking about oneself and one's political identity on this account is a kind of dancing, then we can move to understand Nietzschean subjectivity and its political dimensions as a lifelong project of continuous development, growth, self-cultivation, and self-care in which subjects, and their subjective senses of themselves as well as their political identities, are constantly in motion.

There are some distinct advantages to thinking of selves, and the relationship of selves to themselves and others in multicultural contexts, using Nietzschean resources. First, doing so helps to make it clearer why people with mixed identities who live in multicultural contexts do not need to be burdened with the sense that they are pathological by virtue of their ambiguity to themselves and to others. Ambiguity or diversity is no longer treated as a negative on a Nietzschean account. If a healthy self is not considered to be fixed and stable but is rather taken to be plural and dynamic, open to changes of attachment and value, and concerned with the healthy development of itself and others, then mixed identities may consider themselves to be already healthy. Mixed identities would no longer be incoherent, or problematically ambiguous, or pathological: they may see their competing and diverse attachments, and their work to navigate these, as positive and life affirming. A mixed identity's sense of self can, on a Nietzschean account, be healthy *by virtue* of its dynamic pluralism.

Second, the same argument also carries important consequences for people whose conception of themselves is framed in terms of attachment to a single cultural group (Gutmann 1993). So-called 'pure' identities may also be fossilized and fetishized, to use the terminology provided by Alcoff in her account of mixed identity (2000), by themselves as well as by others. A person of non-mixed identity who is living in a multicultural context may have a relationship with herself that is unhealthy, because she understands her own identity in insufficiently plural terms. For instance, such a person may think that by virtue of her strong attachment to a single cultural group, she cannot explore or develop new attachments to people or to values from other cultural groups within her geographical location. This kind of self-limiting behavior may quickly turn into a problematic stereotyping of oneself or others, and may support an understanding of oneself or others as committed to performing or perpetuating forms of injustice against other individuals or groups within a multicultural community.

If this is right, then the advantages of Nietzschean thinking with respect to identity in multicultural contexts may indeed prove to be significant. We could move to a new way thinking about identity, in which *everyone's* identity could be viewed as dynamic and plural. Doing so would enable people with strong attachments to only one culture, as well as people of diverse mixed identities, to develop and sustain more positive and healthy ways of understanding themselves and of relating to others within their communities. Moreover, this would support ongoing efforts by governments, institutions, and non-governmental organizations to combat racism, xenophobia, and other forms of injustice arising within multicultural communities by opening up the possibility of developing and incorporating new and different, health-promoting, values. While conflicts between different cultural values would not be eliminated, the process of recognizing and navigating such conflicts could be rendered commensurate with the broader aims of political liberation projects if we retain (i) the commitment to truth and knowledge as perspectival and the process of incorporating truth as open-ended, and (ii) understanding all identities as plural and dynamic.

Those who are less familiar with Nietzsche's philosophy might initially worry that his work seems like an unwise or unlikely choice of philosophical resource with which to engage in the project of thinking critically about multiculturalism, especially if this task is conceived as part of pursuing justice within and across regional, national, and global multicultural communities. Moreover, we must acknowledge some of Nietzsche's own thinking on social and political issues does incorporate sexist, racist, and colonialist commitments (e.g., Acampora 2006; Bamford 2014a). Because of these problematic commitments, and because forms of oppression and their consequences – both historical and contemporary – continue to shape and direct the lives of so many people, it is right that we should adopt a cautious attitude with respect to how we read the history of philosophy and to how we put the history of the discipline to work in contemporary ethical and political contexts.

However, in response to such concerns, and to echo previous calls for pragmatism in our assessment of Nietzsche's philosophy, appropriate caution with respect to the oppressive dimensions of the history of philosophy should not be taken to an extreme, in which all engagement with potentially highly useful critical tools from this history is curtailed (Hatab 1995; Schutte 2004). At a minimum, we can affirm that it is defensible to continue to look in detail at Nietzsche's philosophy to see whether we can find conceptual tools in his writing that are helpful to the task of pursuing an account of multicultural justice. I have made a stronger and more specific claim in my discussion in this essay: Nietzsche's philosophy provides our

58 *Rebecca Bamford*

ongoing discussion of multiculturalism and of justice in multicultural contexts with some helpful resources, specifically a conception of pluralism in which the perspectives from which truth and knowledge are arrived at are integrated with a developmental and dynamic conception of self.

Conclusion

As I have suggested, Nietzsche's writing makes it clearer why simple appeals to liberalism are not sufficient to ground the kind of pluralism that is necessary for justice within multicultural contexts. If we accept Nietzsche's view that the task of philosophy is to be concerned with promotion of human health and flourishing, and that such flourishing involves the conditions of contest and struggle, then liberalism may prove to be harmful to pursuit of our health and flourishing. By offering a critique of liberalism and a broader account of truth and knowledge as perspectival that aim to support human health and flourishing, Nietzsche's work enables us to pursue more nuanced ways in which to think about pluralism, especially in multicultural contexts. Instead of pluralism as a fixed range of possible perspectives or identities that may further entrench injustices, Nietzsche opens up ways for us to understand pluralism as dynamic and open-ended: the range of possible perspectives is not finite, and our sense of ourselves – whatever our cultural and value attachments – can be fluid and developmental.

While I have argued that Nietzschean pluralism can be helpful to pursuit of multicultural justice, more research still remains to be done in order to establish the kind of contributions that Nietzschean perspectives may open up for enhancing our understanding of multiculturalism. Future investigations might, first, expand on the ways in which Nietzschean resources may provide pragmatic support for developing positive affirmations of mixed identities within specific multicultural contexts. In particular, the question of whether adopting a Nietzschean approach would place an excessive burden on people already dealing with oppression requires further attention. Second, such investigations might explore in greater depth the extent to which Nietzsche's own thinking on issues of justice is commensurate with the concept of dynamic pluralism that I have discussed here. Third, such investigations might explore the potential for dynamic pluralism to contribute to analysis of epistemic injustice (Fricker 2007). Meantime, I think we may affirm the value of Nietzsche's perspectivism – and his thinking on subjectivity and identity – as important resources for grounding the kind of pluralism that is required to sustain multicultural justice.

Bibliography

Acampora, C. D. (2006) 'Unlikely Illuminations: Nietzsche and Frederick Douglass on Power, Struggle, and the *Aisthesis* of Freedom', in J. Scott and A. T. Franklin (eds.) *Critical Affinities: Nietzsche and African-American Thought*, Albany: State University of New York Press, 175–202.

Acampora, C. D. and Ansell-Pearson, K. (2011) *Nietzsche's 'Beyond Good and Evil': A Reader's Guide*, London: Bloomsbury.

Alcoff, L. M. 2000 (1995) 'Mestizo Identity', in R. Bernasconi and T. Lott (eds.) *The Idea of Race*, Indianapolis: Hackett, 139–160.

Alcoff, L. M. (2004) 'Schutte's Nietzschean Postcolonial Politics', *Hypatia* 19(3): 144–156.

Alcoff, L. M. (2006) *Visible Identities: Race, Gender and the Self*, Oxford: Oxford University Press.

Anker, E. S. (2014) *Orgies of Feeling: Melodrama and the Politics of Freedom*, Durham: Duke University Press.

Babich, B. E. (1994) *Nietzsche's Philosophy of Science: Reflecting Science on the Ground of Art and Life*, Albany: State University of New York Press.

Bamford, R. (2005) 'Nietzsche, Science, and Philosophical Nihilism', *South African Journal of Philosophy* 24(4): 241–259.

Bamford, R. (2007) 'Nietzsche and *Ubuntu*', *South African Journal of Philosophy* 26(1): 85–97.

Bamford, R. (2014a) 'The Liberatory Limits of Nietzsche's Colonial Imagination in *Dawn* 206', in B. Stocker and M. Knoll (eds.) *Nietzsche as Political Philosopher*, Berlin: Walter de Gruyter, 59–76.

Bamford, R. (2014b) 'Mood and Aphorism in Nietzsche's Campaign Against Morality', *Pli: The Warwick Journal of Philosophy* 25: 55–76.

Bamford, R. (2015a) 'Health and Self-Cultivation in *Dawn*', in Rebecca Bamford (ed.) *Nietzsche's Free Spirit Philosophy*, London: Rowman and Littlefield International, 85–109.

Bamford, R. (2015b) 'The Ethos of Inquiry: Nietzsche on Experience, Naturalism, and Experimentalism', *Journal of Nietzsche Studies* 46(3).

Brown, K. (2006) *Nietzsche and Embodiment: Discerning Bodies and Non-dualism*, Albany: State University of New York Press.

Brown, W. (1995) *States of Injury: Power and Freedom in Late Modernity*, Princeton: Princeton University Press.

Connolly, W. E. (2002) *Neuropolitics*, Minneapolis: University of Minnesota Press.

Daigle, C. (2015) 'The Ethical Ideal of the Free Spirit in *Human*', in Rebecca Bamford (ed.) *All Too Human*, in *Nietzsche's Free Spirit Philosophy*, London: Rowman & Littlefield International, 33–48.

Di Martino, C. 2014 (2008) 'The Encounter and Emergence of Human Nature', in A. López and J. Prades (eds.), trans. Mariangela Sullivan, *Retrieving Origins and the Claim of Multiculturalism*, Grand Rapids and Cambridge: William B. Eerdmans Publishing Company.

Fricker, M. (2007) *Epistemic Injustice: Power and the Ethics of Knowing*, Oxford: Oxford University Press.

Gooding-Williams, R. (1998) 'Race, Multiculturalism, Democracy', *Constellations* 5(1): 18–41.

Gutmann, A. (1993) 'The Challenge of Multiculturalism in Political Ethics', *Philosophy & Public Affairs* 22(3): 171–206.

Hatab, L. (1995) *A Nietzschean Defense of Democracy: An Experiment in Postmodern Politics*, Chicago and La Salle: Open Court.

Madelon-Wienand, I. (1998) 'Remarks about the Nietzschean Dancing God', *South African Journal of Philosophy* 17(3): 301–312.

60 *Rebecca Bamford*

Mitcheson, K. (2015) 'The Experiment of Incorporating Unbounded Truth', in Rebecca Bamford (ed.) *Nietzsche's Free Spirit Philosophy*, London: Rowman and Littlefield International, 139–156.

Nietzsche, F. (1974) *The Gay Science. With a Prelude in Rhymes and an Appendix of Songs*, trans. Walter Kaufmann, New York: Vintage Books.

Nietzsche, F. (1996a) *Human, All Too Human: A Book for Free Spirits*, trans. R. J. Hollingdale, Cambridge: Cambridge University Press.

Nietzsche, F. (1996b) *On the Genealogy of Morals*, trans. Douglas Smith, Oxford: Oxford University Press.

Nietzsche, F. (1998a) *Beyond Good and Evil*, trans. Marion Faber, Oxford: Oxford University Press.

Nietzsche, F. (1998b) *Twilight of the Idols*, trans. Duncan Large, Oxford: Oxford University Press.

Nietzsche, F. (2007) *Ecce Homo: How to Become What You Are*, trans. Duncan Large, Oxford and New York: Oxford University Press.

Nietzsche, F. (2011) *Dawn: Thoughts on the Presumptions of Morality*, trans. Brittain Smith, Stanford: Stanford University Press.

Nlandu, T. (2001) 'The Fallacy of Universalism: The Nature and Status of African Philosophy Revisited', *International Studies in Philosophy* 33(1): 83–104.

Owen, D. (2008) 'Pluralism and the Pathos of Distance (or How to Relax with Style): Connolly, Agonistic Respect and the Limits of Political Theory', *British Journal of Politics and International Relations* 10(2): 210–226.

Pugliese, J. (1996) 'Rationalized Violence and Legal Colonialism: Nietzsche "contra" Nietzsche', *Cardozo Studies in Law and Literature* 8(2): 277–293.

Sachs, C. B. (2008) 'Nietzsche's *Daybreak*: Toward a Naturalized Theory of Autonomy', *Epoché* 13(1): 81–100.

Schmidt, W. E. (1992) 'European Unity: Reaffirming Respect for Diversity', *New York Times*, 18 October. Available at http://www.nytimes.com (Accessed 18 October 1992).

Schrift, A. (2000) 'Nietzsche for Democracy?' *Nietzsche-Studien* 29: 220–233.

Schutte, O. (1984) *Beyond Nihilism: Nietzsche Without Masks*, Chicago: University of Chicago Press.

Schutte, O. (1993) *Cultural Identity and Social Liberation in Latin American Thought*, Albany: State University of New York Press.

Schutte, O. (2000) 'Continental Philosophy and Postcolonial Subjects', *Philosophy Today* 44 (SPEP Supplement): 8–17.

Schutte, O. (2004) 'Response to Alcoff, Ferguson, and Bergoffen', *Hypatia* 19(3): 182–202.

Wolf, S. (1994) 'Comment', in Amy Gutmann (ed.) *Multiculturalism: Examining the Politics of Recognition*, Princeton: Princeton University Press, 75–86.

Young, I. M. 2011 (1990) *Justice and the Politics of Difference*, Princeton: Princeton University Press.

Section 2

Multiculturalism and Western contemporary political theory

4 Anarchism and multiculturalism

Uri Gordon

This chapter examines anarchist approaches to ethno-cultural difference,[1] offering three main arguments. The first is that anarchists were early and consistent opponents of racism and imperialism, both in advanced capitalist countries and in the colonial and post-colonial world, reflecting the movement's transnational connections and internationalist outlook. While anarchists remain at the front lines of anti-racist and anti-colonial politics worldwide, the universalist terms in which their predecessors constructed their cosmopolitanism have come into question, as anarchists increasingly express intersectionalist critiques of domination with distinct post-colonial and poststructuralist resonances. The second argument is that anarchists share the wider radical Left critique of multicultural policies, which obscure systemic racial and class inequality while promoting monolithic and elite-driven representations of minorities. Anarchists may also conceptualise multiculturalism as a specific case of the state's general manner of upholding forms of domination by ameliorating their worst excesses in response to resistance. Thirdly, I argue that in order to offer a revolutionary alternative to state multiculturalism, anarchists should further develop their engagement with radical decolonial approaches. These place systemic racism at the centre of social critique, and in the context of past and present dispossession of peoples from land through military occupation, economic dominance, slavery, ethnic cleansing and genocide. Theoretically, this approach integrates critiques of racialisation and capitalism without recourse to essentialism or class reductionism. Ethically, it places the onus on white activists to offer active solidarity to struggles against racism and colonialism, while deconstructing their own privileged identities and behaviours.

A preliminary word on anarchism: I use the term to refer to a global network of activist groups, with their political cultures and discourses, which actively resist all forms of domination in society through means that already embody a non-hierarchical alternative (Gordon 2007, 2008; Amster 2012; Kinna 2012; Shantz 2013). Anarchist critique typically views societies as inherently constituted by systemic and intersecting regimes of domination along lines of ability, age, class, gender, race, sexuality and species. Anarchists think these regimes cannot be transformed through legal or policy

64   Uri Gordon

measures, requiring instead revolutionary change in the basic structures of society. This means challenging, eroding and eventually abolishing all institutions that promote and underwrite regimes of domination – including the state, capitalist and feudal systems of production, and hierarchical variants of family, educational and religious institutions. Anarchism promotes direct action in any given struggle; that is, action without intermediaries, which seeks to directly achieve and defend goals rather than issue demands to established authorities (and thus legitimate them). This could include the use of disruptive means such as blockades, tree-sits, sabotage and street confrontation but also – just as importantly – the constructive task of creating "a new society within the shell of the old" through self-organised communes and cooperatives, practical sustainability initiatives, grassroots transport and energy alternatives, public art practices and more.

In view of the decolonial perspectives discussed later in this chapter, I should also be upfront about my own position as an individual who benefits from a host of privileges: able-bodied, cis-male, educated, hetero and white Jewish Israeli. In consequence, I should not only take special care to question any assumptions and arguments that might self-servingly legitimate my privilege, but also be aware of my limited ability to speak to the struggles of those who lack any or all of these. That said, the overwhelming whiteness of radical movements in advanced capitalist countries means that at least in this respect my positionality is not unrepresentative. As a result, the critical reflections offered here may be relevant to a wider audience.

Ethno-cultural diversity in the anarchist tradition

There are many engagements with topics akin to multiculturalism in 19th and early 20th century anarchist literature, albeit usually in terms of "nations", "nationalities" or "peoples". The prevalent distinction made in this context was the one between "the nation" as an artificial entity constructed by the state and "peoples" as factual entities based on common geographical, linguistic and ancestral features. Rudolf Rocker argued that nationalism had replaced religion as the chief ideological tool of legitimation for the ruling classes. In *Nationalism and Culture* he wrote that "the nation is not the cause, but the result of the state. It is the state that creates the nation, not the nation the state", whereas a "people" is "the natural result of social union, a mutual association of men brought about by a certain similarity of external conditions of living, a common language, and special characteristics due to climate and geographic environment" (Rocker 1938: 200–201).

Kropotkin had taken a similar view in his article on rising Finnish nationalism, emphasising alongside heritage and language the role of "union between the people and the territory it occupies, from which territory it receives its national character and on which it impresses its own stamp, so as to make an indivisible whole both men and territory" (Kropotkin 1885).

Anarchism and multiculturalism   65

Rocker's naturalism in this regard was far more circumscribed – he clarifies that peoples can only be spoken of in place- and time-specific terms, since "cultural reconstructions and social stimulation always occur when different peoples and races come into closer union. Every new culture is begun by such a fusion of different folk elements and takes its special shape from this" (op. cit. 346).

Anarchists thus universally opposed the nationalism promoted by existing states, which instils in the workers a false sense of common identity and interest with their exploiters (Cahm 1978). At the same time, they could celebrate the diversity of culture and language among the world's different peoples. In the words of Gustav Landauer:

> I am happy about every imponderable and ineffable thing that brings about exclusive bonds, unities, and also differentiations within humanity. If I want to transform patriotism then I do not proceed in the slightest against the fine fact of the nation . . . but against the mixing up of the nation and the state, against the confusion of differentiation and opposition.
>
> (Landauer 1973/1910: 263; cf. Landauer 1907)

More recently, Murray Bookchin (1994) wrote:

> That specific peoples should be free to fully develop their own cultural capacities is not merely a right but a desideratum. The world will be a drab place indeed if a magnificent mosaic of different cultures do not replace the largely deculturated and homogenized world created by modern capitalism. But by the same token, the world will be completely divided and peoples will be chronically at odds with one another if their cultural differences are parochialized and if seeming "cultural differences" are rooted in biologistic notions of gender, racial, and physical superiority.

The internationalist and cosmopolitan approach taken by anarchists was only to be expected, in view of the movement's own composition. The commonplace Eurocentric view of anarchism notwithstanding, it developed from the start as a transnational network, marked by "supranational connections and multidirectional flows of . . . ideas, people, finances and organisational structures" (Hirsch and van der Walt 2011: xxxii). Anarchists were active in Argentina, Cuba and Egypt as early as the 1870s, while the first two decades of the 20th century saw sophisticated anarchist movements emerge from the Philippines, Peru and Japan to South Africa, Chile and Turkey. Transnational networks among these movements "were often built upon migratory diasporas and were reinforced by the movement's press and the travels of major activists" as well as international campaigns (op. cit.; cf. Turcato 2007; Khuri-Makdisi 2010; Ramnath 2011; Bantman 2013). In Britain and

66   Uri Gordon

North America, the influx of Jewish, Italian and Irish immigrants in the late 19th and early 20th century created multicultural working class communities in which a radical cosmopolitan outlook took hold, embracing diversity and solidarity across ethnic and cultural lines (cf. Fishman 1975; Katz 2011; Zimmer 2015).

Numerous anarchists vocally opposed American slavery and segregation. Joseph Déjacque, an early French anarchist active for several years in New Orleans, looked forward to a revolutionary alliance between black slaves and white proletarians, and favourably compared John Brown to Spartacus. He expected that the "monstrous American Union, the fossil Republic, will disappear" in the cataclysm of revolution, creating a "Social Republic" wherein "Blacks and whites, creoles and redskins will fraternize . . . and will found one single race. The killers of Negros and proletarians, the amphibians of liberalism and the carnivores of privilege will withdraw like the caymans . . . to the most remote parts of the bayous" (Déjacque 1858/2013). Kropotkin too declared, "All my sympathies lie with the blacks in America", whom despite emancipation he continued to consider as a people under occupation, on par with "the Armenians in Turkey, the Finns and Poles in Russia, etc." (Kropotkin 1897/2014: 140). During the height of lynching murders in the South, the anarchist James F. Morton wrote an extensive pamphlet against racism and its use to dehumanise and justify atrocities. "The blind stupidity of racial prejudice is simply unfathomable", he wrote, "it acts in mad disregard of all logical considerations, and when challenged can give no coherent account of itself . . . it stops its ears in blind rage" (Morton 1906: 31; cf. Damiani 1939).

Jean Grave was perhaps the most eloquent among the many outspoken anarchist critics of colonialism. As part of his wider critique of social hierarchy, and especially of nationalism and militarism, Grave disparaged both the irrationality of notions of racial and cultural superiority and their insidious role in causing workers to legitimate their own exploitation. In *Moribund Society and Anarchy*, he strongly condemned colonisation as robbery and murder writ large, poured derision on its claims to be a "civilising" force and supported the revolts of colonised peoples. In a chapter titled "There are no inferior races", he repudiates a series of then-common arguments about the inferiority of non-Europeans and draws a parallel between racism and the self-serving bourgeois designation of the poor as inherently inferior. Although he did not question the prevailing view of technological sophistication and social complexity as marks of a higher stage of development, Grave argued that colonialism stymied this development in peoples – rather than being justified by its impossibility.

> By what right do we speak of the inferiority of other races when their present condition proceeds from our barbarous persecutions? . . . the aboriginal civilizations which were developing at the time of the European conquests were destroyed by their invaders. . . . Highly flourishing

civilizations thus disappeared, no one knowing what they might have brought forth. . . . Certainly we do not want to assert that all races are absolutely identical; but we are persuaded that all have certain aptitudes, certain moral, intellectual, and physical qualities, which, had they been allowed to evolve freely, would have enabled them to take their part in the labor of human civilization.

(Grave 1899: 105–110; cf. Porter)

Anarchists' responses to national liberation movements were less univocal. Some, like Kropotkin, saw national liberation movements positively, arguing that the removal of foreign domination was a precondition to social revolution (Grauer 1994). On the other hand, anarchists such as Proudhon and Bakunin opposed the elite-led national liberation agendas of their day, such as the Polish national movement. In the 20th century, anarchists distanced themselves from Marxists' often uncritical championing of oppressive regimes in former colonies in Africa and south Asia instrumental, and from their instrumental support for new centralised nation states that would fulfil the program of capitalist development (cf. Bonanno 1976). During the Algerian independence war, French anarchists engaged in heated debate around its various aspects. According to Porter (2011: 487),

> some French anarchists, like Camus, Joyeux, Guerin, and those in *Noir et Rouge*, openly criticized actions and orientations of the FLN while also supporting the principle of ending colonial rule. Guerin, *Noir et Rouge*, and *Tribune Anarchiste Communiste* publicized, supported, and also offered detailed critiques of Algerian *autogestion* ["self-organisation", U. G.] to an extent not easily found elsewhere at the time in the French left, let alone in the mainstream press. While the Berber Spring and urban upheavals of the 1980s received some coverage elsewhere, the particular anarchist emphasis on the anti-authoritarian content of these developments was rather unique.

More recently, Hakim Bey saw revolutionary potential in nationalism's collision with neoliberal capitalism, inasmuch as "the nation as zone of resistance" could "launch its revolt . . . from the left (as 'non-hegemonic particularity')" rather than from the right. Thus a secession movement would deserve anarchists' support "to the extent that it does not seek power at the expense of others' misery. No State can ever achieve this ideal – but some 'national struggles' can be considered objectively revolutionary provided they meet basic minimal requirements – i.e. that they be both non-hegemonic & anti-Capitalist". His tentative candidates for this category include Kurdish, Sahrawi, Hawaiian and Puerto Rican independence movements, movements seeking "maximum autonomy for Native-american 'nations'", the Mexican Zapatistas, and "at least in theory the bioregionalist movement in the US" (Bey 1996: 49).

68   *Uri Gordon*

Most of the historical anarchist approaches to nationalism were grounded in a universalist ethics of humanism and rationalism. While positively encouraging cultural diversity, they sought a continuum leading from the individual through the ethno-cultural group and on to the entire human species. This amounts to a "belief in the shared humanity of people regardless of their membership in different cultural, ethnic, and gender groups, and their complementary affinities in a free society as rational human beings" (Bookchin, op. cit.). The commitment to universalism occasionally involved wishful thinking about the eventual intermingling of all peoples into a single humanity – explicitly in the above quote from Déjacque, as well as in the work of Jean Grave, who was convinced that "races are bound to disappear by fusing, missing with each other through intercrossings; that is the very reason we are choked with indignation at seeing entire tribes disappear before they have been able to contribute to our civilization the original share which they may have potentially possess" (op. cit. 110).

Yet the appeal to universalism has become increasingly problematic, as anarchists come to emphasise post-modern and post-colonial critiques of humanism and universality (cf. Newman 2007; Jun 2012). For American anarchist of colour Roger White,

> European universalism has never truly been about the recognition of our common humanity. In practice it's been about forcing the particular norms, prejudices and ideals of white, Christian cultures on the rest of the peoples of the earth, sometimes through economic domination, sometimes through cultural imperialism, sometimes through force. . . . For left internationalists, universalism provided a nice humanitarian cover for a massive social engineering project that sought to strip the masses of their national and communal identities in exchange for a workerist one.
>
> (White 2004: 15. cf. Alston 1999)

Insights such as these form a parallel, in the area of race, to the experience of feminist movements, who came to critique universalism as an expression and masking of gendered power relations. As a result, universalism fails to "provide adequate grounding for political action in a situation where dominant values masquerade as everyone's values and where opposing identities (and the values and practices associated with them) are necessarily multiple, fragmented, and at best provisional" (Ackelsberg 1996: 93). The anarchist emphasis on intersecting regimes of domination (Shannon and Rogue 2009), which avoids granting any of these regimes analytical primacy, is in this sense much more productive than class reductionism for examining the power dynamics surrounding race and culture. I return to some consequences of this position in the final section of this chapter.

Critique of multiculturalism

Anarchist critiques of multiculturalism are primarily directed at actually existing multicultural policies and discourses, rather than at the arguments found in the works normative multicultural theorists (cf. Kymlicka 1995; Modood 2013). Of the latter, there is little to say from an anarchist perspective except that it has never (at least to my knowledge) questioned the legitimacy of the state. To the contrary, multicultural theory universally "assumes the existence of the state as a neutral arbiter, a monological consciousness that, upon request, dispenses rights and privileges in the form of a gift" (Day 2005: 80). This amounts to yet another instance of the "politics of demand . . . oriented to improving existing institutions and everyday experiences by appealing to the benevolence of hegemonic forces" (Day 2005: 80) – an approach alien to anarchists. So comprehensive is the liberal reliance on the state as the arbiter of collective claims that its presence is sometimes elided altogether. Thus Parekh (2006: 196) allows the terms "society" and "community" to stand in for the state when asserting that a "multicultural society . . . should foster a strong sense of unity and common belonging among its citizens, as otherwise it cannot act as a united community able to take and enforce collectively-binding decisions and regulate and resolve conflicts". In its consistent failure to problematize the legitimacy of the state and seriously challenge hierarchical power, mainline multicultural theory suffers from the same blind spot that afflicts moral-cum-political theory in general: the assumption that the state is, or could potentially be, a vehicle for the operationalization of moral reasoning. Thus moral "ought" statements are cloaked in language which not only assumes the desirability and continued existence of the state, but also rather naively constructs an unproblematic continuum between morally correct positions and what the state is supposed to implement.

Moral theorists might, of course, object that it is not their job to disentangle the real-world political obstacles to the implementation of morally correct policies; it is a job for political scientists and policy analysis, rather than for moral philosophers, to identify these obstacles and suggest ways to overcome them. But the question here is not technical but ontological; it involves the assumption that the state is potentially a neutral tool which can be made subservient to social agendas (presumably through democratic representation). An anarchist approach, in distinction, is informed by a critique of the state as the custodian of a hierarchical society and the institution that legitimates and ultimately underwrites manifold forms of domination. That some states also work to ameliorate some of the excesses of otherwise unregulated systems of capitalist, racist and sexist exploitation (to name a few) is seen not as a virtuous function but as the result of forced historical compromises with liberation movements of the oppressed, an attempt to stave off more thoroughgoing social transformation by curbing the worst excesses of injustice as a way of guaranteeing the continuation of the basic logic of domination. The state, on this account, always tends towards autonomy – that is, to ruling on behalf of itself (Oppenheimer 2007: 8ff.).

Hence, the critiques pursued here focus on "really existing" multiculturalism. Most of these critiques are not idiosyncratically anarchist, but shared with a broader spectrum of the radical left. Perhaps the most prominent one

70   *Uri Gordon*

regards mainline multicultural policy's role in defusing social dissent. This is done by redefining socio-political antagonisms as stemming, not from *inequalities* attached to race, class and gender, but from forms of *difference* among cultural communities inhabiting an allegedly horizontal plane. This conception actively obscures forms of social stratification, while effectively limiting the legitimate use of the term racism to manifestations of individual bigotry. According to Lentin (2005: 381–382),

> As a policy, multiculturalism would have us see our societies as 'race-free' and culturally rich . . . [this] often serves to mask the persistence of ra*cism* in what is widely believed to be a post-racial age. . . . While we may accept that individual institutions contain racist elements or have even become steeped in a culture of racism, extending this to the idea that the state itself may be structured by racism is generally considered to be an extremist position . . . the constant identification of racism with the actions of the politically marginal enables the apparently more banal, everyday racism experienced by the racialized in all social, political, economic and private spheres to be played down.

In the UK, the antifascist group Red Action – which was largely Marxist but included anarchist sympathizers – added a sustained class dimension to this critique. Multiculturalism is here approached as "an alternative and bulwark against" social change, since under its premises "social antagonisms historically on a vertical trajectory are thereafter directed horizontally" (O'Halloran 1998). Multiculturalism dissolves the potential for solidarities that would challenge extant social hierarchies, by redefining which identities enjoy first-order relevance (namely, ethnic or religious ones) and allowing the state, and its coercive technocracy of urban governance, to engage with groups (or their declared leaders) on that basis. Hence multiculturalism is primarily a subsidiary for state-driven population and immigration management, which rewards "ethnic entrepreneurs" (Kymlicka 2010) for representing "their" "community" in ways which either do nothing to challenge inequalities, or do so within the boundaries circumscribed by the state.

To extend this point, anarchists might argue that beneath the rationale of extending recognition and certain collective rights to cultural and racial minorities, the state re-asserts its hegemony over the categorisation and management of its population. The determination of which groups are to be legitimately considered minorities for the purpose of legal and policy entitlements, as well as the substantive characterisation of these groups, becomes the purview of state officials and proceeds through fixed categories tied to ancestry or the profession of religious doctrine. Moreover, under the guise of providing equal attention to diverse cultures, the multicultural paradigm adopted by states (and often integrated by corporations and NGOs) defines and compartmentalises these differences in ways which reinforce state power as well as the neoliberal project. On this view, liberal

Anarchism and multiculturalism 71

multiculturalism "institutes a separate sphere in society where the political antagonisms arising from cultural differences are policed in para-political fashion . . . by incorporating them in the social order as 'competencies' to be developed by individual citizens, 'human capital' to be managed by organizations and 'assets' that enrich society. The move away from concerns with discrimination and structural disadvantage of ethnic minorities and towards organizational efficiency effectively forecloses the invocation of the equality of humans as cultural beings" (Van Puymbroeck and Oosterlynck 2014: 101).

In a similar vein, Sunera Thobani argues that in Canada, multiculturalism has functioned to displace anti-racist discourse and has "allowed for certain communities – people of colour – to be constructed as cultural communities . . . defined in very Orientalist and colonial ways – as static" (Thobani 2008). The policies and discourses of multiculturalism thus continue to construct minorities as opposed to white Canadians, both English- and French-speaking. Averting attention from the continued reproduction of deep racial inequalities, multiculturalism "has become a policy of governing and managing communities of colour, so that those politics only get articulated in the name of culture, and culture is defined in highly patriarchal terms" (Thobani 2008).

Multiculturalism in its state-sponsored rhetorical guise has also been criticized for aggressively painting the white working class as inherently racist, despite phenomena such as interracial relationships being almost entirely a working class phenomenon. According to this point of view, the alienating and artificial ways in which the state promoted its multicultural agenda, and the socially enforced expectation that citizens profess their pride in it (cf. Fortier 2005), has actually played a part in pushing sections of the white working class "left behind" by neoliberal globalisation increasingly to the right. According to Riley (2001), another Red Action writer, the "determination to focus on minority rights and the subsequent racialising of political situations inevitably leads to an 'us or them' scenario . . . the determined air brushing of the working class out of any serious political equation" contributes to a "carefully cultivated myth that anti-racism is the preserve of [privileged] social groups . . . for many, to be properly anti-racist it is necessary to be anti-working class". This amounts to "placing race at the heart of the debate; then denying the political existence of the working class, prior to being forced to seek allies against them".

Thus multiculturalism comes to serve as a lightning-rod for right-wing politicians, who portray it as a failed project of Leftist imposition, blamed "for everything from parallel societies to gendered horror to the incubation of terrorism" (Lentin and Titley 2012: 3). This view, which has rapidly bled over from far right groups into the "centre right" of leaders such as Angela Merkel and David Cameron, constructs multiculturalism as a policy fuelled by guilt and characterised by doctrinaire tolerance towards the illiberalism and intolerance of (always implicitly Muslim) minorities. Surveying the "the

72   *Uri Gordon*

death of multiculturalism" trope in the British, Dutch and German press in 2010–11, Ossewaarde concludes that despite some national differences in the "rhetorical usages of national legacies", its overall context remained "an attempt to reinforce particular monoculturalist visions of a national identity through the sociocultural construction of the other, the Muslims", and the portrayal of Islam as an essentially unenlightened, totalitarian and imperialist ideology (Ossewaarde 2014: 174).

The opposition is often staked out in very similar terms to those used by the white-American right against the bogeyman of "political correctness": as a coercive, state-led project to promote the acceptance of other cultures at the expense of white liberal identities, and to police the language and behaviour of the white majority, which is supposedly now scared to criticise racism and exclusionism when these come from minorities (cf. Gilroy 2012). As Lentin and Titley (2012: 3) argue, the fact that no state multicultural project has ever done any of these things is largely irrelevant, since multiculturalism is used here as "a mobilising metaphor for a spectrum of political aversion and racism that . . . allows for securitised migration regimes, assimilative integrationism and neo-nationallist politics to be presented as nothing more than rehabilitative action" (Lentin and Titley 2012: 3). In this context, "the 'liberal cultural agenda' has become a modality of nationalisms that are primarily grounded through attacks on the illiberalism of minority and Muslim populations, and on the 'relativist' license multiculturalism has accorded them" (op. cit.: 6). Rather than imagined terrorists, those bearing the brunt of this shift are refugees and migrants who are in the most vulnerable position in these societies.

An alternative perspective: Decolonial anarchism

Anarchist notions of cultural difference have engaged explicitly with class conflict and structural racial oppression in a way that contemporary liberal conceptions of multiculturalism do not. By amplifying transnational solidarity and an intersectionalist critique of domination, anarchism creates a much more productive polarity with the far right around these issues, of which neither state policies nor mainline multicultural theory are capable.

To consider an alternative, anarchist response to contemporary ethnocultural pluralism does not amount to expounding some blueprint for social relations among diverse groups in the absence of the state. Instead, the focus is on current ethical and strategical questions relevant to social transformation – asking how encounters in mixed communities impact on the political-cultural dynamics that anarchists face in their everyday organising, and how they can use grassroots forms of encounter to push forward radical agendas. The anarchist alternative to what the state hegemonically codes as "multicultural questions" is therefore the living creation of alternative economic and cultural relations of solidarity, which strive for social equality and autonomous collective self-determination. The contours of any multicultural stateless society of the future need to be worked out, not in abstract theory (a stateless mirror-world to mainline multicultural debates), but from practice. To do this, I would argue that solidarities and alliances across ethno-cultural difference should be constructed under a decolonial banner, with attention to asymmetric power relations and colonial legacies, as well as to points of mutual identification.

Decolonial thinking has been described as an act of "epistemic disobedience" whereby people who share the "colonial wound" can carry out a "political and epistemic de-linking" from Western dominance and the ways of thinking it imposes – not in order to compete with it in the geopolitical and neoliberal arena, but to assert an ethic of respect for all life and for oppressed peoples' struggles (Mignolo 2009; cf. De Lissovoy 2010; Sprecher 2011; Grosfoguel 2012; Morgensen 2012). Politically, a decolonial approach may be a promising antidote to the problematic remains of Western universalism in anarchist practice and theory. This requires anarchists to recognise that colonialism is not merely a historical event, but a set of logics that continue to maintain and deepen inequalities and dispossession in advanced capitalist countries. As Ramnath (2011: 21) puts it,

> Where ethnicity is brutalized and culture decimated, it is callous to discount the value of ethnic pride, asserting the right to exist as such – not forgetting that cultural expression must include the right to redefine the practices of one's own culture over time . . . in the colonial context, the defense of ethnic identity and cultural divergence from the dominant is a key component of resistance . . . the decolonization of culture shouldn't mean rewinding to a "pure" original condition but instead restoring the artificially stunted capacity freely to grow and evolve.

This obviously challenges any notion of the anarchist as an abstract ideological subject, judiciously extending support to those movements meeting her or his criteria. Instead, anarchists have an obligation to consider solidarity with sub-national minorities not simply from a position of ideological agreement, but in the context of activists' positionality within a post- and neo-colonial condition of exclusion and exploitation (cf. Barker and Pickerill 2012). According to Harsha Walia (2012), the implication for non-indigenous activists is that "meaningful support for Indigenous struggles cannot be directed by non-natives":

> Taking leadership means being humble and honouring front-line voices of resistance as well as offering tangible solidarity as needed and requested. Specifically, this translates to taking initiative for self-education about the specific histories of the lands we reside upon, organizing support with the clear consent and guidance of an Indigenous community or group, building long-term relationships of accountability and never assuming or taking for granted the personal and political trust that non-natives may earn from Indigenous peoples over time.

74   *Uri Gordon*

In practice, this has led some anarchists practicing decolonial solidarity to carry out joint work under specific principles. As articulated by a long-term activist in the Israeli group *Anarchists Against the Wall*,

> The first principle is that although the struggle is joint, Palestinians are affected more by the decisions taken within it, and therefore are the ones who should make the important decisions. Second, Israelis have a special responsibility to respect Palestinian self-determination, including respecting social customs and keeping out of internal Palestinian politics . . . it would be far more repressive to try to codify what constitutes appropriate social ties, let alone demand it of individuals. The only principle is the general policy of respecting requests by Palestinian popular committees in this regard as well.
>
> (Snitz 2013: 57–58)

Abdou et al. (2009) suggest a similar conception in considering radical settler-indigenous alliances in Canada. Drawing on Levinas, they promote an ethic of encounter between settler and indigenous activists which builds solidarity through honesty and mutual responsibility. In this ethic, recognition "requires that the settler disrupt his or her colonial (dis)orientation to the other" and adopt a disposition that includes "acceptance of the unknown – a lack of anticipation of the other's essence; a knowledge of self-identity incorporating an understanding of infinite responsibility; a willingness to accept difference and avoid the tendency to subsume the other into the same; and finally, a humility in the face of the other, which implies having the courage and willingness necessary to learn from the other" (215–216).

Here, the deconstruction of one's own identity becomes an essential part of radical action. As Ackelsberg (1996: 98) argues,

> since identities – particularly group identities – are not something we develop independently of politics and then bring fully formed into the political arena but, rather, are constructed precisely in and through politics, it is not only reasonable but necessary to look to politics as the ground on which our differences might finally be constructively addressed. If we can begin to understand coalition-building as a process through which we not only act together with others but develop and change our own identities at the same time, we may open up new possibilities both for identity and for politics.

This has two implications. First, that anarchist struggles must shed any universalist premises, instead striving to empower and defend the spontaneous development of identities in the context of egalitarian economic relations based on commons. Second, that the celebration of diversity and difference could be extended from culture to other aspects of identity, including gender and sexuality. These could also be informed by a queer anarchist logic

Anarchism and multiculturalism 75

(Daring et al. 2012) which seeks fluidity and the defying of fixed categories, as long as there is explicit attention to issues of power and privilege that would work against dynamics such as cultural appropriation.

A decolonial logic is not only relevant to current and former settler-colonial states in the Americas, Oceania, southern Africa and the Middle East. It operates on a continuum from Palestine and Tibet (peoples under military occupation) through America (systemic racism) to Europe's processes of immigration absorption, rejection and securitisation. In the European context, the demographics of inequality continue to carry the legacies of colonialism and the effects of current imperialism, while the exclusionary policies of neoliberal "Fortress Europe" disadvantage precisely those who have borne the brunt of both. For European anarchists, solidarity with migrants and refugees is already an important activity, part of a transnational No Borders movement against migration controls. In Calais, a permanent presence of European activists has for six years been resisting the police harassment of migrants, supporting camps and squats, and raising awareness. In Turin, the Refugees and Migrants Solidarity Committee has squatted the abandoned Olympic village and a second site, where Italian-born and migrant activists have seen through eviction attempts to sustain self-organised communities. Israel Jewish anarchists have supported not only the Palestinian popular struggle but also asylum seekers from Eritrea and Sudan who organised to resist deportations, internment and rampant racism. These and other initiatives share the ethos of taking leadership from self-organised movements of refugees and migrants, and of avoiding both a saviour mentality and the condescension of revolutionary tutelage. As such, they have the potential to generate "an antagonistic struggle which does not take place between particular communities, but splits from within each community, so that the 'trans-cultural' link between communities is that of a shared struggle" (Zizek 2009).

Conclusion

This chapter has emphasised the egalitarian and anti-systemic underpinnings of anarchist engagements with ethno-cultural difference. While anarchists have celebrated cultural diversity and offered critical support to the liberation struggles of peoples under foreign rule, this was always within the context of a revolutionary project to abolish domination and the institutions that maintain it. As a result, anarchists' more recent appreciations of post-colonial and poststructuralist critique have led them to re-evaluate universalist and humanist premises on terms much more profound than those found in liberal re-evaluations. The emergent anarchist analysis, which binds an intersectionalist critique of power with the rejection of state and capital, is deeply indebted to the contributions of anarchists of colour.

With regard to modern multicultural realities, anarchists focus not on how to best manage cultural difference within the confines of the state, but

76   Uri Gordon

on how to relate to such difference in the process of revolutionary struggle. State multicultural policies have thus come under heavy criticism from anarchists and their allies, who view them as veiled strategies for inequality management. In drawing attention away from enduring forms of stratification and discrimination, and in allowing the state to function as an arbiter of recognition, multiculturalism on this view plays an active role in stifling social antagonisms.

From an anarchist perspective, the decolonial approach offers the most promising alternative to mainline multiculturalism. This approach recognises not only the colonial foundation of advanced capitalist societies, but also the ongoing dispossession of indigenous peoples by settler-colonial states and the neo-colonial nature of neoliberal economic dominance. Put together, these recognitions add a crucial dimension to anrchists' intersectional analysis of contemporary hierarchies, while placing the onus on white anarchists to offer active solidarity to the self-organised struggles of indigenous peoples, migrants and refugees – taking leadership from these struggles while deconstructing their own privileged positionalities. The integration of a decolonial approach into anarchist activities is far from complete; yet the advances it has been making in recent years offer an encouraging reminder of anarchism's continuing vitality and of its ability to self-critically transform and reformulate itself in response to new practical and theoretical challenges.

Note

1   Since the concept of multiculturalism is alien to the anarchist tradition, I am using alternative terminology here. In line with the critique of universalism discussed later on, the term "ethno-cultural difference" refers to a perception of such difference, however construed, rather than implying any objective premises. The term logically precedes the "factual" sense of the word "multiculturalism", since the perception of difference obtains whether or not the groups in question inhabit the same geographical space. The term multiculturalism, whose -ism suffix normally indicates a tendentious position rather than a factual description, is reserved here for the policies and rhetoric that normally go by that name.

References

Abdou, M., Day, R. J. F. and Haberle, S. (2009) 'Can There Be a Grassroots Multiculturalism? Some Notes Toward a Genealogical Analysis of Solidarity Practices in Canadian Activism Today', in S. Bolaria, S. P. Hier and D. Lett (eds.) *Racism and Justice*, Winnipeg, MB: Fernwood.

Ackelsberg, M. A. (1996) 'Identity Politics, Political Identities: Thoughts Toward a Multicultural Politics', *Frontiers: A Journal of Women Studies* 87–100.

Alston, A. (1999) 'Beyond Nationalism, But Not Without It', *Anarchist Panther* 1: 1. Available at http://anarchistpanther.net/writings/writing4.html

Amster, R. (2012) *Anarchism Today*, New York: Praeger.

Bantman, C. (2013) *The French Anarchists in London, 1880–1914. Exile and Transnationalism in the First Globalisation*, Liverpool: Liverpool University Press.

Barker, A. J. and Pickerill, J. (2012) 'Radicalizing Relationships to and through Shared Geographies: Why Anarchists Need to Understand Indigenous Connections to Land and Place', *Antipode* 44(5): 1705–1725.

Bonanno, A. M. (1976) *Anarchism and the National Liberation Struggle*, London: Bratach Dubh.

Bookchin, M. (1994) 'Nationalism and the "National Question"', *Democracy and Nature* 2: 2. Available at http://www.democracynature.org/vol2/bookchin_nationalism.htm#_ednref7

Cahm, J. C. (1978) '"Bakunin" and "Kropotkin and the Anarchist Movement"', in E. Cahm and V. C. Fišera (eds.) *Socialism and Nationalism* (vol. 1), Nottingham: Spokesman.

Damiani, G. (1939) *Razzismo e anarchismo*, Newark, NJ: Biblioteca de l'Adunata dei refrattari.

Daring, C. B., Rogue, J., Shannon, D. and Volcano, A. (eds.) (2012) *Queering Anarchism: Addressing and Undressing Power and Desire*, Oakland: AK Press.

Day, R. J. F. (2005) *Gramsci Is Dead: Anarchist Currents in the Newest Social Movements*, London: Pluto.

De Lissovoy, N. (2010) 'Decolonial Pedagogy and the Ethics of the Global', *Discourse: Studies in the Cultural Politics of Education* 31(3): 279–293.

Déjacque, J. (1858/2013) *The Humanisphere: Anarchic Utopia*, trans. S. Wilbur. Available at http://workingtranslations.blogspot.com/p/blog-page.html

Fishman, W. J. (1975/2005) *East End Jewish Radicals 1875–1914*, Nottingham: Five Leaves.

Fortier, A-M. (2005) 'Pride Politics and Multiculturalist Citizenship', *Ethnic and Racial Studies* 28(3): 559–578.

Gilroy, P. (2012) '"My Britain Is Fuck All": Zombie Multiculturalism and the Race Politics of Citizenship', *Identities* 19(4): 380–397.

Gordon, U. (2007) 'Anarchism Reloaded', *The Journal of Political Ideologies* 12(1).

Gordon, U. (2008) *Anarchy Alive! Anti-authoritarian Politics from Practice to Theory*, London: Pluto.

Grauer, M. (1994) 'Anarcho-Nationalism: Anarchist Attitudes Towards Jewish Nationalism and Zionism', *Modern Judaism* 14(1): 1–19.

Grave, J. (1899) *Moribund Society and Anarchy*, trans. V. De Cleyre, San Francisco, CA: Free Society Library.

Grosfoguel, R. (2012) 'The Dilemmas of Ethnic Studies in the United States: Between Liberal Multiculturalism, Identity Politics, Disciplinary Colonization, and Decolonial Epistemologies', *Human Architecture: Journal of the Sociology of Self-Knowledge* 10(1).

Hakim Bey (1996) 'Notes on Nationalism', in *Millennium*, Brooklyn: Autonomedia.

Hirsch, S. and van der Walt, L. (eds.) (2011) *Anarchism and Syndicalism in the Colonial and Postcolonial World, 1880–1940*, Leiden: Brill.

Jun, N. (2012) *Anarchism and Political Modernity*, New York: Continuum.

Katz, D. (2011) *All Together Different: Yiddish Socialists, Garment Workers, and the Labor Roots of Multiculturalism*, New York: NYU Press.

Kinna, R. (2012) *Anarchism: A Beginner's Guide*, London: Oneworld Publications.

Kropotkin, P. (1885) 'Finland: A Rising Nationality', *The Nineteenth Century*, March, 527–546. Available at http://dwardmac.pitzer.edu/Anarchist_Archives/kropotkin/Finland/Finland.html

78   *Uri Gordon*

Kropotkin, P. (1897/2014) 'Letter to Maria Isidine Goldsmith', in Iain McKay (ed.), trans. P. Sharkey, *Direct Struggle Against Capital: A Peter Kropotkin Anthology*, Oakland: AK Press.

Khuri-Makdisi, I. (2010) *The Eastern Mediterranean and the Making of Global Radicalism, 1860–1914*, Berkeley: University of California Press.

Kymlicka, W. (1995) *Multicultural Citizenship: A Liberal Theory of Minority Rights*, Oxford: Clarendon.

Kymlicka, W. (2010) 'Testing the Liberal Multiculturalist Hypothesis: Normative Theories and Social Science Evidence', *Canadian Journal of Political Science* 43(2): 257–271.

Landauer, G. (1907) 'Volk und Land. Dreissig sozialistische Thesen', *Die Zukunft* 58: 56–67.

Lentin, A. (2005) 'Replacing "Race": Historizing the "Culture" in the Multiculturalism', *Patterns of Prejudice* 39(4): 379–396.

Lentin, A. and Titley, G. (2012) *The Crises of Multiculturalism: Racism in a Neoliberal Age*, New York: Zed.

Mignolo, W. (2009) 'Epistemic Disobedience, Independent Thought and Decolonial Freedom', *Theory, Culture & Society* 26: 159–181.

Modood, T. (2013) *Multiculturalism*, Hoboken, NJ: Wiley.

Morgensen, S. L. (2012) 'Destabilizing the Settler Academy: The Decolonial Effects of Indigenous Methodologies', *American Quarterly* 64(4): 805–808.

Morton, J. F. (1906) *The Curse of Race Prejudice*, New York: Self-published. Available at http://catalog.hathitrust.org/Record/000339229

Newman, S. (2007) *Unstable Universalities: Poststructuralism and Radical Politics*, Manchester: Manchester University Press.

O'Halloran, G. (1998) 'Branded', *Red Action* 3(2). Available at http://www.redactionarchive.org/2012/02/branded.html

O'Halloran, G. (1999) 'Race Attack', *Red Action* 3(5). Available at http://www.redactionarchive.org/2012/02/race-attack.html

Oppenheimer, F. (1922/2008) *The State*, Montreal: Black Rose.

Ossewaarde, M. (2014) 'The National Identities of the "Death Of Multiculturalism" Discourse in Western Europe', *Journal of Multicultural Discourses* 9(3): 173–189.

Parekh, B. (2006) *Rethinking Multiculturalism* (2nd edn), London: Palgrave Macmillan.

Porter, D. (2011) *Eyes to the South: French Anarchists and Algeria*, Oakland: AK Press.

Ramnath, M. (2011) *Decolonizing Anarchism*, Oakland: AK Press.

Riley, J. (2001) 'Time "To Dump" Multiculturalism', *Red Action* 4(12). Available at http://www.redactionarchive.org/2012/02/time-to-dump-multiculturalism.html

Rocker, R. (1938) *Nationalism and Culture*. New York: Covici.

Shannon, D. and Rogue, J. (2009) *Refusing to Wait: Anarchism & Intersectionality*, Johannesburg: Zabalaza Books.

Shantz, J. (2013) *Constructive Anarchy: Building Infrastructures of Resistance*, Aldershot: Ashgate.

Snitz, K. (2013) 'Tear Gas and Tea', in U. Gordon and O. Grietzer (eds.) *Anarchists Against the Wall: Direct Action and Solidarity with the Palestinian Popular Struggle*, Oakland: AK Press.

Sprecher, K. M. (2011) 'Decolonial Multiculturalism and Local-Global Contexts: A Postcritical Feminist Bricolage for Developing New Praxes in Education', PhD dissertation, University of Tennessee.

Thobani, S. (2008) 'Multiculturalism', *Talk at World Peace Forum Teach-In*, Video. Available at https://www.youtube.com/watch?v=hh3X1rzv0uc

Turcato, D. (2007) Italian Anarchism as a Transnational Movement, 1885–1915, *International Review of Social History* 52(3): 407–444.

Van Puymbroeck, N. and Oosterlynck, S. (2014) 'Opening Up the Post-Political Condition: Rancière and the Multiple Tactics of Depoliticization', in *The Post-Political and Its Discontents: Spaces of Depoliticization, Spectres of Radical Politics*, Edinburgh: Edinburgh University Press.

Walia, H. (2012) 'Decolonizing Together: Moving Beyond a Politics of Solidarity Toward a Practice of Decolonization', *Briarpatch Magazine*, 1 January. Available at http://briarpatchmagazine.com/articles/view/decolonizing-together

White, R. (2004) *Post Colonial Anarchism*, Oakland, CA: Jailbreak Press.

Zimmer, K. (2015) *Immigrants Against the State: Yiddish and Italian Anarchism in America*, Champaign, IL: University of Illinois Press.

Žižek, S. (2009) 'Appendix: Multiculturalism, the Reality of an Illusion', *Lacan.com*. Available at http://www.lacan.com/essays/?page_id=454

5 Multiculturalism and oppression
The Marxist perspectives of Fraser, Lenin, and Fanon

Andrew Ryder

Drawing on Nancy Fraser's critique of mainstream multiculturalism, this essay draws out an approach rooted in the distinctive revolutionary Marxist tradition. It is first worth revisiting Fraser's insights regarding the shortcomings of the programs offered by the liberal welfare state, as well as her identification of the tendency to reify difference, evident in many of the civic and social proposals to redress prejudice on the basis of race, gender, and sexuality. However, we can also identify a consistently Marxist approach to these questions that precedes Fraser's intervention. I draw this out by means of engagement with the history of Marxist positions on the national question, as presented in particular by V. I. Lenin, and the decolonizing and anti-racist practice of subsequent Marxist figures. In particular, I emphasize the work of a heterodox Marxist, Frantz Fanon, in extending the tradition's relevance to questions of cultural oppression.

Mainstream liberal multiculturalism tends to reify distinctions between cultures and to present their definition and needs as static. Further, it tends to privilege matters of cultural expression over egalitarian change in economic relations. Last, it can commodify and exoticize the products of diverse groups, making them simply another participant in the diversity of the marketplace. The Marxist viewpoint supports multiculturalism in that it recognizes the need to defend marginalized groups from oppression by the dominant culture. Further, Marxism recognizes the role of chauvinist ideology in enforcing uniform national allegiance above class solidarity. For this reason, revolutionary Marxists have argued for a transformative understanding of the multiplicity of cultures, first in consideration of the national question, and subsequently in anti-racist practice, decolonization struggles, and contemporary social movements. Marxism consistently understands oppression as the primary criteria of the imperative towards a defense of cultural pluralism. A double movement of defense against oppression by dominant ideology, as well as a dynamic and transformative approach to cultural identity, appears throughout the work of Lenin, Fanon, and Fraser.

Fraser argues that the site of collective struggle, after the end of the Cold War, seemed to have migrated from redistribution to recognition (identity politics rather than egalitarianism). She suggests that both redistribution

Multiculturalism and oppression 81

and recognition are necessary to a contemporary socialist politics, but that they should be understood differently than the dominant liberal paradigm of the 1990s. In constructing this argument, she says that the traditional definition of the proletariat is the clearest example of a purely redistributive movement, because the working class (in the Marxian understanding) does not want recognition of its distinct cultural identity and practices at all; rather, it works towards its own abolition. In searching for a contrary pole, a political movement that would be entirely organized around recognition with no commitment to economic equality, she takes the example of gays and lesbians. She says that most social movements combine both these demands – partly for respect and dignity, and also for material needs. However, in her view, the typical approach to these movements has unintended negative consequences, because it constructs these diverse cultural groups as fixed and enclosed, as well as continually deficient. In opposition to this, Fraser argues for a more transformative approach that will emphasize the dynamic, mutual, and co-implicating aspects of cultural difference, as well as a broadly egalitarian economic program that addresses the majority as well as minorities.

I argue that this is consistent with the approach to the national question developed by revolutionary Marxists in the early twentieth century, with Lenin the most famous among them. Lenin understood class struggle as mediated by cultural oppression, particularly of national minorities. He argued for the need to support national liberation struggles that combat domination by more powerful nation-states, but that the criteria for this commitment should be the question of oppression – such a principle is primarily defensive. He argued that cultural difference was not something to be championed as an intrinsic good, but rather as a strategic necessity to agitate against the imperialism of dominant cultures, and that this protection of cultural autonomy should take place alongside a project for the drastic reorganization of class society. I argue that this presents a basic forerunner of Fraser's argument, in that both Fraser and Lenin argue for cultural multiplicity as an element of a broader political transformation.

Last, I discuss Fanon's work on anti-racism and decolonization, which articulates a position broadly consistent with Lenin's and Fraser's. He argues for the necessity of a cultural transformation of the oppressed, in order to reject the learned inferiority produced by the dominant group. This project will re-valorize the marginalized and impoverished, as well as produce a new cultural unity on the basis of revolutionary egalitarian change. This is consistent with Lenin's demand for resistance to national oppression as a concomitant effort with socialist agitation, as well as with Fraser's emphasis on redistribution. Fanon wrote detailed descriptions of the lived experience of oppression by racialized individuals and groups, but he is also insistent that commitment to egalitarian change is the primary criteria of participation in the project of cultural and economic transformation. Ethnic or traditional authenticity is not fundamental or desirable

82 *Andrew Ryder*

for him. In his view, the rejection of the dominant culture is part of the creation of a new egalitarian society, and so in principle anyone at all could take part. This insistence on the dynamic and constructed nature of group identity anticipates Fraser's thesis as well as extends Lenin. Taken together, these three figures – an American, a Russian, and a Martinican Frenchman who became Algerian – provide the basic lineaments of a Marxist approach to multiculturalism.

Fraser's critique of liberal multiculturalism

Fraser's essay of 1995, "From Redistribution to Recognition?: Dilemmas of Justice in a 'Post-Socialist' Age", is among the most elegant responses to liberal multiculturalism, from a leftist point of view. She contends that the new social movements who hold political prominence in the contemporary period emphasize group identity rather than class consciousness, and aim for "cultural recognition" rather than overcoming economic exploitation (Fraser 1995: 68). She argues, however, that this collective desire for recognition coexists with an awareness of inequality and injustice suffered by marginalized groups. For this reason, Fraser argues for a *"critical* theory of recognition" that will combine identity politics with comprehensive egalitarian social change. She destabilizes permanent or static divisions between cultures, arguing for an approach similar to the deconstruction of gay identity advocated by queer theory.

In part, Fraser is responding to the liberal multiculturalism of Will Kymlicka, who argued for a civic understanding of group rights, rooted in the social reforms enacted in Canada in order to address the needs of French, indigenous, and immigrant Canadians (Kymlicka 1995). Kymlicka's approach to multiculturalism argues for legal recognition of certain rights to linguistic expression, territory, and cultural autonomy, and maintains that this is compatible with liberal goals and concepts. In order to do this, he argues that any group practices that violate basic human rights will not receive protection, but that incorporation of diverse cultural experience will enhance the universality of ethical and legal prescriptions for society as a whole. Fraser agrees with this aspect of Kymlicka's argument, saying "no identity politics is acceptable that fails to respect fundamental human rights of the sort usually championed by left-wing liberals" (Fraser 1995: 70).

However, Fraser rejects certain foundational claims for liberal multiculturalism. Most importantly, she insists on an "understanding of socioeconomic injustice informed by a commitment to egalitarianism" as a basic principle (Fraser 1995: 71). Fraser does not insist on an orthodox Marxist approach to this question, and contends that left-liberals such as John Rawls, Amartya Sen, and Ronald Dworkin can equally be enlisted in support of this insight. However, her emphasis on this basic need, and criticism of the growing inequalities of capitalist society, leads her to criticize the liberal multicultural framework as hindered and limited by its focus

Multiculturalism and oppression 83

on cultural recognition, without a fully articulated comprehension and response to poverty and material deprivation.

Liberal multiculturalism often proposes specific remedies for discrimination, in the form of affirmative action programs or special social services. Fraser identifies these forms of "affirmative redistribution remedies" as primarily comprised of programs that cover some of the costs of social reproduction for workers (such as childcare) and public-assistance programs for those who are unemployed or underemployed (what Marxist theory considers the "reserve army" of labor) (Fraser 1995: 85). Fraser argues that this approach, when it is targeted at distinct cultural groups, actually tends to practically undergird a stigmatizing and oppressive approach to difference, because the cultural group is defined as uniquely deficient, seemingly permanently. Fraser argues that in place of this approach to redistribution, political action should aim towards "transformative remedies" that will abolish the distinct hindrances that define a particular group and establish a framework for redistribution that addresses a shared experience of deprivation across the working class as a whole (Fraser 1995: 86).

On the level of culture, Fraser draws out a distinction between the different struggles for recognition – often on the level of race, gender, or sexuality – and the more traditional understanding of working-class political action. Marxism holds that the liberation of the proletariat will also be its abolition. The end of exploitation will end the distinct condition of the working class, bringing true universalism into the social horizon (Fraser 1995: 76). In contrast, recognition struggles desire the continuing presence and respect for the group identity as separate. Fraser takes her primary example as gays and lesbians. In Fraser's view, these "despised sexualities" face cultural misunderstanding and denigration, without an unusual or distinct material hardship (Fraser 1995: 77). While Judith Butler famously criticizes this designation in her essay, "Merely Cultural", Fraser's example is meant to illustrate the distinction between a recognition claim and a redistribution claim, rather than to enforce a definition of the exact oppression faced by lesbians, gays, and bisexuals. Her point is that a certain form of violence and injustice can be isolated that is rooted in a "cultural-valuational structure" rather than in relations of production. This is, then, a form of oppression primarily combated by social change at the level of understanding, rather than material restructuring. The oppression of women and racialized groups, in her view, are "bivalent collectivities" that share some of the features of material deprivation described by Marx's understanding of the proletariat, as well as many of the cultural prejudices and distinctions in self-understanding that Fraser associates with gay and lesbian communities.

In her understanding of this cultural form of injustice, Fraser draws on the distinction between gay-identity politics, which insists on the revaluation of a stable group identity for gays and lesbians, and the contrary theoretical outlook presented by queer theory (Fraser 1995: 83). While a gay identity politics would insist on respect and social acknowledgment of the

84   Andrew Ryder

distinct traditions of gay and lesbian people (their great representatives in history, their aesthetic contributions, shared social practices), queer theory aims to destabilize the "homo-hetero dichotomy", refusing fixed boundaries between gay and straight identity and experience. Fraser indicates that this model could perhaps be partly generalized, then, towards the questions of race and gender. That is to say, the feminist struggle for recognition could take the form not of a radical feminism that insists on the sharp distinction between the standpoints of men and women, but rather it could emphasize the instability of definitions of the feminine and the way that conventionally understood approaches to masculinity (including on the political level of citizenship and governance) might recognize disavowed roots in women's experience and practice. Or, she indicates, the recognition of racial difference may not best be enacted by a separatist cultural nationalism or an integrationist approach to the distinct contributions, history, heroes, and struggles of non-white populations (Fraser 1995: 90). This might only serve to reify group identity in a manner that is basically patronizing, as well as artificially fixed. Instead, Fraser proposes a political strategy that deconstructs racial difference, bringing its instability and artificiality into view.

To conclude, Fraser contends that the best solution to problems of redistribution and recognition is "socialism in the economy plus deconstruction in the culture" (Fraser 1995: 91). She argues that the contemporary approach of the center left, in contrast, is a "combination of the liberal welfare state plus mainstream multiculturalism" (Fraser 1995: 93). This liberal multiculturalism, in her view, offers inadequate affirmative redistribution programs that maintain the dependency and marginalization of oppressed groups, alongside a rather fixed and crude performance of respect for cultural difference. In this regard, Fraser is in accord with a later perspective, articulated by Richard Seymour (2010):

> Multiculturalism, though challenging spurious conceptions of an ethnically 'pure' nationhood, has its weaknesses as a response to racism. It fails seriously to address the systemic roots of racial discrimination. And in attempting to 'celebrate' diverse cultures in a depoliticised fashion, it transforms culture from a process in which one might participate into a static object to be passively observed and enjoyed.

In contrast, Fraser argues for the necessity of a political approach that understands the artificiality and instability of boundaries, as well as the need for a radical change in economic relations of production that benefits the entirety of the working class. In her conclusion, Fraser comes very close to restoring a revolutionary Marxist approach to multiculturalism, although she begins the essay by acknowledging the failure of the traditional socialist project and the apparent obsolescence of the orthodox approach. However, I argue that Fraser's broad understanding of redistribution, which aims to reconcile the basic outlook of Marx with that of liberals like John Rawls, somewhat adulterates the precision of her argument. I think that an account can be developed that builds on the strengths of Fraser's critique of liberal multiculturalism, while more closely adhering to the positions presented by the revolutionary Marxist tradition.

The most evident way to do this is by means of the national question. Fraser's critique of liberal multiculturalism avoids the question of national difference (Fraser 1995: 69). This is doubly ironic, because of the historical origins of multicultural thought in the approach to Canadian (and later Australian) national minorities. Moreover, the Marxist tradition has presented a uniquely rich history of debates on precisely this question, as well as great practical experience in the period of decolonization. Fraser sidelines this question partly because of the greater significance of race, gender, and sexuality in U.S. politics, as well as the desire to avoid the stale prescriptions about oppressed nations found in the Stalinist tradition. However, I argue that a consultation of the Marxist approach to the self-determination of national groups offers us further insight into a contemporary, and truly socialist, multiculturalism.

Marxism and the national question

Lenin's approach to the national question anticipates many of the contemporary debates regarding multiculturalism. Indeed, prior to the Canadian civic definition of multiculturalism, Lenin already attempted to implement such a strategy, in his writings as a revolutionary and to some extent after the victory of 1917.[1] Lenin extended the approach to national differences already present in classical Marxism and integrated it with the crucial emphasis on working-class solidarity. For this reason, his place in the Marxist tradition cannot be neglected in a study of multiculturalism.

Multiculturalism posits the desirability of the coexistence of different cultural groups. In contrast, the classical Marxist tradition is often thought to practice a reductive account of interest and identity on the basis of economic class. It is true that Karl Marx and Frederick Engels were concerned with class consciousness above all of other forms of identity. With the famous statement, "the proletarians of the world have nothing to lose but their chains", they affirm a unity of all the individuals of a certain class, a class defined by its place in the mode of production (Marx and Engels 1969: 137). Concretely, this means that a twelve-year-old assembly line worker in Korea and a forty-five-year-old construction worker in Italy, as two arbitrary examples, are bound across space in their political interests, whether they know it or not. Marxist activists aim to bring this unconscious affinity to light. The revolutionary Marxist tradition, however, extends the notion of comradeship throughout other oppressed and potentially powerful elements of the population: most famously the peasantry, but eventually the "new social movements" of feminism, anti-racism, and national self-determination struggles. While Marx and Engels were not silent on these

86   *Andrew Ryder*

subjects, subsequent thinkers in the tradition have provided rich analyses that extend their initial viewpoint.[2] Marx and Engels were aware of the role of national and racial oppression in enforcing class domination. For this reason, they were involved in the movement against slavery and for national self-determination of Ireland. However, they did not elucidate general principles in this matter, and these must be extrapolated from their practical historical analyses.[3]

These extensions of the tradition are largely defined by the work of the famous Russian revolutionary, V.I. Lenin. His classic early work on the organization and role of the party, *What Is to Be Done?*, provides an account of how Marxist political action ought to proceed, both for the specific Russian context and more broadly.[4] Lenin saw the party as acting outside the purely economic arena, rather, operating in the "sphere of relationships between *all* the various classes and strata and the state and the government – the sphere of the interrelations between *all* the various classes" (Lenin 1966: 112). The imperative for the Party-member is to "*go among all classes of the population*" (Lenin 1966: 112). His duty is to "react to every manifestation of tyranny and oppression, no matter where it takes place, no matter what stratum or class of the people if affects; he must be able to group all these manifestations into a single picture of police violence and capitalist exploitation" (Lenin 1966: 113). This is the articulation of a common interest among the exploited proletariat and all other marginalized members of society.

This mediated, dialectical understanding of class struggle in the context of social totality led Lenin to develop a complex and influential understanding of the national question, which he understood in terms of national self-determination struggles against imperialism. Kevin B. Anderson argues that Lenin developed an understanding of the significance of oppressed nationalities during World War I, during and subsequent to his close study of G.W.F. Hegel's *Logic* (Anderson 1995). In contrast, Lars Lih has argued that this attention to the significance of national self-determination precedes this period, and is present already in the work of Lenin's predecessor, Karl Kautsky (Lih 2011). A third perspective has been offered by Eric Blanc, who argues that the decisive concern with national self-determination was really developed between Kautsky's orthodoxy and Lenin's new pre-eminence, by the "borderland Marxists" of Poland, Georgia, Lithuania, Finland, Ukraine, Latvia, Armenia, and Russia (Blanc 2014).

In any case, Lenin's strong support for the rights of oppressed nations to liberate themselves from the control of larger empires, including by the formation of separate nation-states, was the occasion of continuing controversy. Famously, Rosa Luxemburg opposed this perspective, arguing that capitalism had pre-empted political means of subordination; in her view, secession would only lead to bourgeois nationalism (Löwy 1976: 81–99; Mattick 1978). Subsequently, other Bolsheviks, in particular Nikolai Bukharin, opposed the relevance of Lenin's support for the independence of national minorities, at least in the former Russian empire (Lewis 2000a). I argue that Lenin's distinct approach to national self-determination was a crucial step in a Marxist theory of multiculturalism. While this is not a concept that he explicitly names, Lenin's dialectical approach to nationhood has the merit of a materialist approach to the coexistence of cultures and the inequalities of power among them. Tom Lewis summarizes Lenin's point of view in the following manner:

> In a world defined by the existence of richer and poorer nations, not only do 'nationalisms of the oppressed' emerge as agents of struggle against global capitalism; 'nationalisms of the oppressor' emerge as well and are used by bosses and politicians in the strong nations to justify the imperialist system. Moreover, a layer of workers in the dominant nations actually comes to think that workers, too, stand to gain from imperialism's oppression of the weaker nations. These nationalisms of the oppressor represent formidable obstacles to building the international solidarity among workers that is needed in order to succeed in the fight against global capitalism.
>
> (Lewis 2000a)

Lenin believed that the nationalism of the oppressed would lead them to fight against the imperialist ruling class. In keeping with the perspective previously outlined in *What Is to Be Done?*, he saw socialist action as necessarily engaged in a popular fight against all forms of oppression. For him, this question was bound to the consideration of power. He wrote, "Combat all national oppression? Yes, of course! Fight for any kind of national development, for 'national culture' in general? Of course not!" (Lenin 1972: 17–51). National culture, then, served the role of a struggle against material domination; it was not considered as maintaining an intrinsic value, but rather as serving a role in combating oppression and striking at imperialism. In Lenin's view, this struggle for national expression could never truly succeed under conditions of global capitalism, and as a result would necessarily imply an eventual contribution to revolutionary struggle. In a manner of speaking, then, Lenin anticipated Fraser's prescription of a struggle for socialism in the economy alongside the recognition of cultural difference as inherently unstable and dynamic.

While Lenin and other Bolsheviks were concerned about racial oppression, and in particular the condition of African-Americans, they saw this in terms of the national question and lacked a general theory of racism. Indeed, as Robert Carter points out, Marxists have rarely presented a distinct analysis of race as such, and often accepted it as given (Carter 2008: 431). Fraser, then, as the merit of suggesting approach that emphasizes racism as a bivalent oppression, combining demeaning misrecognition with material deprivation (Fraser 1995: 81). However, long before Fraser, the North American Black radical tradition often understood anti-racist practice through an extension of the Marxist tradition. As Cedric Robinson writes, for figures such as W. E. B. DuBois, C. L. R. James, and Richard Wright, "Marxism had been the prior commitment, the first encompassing and conscious experience of organized opposition to racism, exploitation, and domination" (Robinson 2000: 5). While all three of these figures took clear influence from Lenin as well as Marx, their perspective was often heterodox. Carter emphasizes O. C. Cox as presenting a particularly influential account of racism for traditional Marxists. In Cox's view, racism was entirely a product of ruling-class manipulation and was primarily defined by its function, rationalizing exploitation and dividing the working class (Carter 2008: 433). Carter argues that the parameters of this understanding were greatly expanded by Stuart Hall and Paul Gilroy, who drew on Antonio Gramsci's sophisticated understanding of the relationship between economy and culture (Carter 2008: 435–437). Subsequent social scientists tended to dismiss Marxism as economically reductionist, nonetheless.

I will now discuss another figure, Frantz Fanon, who contributed classic studies of racism and colonization, from a perspective decisively informed by the strategies of Marx and Lenin presented earlier in this essay. I am not concerned with claiming Fanon's approach to revolutionary strategy and class relations as purely Marxist, but rather with drawing out his particular analysis in terms of oppression, and linking it both to the Leninist conception of national determination and to the distinctly egalitarian approach to multiculturalism elucidated by Fraser.

Fanon's approach to national oppression and racism

Frantz Fanon is widely influential in his understanding of racism and national oppression, understood as linked processes. He gives a thorough and detailed approach to national liberation, specifically regarding the Algerian context, in his book, *Wretched of the Earth*, published in 1961. Fanon's commitment to Marxism is not entirely pure; he famously writes, "Marxist analysis should always be slightly stretched every time we have to do with the colonial problem" (Fanon 1963: 40). However, Fanon's work has largely been incorporated into the Marxist tradition, although not without some controversy. I argue that Fanon fleshes out Lenin's perspective, particularly with regard to the understanding of racism and apartheid structures that appear within colonial situations. In Fanon's view, it is possible for any individual to identify, politically, with the groups who are most exploited. For this reason, he portrays cultures as supple and permeable, and fundamentally from the perspective of egalitarian transformation. While he developed this approach through an analysis of the Algerian war of national liberation, his basic emphasis on a shared project that overcomes original group belonging exceeds this particular instance.

Fanon argues for a reevaluation of national cultures. In his view, the revolution will require a revolution in consciousness, most of all on the part of

Multiculturalism and oppression 89

intellectuals. The colonized mass will collectively reject the values beaten into them by the colonial state (Fanon 1963: 43). Likewise, Fanon argues that the native intellectual will enact an "auto-da-fé", a destruction of his old self-image and individualism (Fanon 1963: 47). However, the revolutionary intellectual must surpass the stage of serving as an uncritical parrot for the masses he agitates as "a kind of yes-man" (Fanon 1963: 49). In Fanon's work, "the *fellah*, the unemployed man, the starving native do not lay a claim to the truth; they do not *say* that they represent the truth, for they *are* the truth" (Fanon 1963: 49). The truth underlies the will of all, as in Rousseau; it is the truth of the nation, exceeding the conscious knowledge of any particular elements of that nation.[5]

Fanon's understanding of national self-determination substantially alters classical Marxist class analysis. While granting that the peasantry are reactionary in the industrialized countries – those who must be represented, in Marx's famous words – Fanon comes close to reversing Marx's class valorization completely in the Algerian context (Fanon 1963: 111). Peasant traditions, rather than a reservoir of nostalgia and conservativism, provide discipline and altruism to the masses (Fanon 1963: 112). Fanon's urban working class has the role of a nationalist bourgeoisie; while Marx dismissed the *lumpenproletariat* as a corrupt tool of counterrevolutionary intrigue, Fanon recasts the criminal class as the "urban spearhead" of the revolution (Fanon 1963: 129). The leader can never "substitute himself for the popular will"; it is the duty of the nation to produce souls capable of freedom (Fanon 1963: 205). He asserts that a revolutionary country "must possess a trustworthy political party", but that this must be a "tool in the hands of the people" rather than the government (Fanon 1963: 185). According to him, the party should be extremely decentralized and spread through the countryside; it will not be an authority, "but an organism through which they as the people exercise their authority and express their will" (Fanon 1963: 185). The masses are capable of governing themselves; to say otherwise is Western, bourgeois, and contemptuous (Fanon 1963: 188).

Fanon's analysis of national self-determination draws on his study of racism, published ten years prior: *Black Skin, White Masks*. Prior to his experience of the Algerian war, Fanon studied racist cultural formation on his native island, Martinique, and in France. His book contributes an understanding of a specific and crucial form of cultural oppression, left under-theorized by the European Marxists of the nineteenth and twentieth centuries. Fanon believes that class conflict is linked to another social split, between white and black. He writes,

> [T]he real Other for the white man [sic] is and will continue to be the black man [sic]. And conversely. Only for the white man the Other is perceived on the level of the body image, absolutely as the not-self – that is, the unidentifiable, the unassimilable.
>
> (Fanon 1967: 161)

90   *Andrew Ryder*

Fanon argues that racism conditions black people to identify with white people. Whites, however, derive their symbolic position through the ability to differentiate themselves from the fantasy of a black Other, the animal-child, who represents all repressed urges. This renders the presence of the black man or woman as a constant nuisance. As Homi K. Bhabha points out, this schema presents a radically anti-essentialist view of race, insofar as blackness is in a sense the truth of whiteness. Those with white skin also wear white masks, no more authentically embodying their role than their black-skinned counterparts.

However, Fanon also insists on the materiality of racism. In his first book, anti-racist struggle is presented as a fundamental priority, before class conflict and nationalism. In *Black Skin, White Masks*, the essential problem is the social understanding of the melanin present in the skin of a black person. However, he says, "historical and economic realities come into the picture" (Fanon 1967: 161). Fanon extends this concern with historical and economic context in his later work on decolonization. His immersion in the struggle of the Algerian people, and the theory and practice of this struggle, leads him to modify the nature of his analysis; race becomes less significant than national oppression. Historical and economic realities conspire to undo the binary opposition between black and white Fanon explores in his first book. After studying the radically different roles of subjective identification present in Africa – Africanism, Arabism, Islamism, bourgeois nationalism, varieties of socialism centered on the urban workers or the rural masses – Fanon adopts a new mode of social practice. In *The Wretched of the Earth*, he de-emphasizes the quality of black skin and champions instead the landless peasantry.

It may seem very counterintuitive to enlist Fanon in the cause of multiculturalism. The Algerian war of liberation led to the expulsion of the settler population, and subsequently to continual civil war concerning the cultural truth of the Algerian population (Stora 2001: 117–213). In this regard, Algeria has emerged as a cautionary tale in the failure to accept the multiplicity of culture. However, Fanon is a singular case, and his theories ought not to be seen as falsified by the tragic failure of the Algerian popular revolution. It is necessary to emphasize Fanon's particular definition of revolutionary nationhood, and its rejection of essentialist dependence on ethnicity or religion. He saw Algerian national identity as open, and indeed himself became Algerian, despite his entirely heterogeneous origins. In this regard, his theories are much more in line with a revolutionary multiculturalism than with the authoritarian uniformity that subsequent leaders have tried to impose on Algeria in the years of independence.

Fanon identifies the revolutionary moment as a mass collective identification with the excluded and exploited of the political situation, in Algeria, the rural masses. It is this rear guard that best symbolizes the whole of the oppressed North African majority. Anyone at all who is present to the Algerian situation is capable of theoretical and practical commitment to the

Multiculturalism and oppression 91

peasantry, and by this commitment, to the promise of the Algerian nation. As Aimé Césaire puts it in his *Notebook of a Return to the Native Land*, "Who and what are we? Excellent question!" (Césaire 1956: 18). Fanon himself, neither Algerian by birth nor belonging to the peasantry by class, took part in this identification. In the words of Césaire again – "He chose. He became Algerian. Lived, fought and died Algerian" (Césaire 1961: 24). This is why Fanon believed that Europeans could play a part in the revolution: "[A]ny individual living in Algeria is an Algerian. In tomorrow's independent Algeria, it will be up to every Algerian to take on Algerian citizenship or to reject it in favor of a different citizenship" (Fanon 1966: 146–147).

The identification with the exploited of the situation, with the rural *nègres* of Algeria, with the wretched of the earth, has certain consequences. In this instance, those consequences include war. This is a war between two distinct positions: the Algerian nationalists and the French colonialists. These two positions have certain racial, religious, and cultural valences to them, which are tactically significant to the hazardous battlefield of Fanon's Algeria. What is the function of this enemy other for him?

Fanon speaks of the colonial system as a self-contained and Manichaen world of internal consistency, in which both the natives and the colonists are enmeshed at the most intimate level: "it is the settler who has brought the native into existence and who perpetuates his existence. The settler owes the very fact of his existence, that is to say, his property, to the colonial system" (Fanon 2002: 40). This statement introduces the basic opponents – the settler *colon*, who gains his status by virtue of his European lineage, white skin, and consequent economic advantage; and the colonized *indigène*, who is coded as French but not quite, the partial absence and distortion of Frenchness, whose identity is produced by differentiation from the colonist and whose body and possessions are rendered inferior. The colonized *nègre* is human in some partial sense, but is not fully accorded an identity. They are born in the native zone, but "it matters little where or how; they die there, it matters not where, nor how" (Fanon 2002: 42). The existence of the natives outside the official registers of birth and death leaves them effectively nameless.

The separation from identity in its full sense produces a constitutive envy: "there is no native who does not dream at least once a day of setting himself up in the settler's place" (Fanon 2002: 43). The identification of the colonial system is produced in a material fashion, both economically and bodily. He says that the effects of colonization are inscribed materially into the body: "every time Western values are mentioned they produce in the native a sort of stiffening or muscular lockjaw" (Fanon 2002: 46). Fanon argues that racist colonial society depicts natives as intrinsically evil: "the native is declared insensible to ethics; he represents not only the absence of values; but also the negation value. He is, let us dare to admit, the enemy of values, and in this sense he is the absolute evil." Social ideology, however, identifies this

92   *Andrew Ryder*

evil with nature. Fanon writes that the Algerians blend in with the natural background of French Algeria (Fanon 2002: 250). Decolonization brings these invisible, absent actors into view, and makes it possible for them to act historically as a collective subject; it "transforms spectators crushed with their inessentiality into privileged actors, with the grandiose glare of history's floodlights upon them" (Fanon 2002: 40).

The basic division between the settler and the native is maintained by naked manifestations of violence: the policeman and the soldier, who, "by their immediate presence and their frequent and direct action maintain contact with the native and advise him by means of rifle butts and napalm not to budge. It is obvious here that the agents of government speak the language of pure force" (Fanon 2002: 42). Fanon's detailed description of the opposing zones of native and settler are deeply intertwined. The settlers cut themselves off from their native counterparts by means of an elaborate identification with a white, French self-image. The native is compelled to aspire to the status of this self-image, but is at the same time repelled from complete access to this realm, being assimilated to the compromise formation of the stereotype. The stereotype allows for some social existence, but also lacks autonomy, being overdetermined by the social imaginaries of both the natives and the settler.

The failure to accomplish any satisfying reconciliation between the lived experience of the natives and the white ideal necessitates the production of an alternative self-image, a cultural project that "invents souls" (Fanon 2002: 187). Fanon describes this cultural transformation as essentially violent and military:

> They won't become reformed characters to please colonial society, fitting in with the morality of its rulers; quite on the contrary, they take for granted the impossibility of their entering the city save by hand grenades and revolvers. These workless less-than-men are rehabilitated in their own eyes and in the eyes of history. The prostitutes too, and the maids who are paid two pounds a month, all the hopeless dregs of humanity, all who turn in circles between suicide and madness, will recover their balance, once more go forward, and march proudly in the great procession of the awakened nation.
>
> (Fanon 2002: 126)

The production of this alternative cultural project, however, carries with it a great uncertainty, which requires its own constant redefinition in terms of the Algerian situation and its determining valences (Islam, pan-Arabism, socialism, Cold War alliances), but most of all the elimination of those social forces which would enforce the content of "Frenchman" as white settler, dominating the Algerian political situation.

The brutality of combat, putting both settlers and natives in the position of desire for the continuation of mere existence, has the consequence of

Multiculturalism and oppression 93

dehumanizing both of the adversaries. However, this is to the advantage of the native, who, never having been privileged with the name of the human even under conditions of peace, and previously at war with herself and her fellow natives, now finds herself at least in the endeavor of establishing a solid identity, mediated by the Algerian nation. This transformation of identity is executed in the demand for property and for land: "for a colonized people, the most essential value, because the most concrete, is first and foremost the land: the land which will bring them bread and, above all, dignity" (Fanon 2002: 47). Just as the settler derives his goods and property from his symbolic position, a product of matter and history (European superiority), the Algerian's ownership of the land allows for "dignity" (Algerian identity) and various social goods (bread). This struggle, then, combines the need for recognition and redistribution, along lines later delineated by Fraser.

Conclusion: Principles of Marxist multiculturalism

We can find points of agreement among Lenin, Fanon, and Fraser. They are rarely read together, and come from very different geographical and historical origins. Lenin was concerned with revolutionary action in the Russian Empire of the early twentieth century; Fanon analyzed racism in the Caribbean and in France, as well as the struggle against colonialism in Algeria; and Fraser provides a conceptual understanding and elaboration of the feminist and queer social movements in the contemporary United States. Nonetheless, we can develop points of agreement that present a consistent Marxist approach to multiculturalism from these three authors. These are:

1   A definition of the defense of minority cultures that identifies oppression as the key political criteria. A cultural distinction that is not subject to oppression has a simple social existence, and lacks political value. The fundamental principle of multiculturalism is not a celebration of diversity for its own sake, but an active defense of groups who are marginalized and silenced as a means of disempowering their expression and political activity.

2   The need for a concept of numerous cultural groups that retains a sense of their instability, flexibility, and contingency, as well as their porous boundaries. From the Marxist viewpoint, it is not legitimate to identify particular traditions as essential, authentic, or timeless. This basic point can avoid many of the controversies regarding the compatibility of multiculturalism and human rights. The revolutionary viewpoint identifies the need to defend cultural minorities, but to do so with an egalitarian project in mind. Unjust hierarchies that persist in the cultures of minority groups can be challenged from within, just as they are in the dominant culture. Further, the Marxist tradition identifies the ability to share positive cultural attributes and experiences, and to change the self-presentation of individuals and groups who originate in the more

94 *Andrew Ryder*

dominant culture. The authors I have discussed present a consistent refusal of fixed boundaries, alongside an imperative to overcome oppressive and denigrating ideas and practices.

3   The fundamental alignment of a project of cultural recognition of the marginalized with a commitment to radical political democracy and economic egalitarianism. The Marxist viewpoint views class exploitation as the primary agent of inequality and injustice in global society. For this reason, any process of cultural valuation will remain very limited, and even counterproductive, if it does not begin to consciously overcome the basic inequality of class society. Cultural autonomy and self-determination are necessary in order to combat oppression by a dominant group, but this oppression is rooted in the division of the working class and the devaluation of certain sectors of labor, in the interests of economic elites. Only the broad empowerment of the working class collectively, against these elites, can end various forms of cultural oppression.

It might be asked whether these authors are suggesting that the eventual goal of a socialist society would present a monoculture, because distinctions based on oppression would vanish. It seems clear to me that Lenin, Fanon, and Fraser take for granted that a diversity of social experience would continue to take place after the end of class society. Certainly individuals would congregate according to preference and interest and would engage in a variety of distinct aesthetic and social projects, some entirely new and others rooted in traditions of the past. However, in such a socialist society, a formal legal framework for multiculturalism, or initiative to respect it, would be superfluous. Such distinctions would be freely chosen and without stigma in a society without class exploitation or oppression.

I have presented here a consistent leftist critique of mainstream multiculturalism that aims to reject any singular or essential definition of a national culture, alongside the insistence on socialist transformation of the economy as the only durable means of maintaining a truly open conception of cultural identity. I have also understood the question of coexistence of cultures as fundamentally rooted in the question of oppression, and developed the conceptual and historical origins of this viewpoint in the consideration of national self-determination developed by the revolutionary Marxist tradition. Further, we can see the effects and fruits of this outlook in the theory and practice of anti-racism and decolonization, as expressed in the theories of Fanon. It is my hope that this study enriches and expands the influential theory presented by Nancy Fraser, and that further study of cultural difference might draw on the principles recovered here.

Notes

1   For a thorough and unusual case study of how this played out in the era subsequent to the revolution, see O'Keeffe (2013).

Multiculturalism and oppression   95

2 For an account of national self-determination and peasant struggles in classical Marxism, see Anderson (2010).
3 For an analysis of the classical texts on this question, see Brewer (1990: 26–57).
4 This book is especially controversial. For a comprehensive and groundbreaking approach to Lenin's precise meaning, see Lih (2008).
5 Arguably, this popular, rather than class-based, theory depends on a viewpoint that is Rousseauian in nature, and not precisely Marxist. See Tamás (2006).

Bibliography

Anderson, K. B. (1995) *Lenin, Hegel, and Western Marxism: A Critical Study*, Evanston: University of Illinois Press.

Anderson, K. B. (2010) *Marx at the Margins: On Nationalism, Ethnicity, and Non-Western Societies*, Chicago: University of Chicago Press.

Blanc, E. (2014) 'National Liberation and Bolshevism Re-Examined: A View from the Borderlands', *Links International Journal of Socialist Renewal*, May 28.

Brewer, A. (1990) *Marxist Theories of Imperialism: A Critical Survey*, London: Routledge.

Butler, J. (1997) 'Merely Cultural', *Social Text* 52–53, Autumn–Winter: 265–277.

Carter, R. (2008) 'Marxism and Theories of Racism', in J. Bidet and S. Kouvelakis (eds.) *Critical Companion to Contemporary Marxism*, Leiden: Brill, 431–452.

Césaire, A. (1956) *Cahier d'un retour au pays natal*, Deuxième édition, Paris: Présence africaine.

Césaire, A. (1961) 'La Révolte de Frantz Fanon', *Jeune Afrique*, 13–19, December 1961. Cited in Macey, D. (2000) *Frantz Fanon: A Life*, London: Granta Books.

Fanon, F. (1963) *The Wretched of the Earth*, trans. Constance Farrington, New York: Grove Press.

Fanon, F. (1966) *Sociologie d'une révolution*, Paris: Maspero, 1966, cited in Macey, D. (2000) *Frantz Fanon: A Life*, London: Granta Books.

Fanon, F. (1967) *Black Skin White Masks*, New York: Grove Press.

Fanon, F. (2002) *Les damnés de la terre*, Paris: La Découverte.

Fraser, N. (1995) 'From Redistribution to Recognition? Dilemmas of Justice in a "Post-Socialist" Age', *New Left Review* I/212, July–August: 68–93.

Kymlicka, W. (1995) *Multicultural Citizenship: A Liberal Theory of Minority Rights*, Oxford: Oxford University Press.

Lenin, V. I. (1966) 'What Is to Be Done?' in Henry M. Christman (ed.) *Essential Works of Lenin*, New York: Bantam.

Lenin, V. I. (1972) 'Critical Remarks on the National Question', in *Lenin Collected Works*, volume 20, Moscow: Progress Publishers, 17–51.

Lewis, T. (2000a) 'Marxism and Nationalism', part 1, *International Socialist Review* 13, August–September.

Lewis, T. (2000b) 'Marxism and Nationalism', part 2, *International Socialist Review* 14, October–November 2000.

Lih, L. T. (2008) *Lenin Rediscovered: What Is to Be Done? In Context*, Chicago: Haymarket.

Lih, L. T. (2011) 'Lenin, Kautsky, and the "New Era of Revolutions"', *Weekly Worker* 22(12): 895.

Löwy, M. (1976) 'Marxists and the National Question", *New Left Review* 96, March–April: 81–99.

Macey, D. (2000) *Frantz Fanon: A Life*, London: Granta Books.

96   *Andrew Ryder*

Marx, K. and Engels, F. (1969) *Manifesto of the Communist Party* in *Selected Works, Vol. 1*, Moscow: Progress Publishers.

Mattick, P. (1978) 'Luxemburg vs. Lenin', in *Anti-Bolshevik Communism*, London: Merlin Press. Available at marxists.org

O'Keeffe, B. (2013) *New Soviet Gypsies: Nationality, Perfomance, and Selfhood in the Early Soviet Union*, Toronto: University of Toronto Press.

Robinson, C. J. (2000) *Black Marxism*, Chapel Hill: University of North Carolina Press.

Seymour, R. (2010) 'The Changing Face of Racism', *International Socialism* 126. Web.

Stora, Benjamin. (2001) *Algeria, 1830–2000: A Short History*, Ithaca: Cornell University Press.

Tamás, G. M. (2006) 'Telling the Truth about Class', *Socialist Register* 42. Web.

6 Associative democracy, heterosexism and sexual orientation

Luís Cordeiro-Rodrigues

Introduction

Contemporary political philosophers who have researched the topic of multiculturalism have faced a paradox. The paradox is that although there are sound normative reasons to provide rights to cultural minorities to sustain their culture, providing such rights may entail providing a form of power to these groups that facilitates the violation of internal minorities. Ayelet Shachar called this the paradox of multicultural vulnerability. Hence, the normative literature on multiculturalism has focused on justice within groups. In particular, the debate has changed to the analysis of the potentially perverse effects of policies to protect minority cultural groups with regard to the members of these minority cultural groups. Most questions have been addressed taking into consideration the situation of women and children. However, lesbian, gay and bisexual (LGB) individuals' vulnerability to abuse within minorities has been largely neglected.

The concern of this chapter is how those policies meant to protect minority cultural groups can potentially impose serious threats and harm the interests and rights of a kind of internal minority that contemporary political philosophers have overlooked; namely, the kind of internal minority that this chapter explores is the practical implication of policies for multiculturalism for LGBs. This is not just a theoretical concern, but an actual real life problem: within some minority cultural groups, LGBs are very disadvantaged by the unintended consequences of multicultural politics (Swaine 2005: 44–45). This form of injustice I call heterosexism. In particular, heterosexism is understood in this chapter as a system of attitudes that discriminates in favor of opposite-sex sexuality and relationships and against same-sex relationships. Heterosexism is a cross-cutting issue in minority cultural groups (and society in general), covering diverse areas of life, ranging from basic freedoms and rights, employment, education, family life, economic and welfare rights to sexual freedom, physical and psychological integrity, safety and so forth. My argument is that the solution for the paradox consists of endorsing an associative democracy model, which I will explain in detail later on.

98   *Luís Cordeiro-Rodrigues*

This chapter is divided into three sections. In section 1, I outline briefly the rights of LGBs. In section 2 I explain what associative democracy is and how it can be good for addressing the violations of LGBs' rights within minorities. Finally, in section 3, I look into some possible objections and respond to them.

1 – The rights of LGBs

In general terms, it can be affirmed that LGBs have an interest in bodily and psychological integrity, sexual freedom, participation in cultural and political life, family life, basic civil and political rights, economic and employment equality and access to welfare provision.

A question that may come up at this point is where the list of LGB interests comes from. That is, the question as to why LGBs have these interests and why these interests are morally relevant needs to be addressed. The reason why these interests matter is because fufilling these interests is indispensable for LGBs' well-being. Such interests refer to what is fundamentally important for the well-being of LGBs. Put differently, such interests are of supreme importance due to the fact that it is necessary that LGB individuals have access to them in order to have a worthwhile life. Hence, these interests are, in part, what fulfills human life because they are how human beings flourish. It is empirically observable that LGB individuals across cultures have these interests and that it is a requirement for them to have access to these interests so as to flourish. Whenever LGB individuals have a realistic option for accessing these interests, they always or usually choose them. However, I do not mean that this list of interests is just a list of interests for LGB individuals. In fact, they are universal interests, but expressed in particular with respect to LGB individuals. In other words, the list of LGBs' interests mentioned above consists of interests that fall within the scope of human universal interests (Lau 2004). In turn, this means that these interests refer to those inalienable rights that individuals have in virtue of being human and that others have to respect them, no matter what. For these rights are fundamental rights that people have, independent of the kind of person they are (e.g., from a different religion, race, etc), and these take precedence over other rights.

From the egalitarian point of view taken in this chapter, the state is duty bound to promote and protect these universal interests. In my interpretation, an egalitarian view of society has at minimum the core goal to guarantee that all human beings have access to, or an equal opportunity to, live a worthwhile or good life. Therefore, due to the fact that access to that inventory of interests is a requirement for flourishing in a way that ensures one will have a worthwhile life, then the state is under a duty to protect those interests. And even if individuals decide not to take advantage of having the right to pursue those interests, owing to the fact that they are so fundamental, the state is under an obligation to offer the possibility of accessing them.

Associative democracy and sexual orientation   99

These characteristics and the capacity to flourish give individuals dignity. Hence, denying such rights that individuals have in virtue of their nature is treating them as somehow below their human dignity.

Sometimes minority groups violate these fundamental interests. One of the LGBs' interests that may be jeopardised is in basic rights and freedoms. Sometimes, LGBs have their freedom of association, opinion, expression, assembly and thought limited (European Union Agency for Fundamental Rights 2009: 50–55). Minority cultural groups can jeopardise these interests due to hierarchies of power within groups. Some groups use a variety of norms of social control; the Hutterites, for example, have monopolised power over economic resources. Also in some groups, participation in political decisions and freedom of expression is culturally determined; for the Hutterites, the right to express one's own opinion and so forth belongs exclusively to the Elders, a group of heterosexual older males in the group. In other cases, groups can coercively discourage and forbid political expression and exit from the group with threats, indoctrination and so forth. Nathan Phelps, a former member of The Westboro Baptist Church, has mentioned in his interviews the fear that the most prominent members of the group instill in others about challenging 'God's views' and exiting the group (Winston 2012). James Schwartz is a gay man and ex–member of an Amish community; in his interviews, he reported that he had no power for participating in the decisions made by his community and, in particular, the decision of being expelled due to his sexual orientation (Huffington Post 2012; HuffPost Live 2012). Moreover, sometimes there is emotional coercion and blackmail exerted on those who decide to stand up for their basic civil and political rights. For example, in some Hutterite communities, those who deviate from the norms set up by the Elders are the target of ostracism, humiliation and shunning. In other cases, members are forced to stay and abide by the norms of the group, against their will. For instance, some lesbian women are forced into marriages with men they do not with to marry.

In some minority cultural groups, LGBs' interest in being free from murder, torture and other cruel, inhuman and degrading treatment is also sometimes violated (European Union Agency for Fundamental Rights 2011: 13–16). Many LGBs are victims of physical and psychological harassment, murder, hate speech, hate crimes, brutal sexual conversion therapies and corrective rape, among other kinds of physical and psychological violence. Some members of the Americans for Truth about Homosexuality, as well as members of the Southern Baptist Church along with some minorities in Ecuador occasionally engage in sexual conversion therapies that involve physical and psychological torture. Take the case of Samuel Brinton, a former gay member of the Southern Baptist Church; his parents, who are ministers of the Church, forced him to attend a form of sexual conversion therapy which involved inflicting electric shocks on his genitals and sticking nails in his fingers, among other inhumane practices (Wareham 2011). Paola Concha, a lesbian from Ecuador, was put in an illegal clinic to change

100   *Luís Cordeiro-Rodrigues*

her sexual orientation where the conditions were unsanitary, and where she was regularly beaten and denied food (Romo 2012). Some individuals of South African origin engage in a practice called corrective rape that consists of sexually abusing LGB individuals, especially lesbian and bisexual women, with the purpose of making them 'become' heterosexual (Carter 2013). Some Muslim groups believe that if they have an LGB individual in their families, they need to murder LGBs to restore family honour (IGLHRC 2010). Take the example of Roşin Ç, a Muslim man who was murdered by his family due to his sexual orientation; his family was ashamed of this, and considered that only his death could restore honour to the family (IGLHRC 2013). Some British Muslims, like Sheik Omar Bakri, and extremist groups, like the Westboro Baptist Church, have demanded the death penalty for LGB individuals (Westboro Baptist Church 2013e).

In other cases, the violence is psychological rather than physical; as mentioned already, in groups like the Hutterites, Amish and Mennonites, there are strategies of shunning and ostracism that may exert a strong negative impact on LGBs. Some LGBs may have strong feelings of guilt, shame, self–hate and so forth as the result of psychological and emotional coercion. For example, James Schwartz, a gay man who is a former member of an Amish community, has affirmed in his interviews that his coming out was a painful experience due to the reactions of the members of his community (HuffPost Live 2012). Some forms of education that are overly focused on promoting heterosexuality may reinforce these feelings.

Some minority groups also neglect their members' interests in sexual freedom. Many groups have norms and beliefs that imply anti-sodomy laws. The term 'sodomy' has had and still has a variety of different meanings. In many cases, sodomy refers to anal intercourse between a man and a woman or two men. More broadly, the term is used to refer to what some consider unnatural homosexual acts. Hence, sodomy sometimes refers to lesbian, bisexual and gay sexuality, which is also the meaning I use in this chapter, although I make no assumptions about sodomy being natural or unnatural. So in this chapter, anti-sodomy laws are laws that criminalise, prohibit or control sexual behaviour and intimacy relating to lesbians, gays and bisexuals. Groups like the Westboro Baptist Church or some British Muslims like Sheik Omar Bakri demand that LGB individuals should be given the death penalty; some Amish and some Hutterites impose practices of ostracism, shunning and excommunication on those who engage in sexual practices with someone from the same sex. Some Mormons, Catholics and Muslims do not deny membership nor discriminate against individuals who have a non-heterosexual sexual orientation if these individuals do not engage in same-sex relations, i.e., if they remain chaste. Hence, some minority cultural groups have practices, beliefs and norms that forbid or discourage same-sex activity.

Some minority cultural groups also sometimes undermine LGBs' interests in economic and welfare rights. In the case of employment, this refers to

Associative democracy and sexual orientation   101

anti-discrimination law in the workplace and in admission for jobs. In some cases, LGBs' freedom and the right to join the armed forces, to work with children, to employment benefits and health insurance for same-sex families are denied. Although not many religious groups have armed forces, this example could apply to the Swiss Army that protects the Vatican. Generally speaking, in the Catholic Church and in Islam, LGBs cannot occupy job positions such as being a Priest or an Imam. Some Catholic Schools and institutions discriminate against LGB individuals because of their sexual orientation. For example, Carla Hale, a lesbian teacher in the United States, was fired from her job because the school board discovered her sexual orientation (Viviano 2013). James Dale, a former Scoutmaster with the Boy Scouts of America, was fired from his post due to the fact that he was gay (Koppelman and Wolff 2009). Some LGBs are denied equality in healthcare; for instance, religiously run hospitals are unlikely to offer sexual health appointments directed to LGBs' sexuality (European Union Agency for Fundamental Rights 2009: 76–82).

LGBs also have an interest in being able to participate in the cultural and political life of their groups. They wish to be involved in the sacraments, cultural activities, decisions about norms and practices, etc. Many groups refuse membership to LGBs and exclude them from the political decision making process as well as cultural activities within the group. For instance, in 1992, when the Irish-American Gay, Lesbian and Bisexual Group of Boston (GLIB) wanted to participate in the St. Patrick's Day organised by other Irish Americans, they were refused on grounds of GLIB having a different cultural identity from the rest of the participants, and that this would send the wrong message about St. Patrick's Day (Koppelman and Wolff 2009). Groups like the Hutterites do not usually include LGBs in the major decision making process of the group.

Finally, some minority cultural groups may discourage or forbid non-heterosexual style families. Some groups may deny LGBs the right to child custody and adoption (Kranz and Cusick 2005: 6–7). For example, the charity Catholic Care, in Leeds, appealed for the right to refuse adoption to same-sex parents (BBC News 2012). Sometimes, minority cultural groups do not have institutions that correspond to same-sex marriage. In general terms, there are no ceremonies for same-sex marriage in Islam and Catholicism. In groups like the Westboro Baptist Church, same-sex marriage is described in a degrading and violent manner; they usually refer to same-sex marriage as 'fag marriage'. This can be extremely discouraging and emotionally coercive for LGB individuals. Taking this on board, there are a number of significant interests of LGBs within minorities that may be threatened by the norms and beliefs of cultural groups. Heterosexism within cultural minorities is a reality that many LGBs challenge.

Indeed, there is a wide list of LGBs' interests that are harmed by some minority cultural groups. However, it is important to point out that not all minority cultural groups are heterosexist. Many Buddhist and Hindu

102 *Luís Cordeiro-Rodrigues*

groups have very positive attitudes towards LGB individuals. In general terms, individuals of Thai nationality accept some forms of homosexuality. Many individuals of Latin-American origin, especially Brazilians, are similarly accepting. Additionally, in some Indigenous tribes, bisexuals are considered sacred (Herdt 1997). It is also important to point out that not all members of heterosexist groups are necessarily heterosexist. As I will point out throughout this chapter, there are Catholic and Muslim theologians, for example, who consider that homosexuality does not go against their religious doctrine. For instance, the British Muslim gay activist Omar Kuddus does not consider that Islam condemns homosexuality (Kuddus 2013a, 2013b). Moreover, many members of minority groups who are LGB, such as James Schwartz, consider themselves good-faith Christians (Huffington Post 2012; HuffPost Live 2012), even though they disagree with their communities' teachings on homosexuality.

2 – What is associative democracy?

My argument is that the best solution for the dilemma of LGBs within minorities is a model of associative democracy that is an institutional pluralist approach; associative democracy is a power-sharing system, while sovereignty is divided and is not exclusively from the state or the majority. That is, there is a decentralisation of powers and a fair amount of autonomy for organisations (Bader 2005: 322–323; Bader 2007d: 186–189). This model is strongly inspired by the works of Bader (2003a, 2003b, 2005, 2007d) and Hirst (1988a, 1994, 1999a, 2000, 2001). This approach has four main characteristics.

First, the institutions and the welfare providers in society should not be only the ones provided by the state and the market; rather, associations should gradually be able to form and maintain their own institutions; furthermore, they should also become the providers of economic and social affairs. Put differently, in associative democracy, associations are, along with the state and the market, the primary means of organising economic and social life. In particular, that means that it will not be only the state and the market, but also associations that provide health care, education and so forth. Associations can also have their own institutions, like their own version of marriage (e.g., polygamous, same-sex, heterosexual). Hence, although the state does not become a secondary public power, it would have to divide power with associations (Cohen and Rogers 1992: 395; Hirst 1994: 19, 2002: 409; Bader 2007d: 189–190). In an associative democracy, most of the institutions available and the welfare provided would come from associations such as ILGA, Queer Nation, the Catholic Church, Al–Fatiha Foundation and so forth. This would permit institutions and welfare providers to reflect the preferences of the consumers and different identities. Hence, there will be a variety of institutions and welfare provisions that are consistent with different kinds of lives (Hirst 1997: 31–33). The Catholic Church can provide a Catholic model of welfare and institutions that correspond to the Catholic

Associative democracy and sexual orientation   103

doctrine. The LGB community can have its own model of welfare and institutions. In short, in an associative democracy, different versions of the good life are provided by a variety of different welfare systems that reflect various ways of life lived by individuals and groups. Hence, associative democracy stimulates minority institutional pluralism (Hirst 1988a: 142; Hirst 2000: 292–293; Hirst 2002: 409; Bader 2005: 322–324). Hence, according to this first characteristic, both the state and groups have the possibility to form their own welfare system and avoid majority bias.

The second characteristic of this style of associative democracy is that there are a variety of mechanisms of public finance available for individuals and associations. Associations would, in general, be publicly funded according to a common per capita formula, i.e., according to the number of people who join and use the services provided by the associations (Hirst 1997: 65–67; Hirst 2000: 292–293). Moreover, in an associative democracy, all individuals would be entitled to a basic universal income. A universal basic income means that individuals are entitled to an amount of income unconditionally, despite their willingness or otherwise to work, group membership, class, family status, etc. (Parijs 1995: 35). On top of this, the model of associative democracy provides a voucher system that gives individuals access to basic welfare provisions. With these vouchers, individuals can gain access to education, health care and other kinds of welfare provision (Hirst 1994: 179; Bader 2005: 334–335; Bader 2007d: 212–214).

The third characteristic of this model is that there are two functions that are exclusively state functions, i.e., they are not the role of associations. First, the state and only the state has the power to secure peace between associations and safeguard the rights of individuals. In other words, only the state has the monopoly on violence and the administration of justice (Hirst 1994: 44–45). Second, the state has the function of collecting taxes and redistributing funds. According to this third characteristic for an associative democracy, this kind of power cannot be delivered to groups because of the potential risks of doing so.

The fourth characteristic of this model is that it makes a distinction between two kinds of associations: these are cultural associations and cultural-based associations. Cultural associations refer to institutions like the Catholic Church, the Westboro Baptist Church, the Southern Baptist Church, the Black Church and so forth. These associations have as their primary purposes the expression of norms of conduct and a system of beliefs, even if a thin one, that works as their guidance. These are groups that are, at least in part, semiotic and normative. Cultural-based associations refer to those institutions that relate to a culture but also have a public function. This public function can be commercial or offer a public service. Some examples are Catholic schools, Catholic adoption services, Mormon hospitals, Muslim health centres, Christian Bed and Breakfasts, etc. This dual typology aims at balancing the associational freedom of groups with the need of anti-discrimination laws to protect LGBs within groups.

104 *Luís Cordeiro-Rodrigues*

In this conception of associative democracy, the rules governing the internal affairs of cultural associations are different from the rules ruling the affairs of the cultural-based associations. Cultural associations cannot violate the basic civil and political rights and freedoms of individuals, neither can they violate members' physical and psychological integrity nor jeopardise members' capacity to exit and deliberative democratic procedures. In practice, what these limitations imposed on cultural associations mean to LGBs within minorities is that torture, corrective rape, honour killings of LGBs, sexual conversion therapies that involve physical and psychological coercion, anti-sodomy laws like the death penalty, corporal punishment and so forth are practices that associations cannot impose on their members. So the therapies Samuel Brinton and Paola Concha were victims of, the ostracism and shunning carried out by some Amish and Hutterite communities and the hate speech used by the Westboro Baptist Church are all practices that are prohibited by this model of associative democracy. Respect for psychological integrity means that groups cannot have practices of ostracism and psychological coercion, as some Hutterites have. In terms of exit capacity, this means that associations cannot impose practices on members that undermine their members' capacity to exit. It also means that basic freedoms of speech, assembly, association and so forth cannot be undermined in any way. Finally, another requirement that should be followed by cultural associations is that all decisions within the group should follow an internal deliberative democratic model. This means that decisions about the norms of the group should follow deliberation on a variety of platforms, with the safe inclusion of all members affected by the norms and also the inclusion of outsiders.[1]

However, cultural associations are free to have internal rules that discriminate against their members; for instance, in job posts that relate to their culture, associations can discriminate according to sexual orientation – for example, the Catholic Church and Islamic groups can discriminate against gay and bisexual men when filling jobs as priests and Imams, respectively. Associations can also have discriminatory membership rules and exclude LGBs, i.e., LGB members can be expelled or denied membership due to their sexual orientation, with the proviso that LGBs' basic rights and freedoms are respected and the process of expelling or of making the discriminatory norm is democratic. The reason why these discriminatory practices are allowed but the others are not is due to the fact that denying these interests does not significantly disadvantage LGBs within minorities in the same way that the violation of other interests does. In the case of same-sex marriage and discriminatory rules of membership, LGBs can simply join another group, form a new group or exit to the larger society, where membership and marriage laws are more egalitarian. With respect to jobs like the priesthood, there should be a balance of associational freedoms and anti-discrimination law, and allowing groups to discriminate in these jobs does not substantially undermine the equal opportunity to find jobs for LGBs. Contrastingly, if

Associative democracy and sexual orientation 105

someone's bodily and psychological integrity, basic civil and political rights, exit capacity and deliberative democracy were violated, this would probably mean they could not go elsewhere. Undermining bodily integrity is a kind of harm that is so basic that it should never be violated. Psychological violence often creates self-hating images, which have a paralysing effect on individuals, undermining their capacity to pursue interests and live a psychologically healthy life. If individuals were denied basic rights (e.g., freedom of association) and capacity to exit, they could not go elsewhere to pursue their interests. If internal deliberative democracy were denied, then LGBs would not have the possibility to fulfill their interest of participating in the political and social life of their culture.

With respect to cultural-based organisations, the requirements of respect for exit, internal deliberative democracy, bodily and psychological integrity and basic rights also have to be followed. Hence, institutions like Exodus International or the Americans for Truth about Homosexuality cannot offer sexual conversion services that violate those rights. Nor can they have norms that undermine the capacity of individuals to exit and deliberate. The difference of these from cultural associations is that these cultural-based associations are semi-public, in the sense that although they are run privately and some rules can be set privately, they, in general terms, are open to everyone. This means that these kinds of organisations cannot discriminate, they cannot select their employees according to sexual orientation, race, gender, etc. Nor can they refuse to allow their service to be used by individuals based on those individuals' identity. This means that Catholic Care, for instance, cannot deny adoption services to same-sex parents. Catholic schools cannot deny education to the daughter of a same-sex couple; nor can Catholic schools deny a teaching job to LGB individuals, as happened in the case of Carla Hale. With regards to health care needs, this means that associations cannot deny medical services or health care support to individuals due to their sexual orientation. Hence, religious hospitals that belong to a heterosexist group cannot refuse, say, cancer treatment, to an individual due to this individual's sexual orientation. Whenever cultural and cultural-based associations violate these norms, the state can legitimately intervene, and whenever necessary those that violate these rights should be taken to court. Total power over employment and welfare could potentially facilitate the imposition of heterosexist practices. Having taken this into consideration, it can be argued that associative democracy provides groups with the power to form their own institutions, but limits the power to discriminate internally.

To understand why this model is good for LGBs within minorities, it is helpful to recall what the interests of LGBs within minorities are. Broadly speaking, LGBs have an interest in family life (marrying, adopting, having child custody rights), in sexual freedom, bodily and psychological integrity; they have an interest in employment, economic opportunities and access to welfare services, an interest in basic civil and political freedoms and an interest in participating in the social and political life of the group.

106 Luís Cordeiro-Rodrigues

Family life interests are protected by the shape of associations, public institutions and the possibility of LGBs forming their own institutions. Cultural-based associations, which are the ones that provide adoption services, cannot discriminate, i.e., they cannot lawfully reject LGBs from using their adoption services. Cultural associations can deny same-sex marriage; however, state institutions can recognise same-sex marriage and LGBs can form their own associations, where same-sex marriage has legal recognition. This contrasts with Kymlicka's interpretation of federal powers and the laissez-faire approach of Kukathas. In both cases, groups can completely ban same-sex marriage without leaving any other option. The interest of LGBs in sexual freedom is also protected. Groups do not have the power to establish anti-sodomy laws, as the administration of justice is a function of the state. The only measure that can resemble an anti-sodomy law is that cultural associations have the right to expel members according to sexual orientation. However, even if this is the case, the process has to be done democratically.

Bodily integrity and the life of LGBs within minorities are protected because the associational autonomy of both cultural and cultural-based associations is limited in the sense that they are prohibited from imposing such practices. Hence, honour killings, sexual conversion therapies, corrective rape, etc. are kinds of practices prohibited by law. Another reason why bodily integrity of LGBs is, broadly speaking, not threatened is due to the fact that the monopoly of violence and administration of justice are not powers that groups have; rather, these are powers that belong to the state.

Psychological integrity is also protected by the limitation of associative power in engaging in psychological violence. As mentioned, neither cultural nor cultural-based associations can engage in such practices, for example, ostracism. As Charles Taylor (1994) rightly points out, misrecognition by significant others can affect one's well-being by creating self-hating images. In the case of LGBs, these individuals can internalise homophobia as a result of these negative attitudes. Stereotypes towards LGBs are an important source of heterosexism in two ways. First, many homophobic attitudes, such as denying employment to LGBs or engaging in hate speech and hate crimes towards them, result from stereotyped views of what LGBs are. Second, stereotypes have a paralysing effect on LGBs, undermining their agency to take advantage of the opportunities available. In addition, they have a negative psychological impact on individuals who are likely to be affected by such attitudes. Because in associative democracy there is internal deliberation, engaging in deliberation has the advantages of helping LGBs to report abuse, increasing the possibility of contact with other individuals who can be supportive, empowering individuals and helping clarifying the meanings of group practices. In an associative democracy, the internal structure of associations ought to follow internal democracy, which grants the inclusion of all members affected by the norms as well as the inclusion of outsiders.

Associative democracy and sexual orientation 107

The interests in participation in social and cultural life are mainly protected by the availability of funds for forming associations and internal deliberative democracy. The availability of funds enables individuals to form associations the way they wish and pursue their lifestyles, costumes, traditions and conception of the good via accessing the funds available for these purposes. Owing to the fact that groups are internally democratic, individuals are able to participate in the construction of norms, veto norms that are undesirable and voice their opinions in general.

The interests of employment and economic opportunities and access to welfare are protected via the mechanisms of public finance, the differentiation between cultural and cultural-based associations, the egalitarian society and the internal deliberative democratic structure of associations. With respect to public finance, the basic universal income alleviates LGBs from economic pressure and creates independence from the group. The voucher system reinforces the economic status by giving LGBs access to public welfare. These two mechanisms are especially helpful in groups like some of the Hutterite communities, where there is no private property. LGBs' economic opportunities are also improved by the shape of associations and the public state institutions available. Cultural-based institutions cannot discriminate in job posts and neither can they reject LGBs from using their services. Jobs and welfare services should also not discriminate according to sexual orientation, so there is also that option as well. Thus, in this model of associative democracy, there are a variety of forms of public finance to form their own institutions, which correspond to LGBs' welfare needs. Deliberation and internal democracy can help make people more sympathetic to LGBs' needs, with LGBs becoming more empowered to contribute to a better welfare system that corresponds to their needs.

Finally, the interest in basic and political freedom is protected because all associations have to respect freedom, and because there are public finance mechanisms which can be used to pursue freedom of association, assembly, etc. For example, LGBs can use public funds for organising LGB parades.

3 – Possible objections to associative democracy and response

In this section, I would like to respond to some possible counter-arguments against the view defended. First, it could be argued that this approach still allows some discrimination towards LGBs within minorities due to the fact that cultural associations can treat LGBs unequally to a certain extent. Although it is true that this is the case, it is important to balance freedom of association with individual rights, and permitting associations to have a degree of associative autonomy that allows them to discriminate is a consequence of actions that individuals are allowed to do. Still, associative democracy is committed to transforming cultures by engaging in regular deliberation and including LGBs in the decisions of the group.

108 *Luís Cordeiro-Rodrigues*

Second, if groups are given the powers of associative democracy, especially the power to provide their own welfare, it could be argued that this would entail associations gaining the power to institutionalise practices that harm LGB interests. Therefore, some health care cultural associations would provide sexual conversion therapies, which go against the interests of LGBs. Hence, the argument is that allowing cultural institutions to have this degree of autonomy would lead to freedom for institutionalising these practices. So, in this case, those clinics in Ecuador, the Americans for the Truth about Homosexuality and Exodus International would be publicly funded to continue these practices. This argument can be understood in two ways. First, that associative democracy implies that groups have the freedom to impose these practices. According to this argument, it is compatible with associative democracy to accept these practices. Second, the power acquired by groups within associative democracy facilitates the institutionalisation of these practices, even if they are not allowed. Hence, in the case of associative democracy, the power to have one's own welfare is the same power that imposes the practices that harm LGBs within minorities.

The first version of the argument is of normative character, whereas the second is a practical matter. To answer the first version of the argument, it is not the case that this is compatible with associative democracy; as explained, bodily integrity is protected no matter what, hence, there is protection of LGBs from those kind of practices. With respect to the second version of the argument, even though it is more difficult to answer it is still possible to counter-argue it. In the case of associative democracy, associations only gain partial power over some affairs, having to be subjected to state law. This partial power makes a significant difference to the kind of practices that can and cannot be imposed. With respect to power over membership, in associative democracy, cultural associations can discriminate against members, but the process has to be democratic, which implies a level of empowerment that federalism lacks. Cultural-based associations cannot discriminate with respect to membership, and for that reason, an associative democracy does not face the problems that these other theories face. With regards to employment and welfare, as explained, cultural-based associations cannot discriminate against LGBs; only cultural associations are allowed to discriminate in employment, and only if the job position is essential to their cultural expression. Cultural associations do have power over important matters of family law, like marriage. However, this does not pose a problem to LGBs within minorities due to the fact that they have a viable realistic alternative to marriage in their community; namely, in associative democracy, as alternatives, LGBs can either be married by state institutions or form associations where marriage is legally recognised. Due to the fact that adoption services are a public service provided by cultural-based associations, then these are not entitled to discriminate against LGBs according to sexual orientation. The administration of justice and decisions in criminal law are areas where, in this model of associative democracy, groups have no

Associative democracy and sexual orientation   109

power and, thereby, cannot undermine LGBs' interests in bodily integrity by making sexual conversion therapies compulsory or lawful.

Third, it could be argued that associative democracy would lead to a series of homophobic tyrannies, where individuals can form their own associations in ways that could be quite discriminatory. Again, this is not the case with associative democracy. For not only is there a mainstream society, where individuals are treated equally, but also the autonomy of associations is limited. In associative democracy, cultural-based institutions are semi-public, which means that they cannot totally exclude individuals.

The fourth possible criticism to the associative democracy welfare system is that it promotes inequalities because it permits different association performances. If a Catholic group is made up of 40 per cent of the population and Muslims only make up 1 per cent, the funds available and the overall performance of the former is likely to be much higher than the latter. Hence, the services provided for Catholics will be much better than those provided for Muslims (Stears 1999: 584). Therefore, associations can be in danger of promoting group inequalities and reinforcing material hierarchies between groups (Amin 1996: 34; Rahman 2002: 23–24). With regards to LGBs within minorities, this would mean mechanisms of public finance are of little or no use to them. This is so because those who wish to form their own welfare system corresponding to their identity and/or those who wish to use the vouchers they hold in order to fulfil their welfare needs would not have a realistic alternative to the welfare and life in the group because they are fewer in number. More precisely, the welfare provided by LGBs would not be sufficiently competitive and would be of lower quality than that provided by those associations which have more members; in addition, there would be very few services available for LGBs where the voucher system could be used.

In response, the inequalities between groups are able to be corrected by the state funding system of associative democracy. As a general principle, associations are funded according to a per capita formula; however, this is not necessary. If there are relevant inequalities, this can be corrected so that associations perform equally (Elstub 2008: 116–117). Moreover, even if the performance is not the same in general, the basic needs of LGBs (which refer to the most relevant inequalities) are all covered by the associations. In other words, not only do the funds have to be sufficient for associations to satisfy the basic needs of their members, but also with regards to the satisfaction of basic needs, it is compulsory that all associations are open to the public (e.g., for medical emergencies). In addition, the alternatives to associative democracy do not necessarily perform better than associative democracy. State-centered welfare and free market welfare also suffer from regional inequalities; the services in London are probably better than in Wigan because there are more funds and investors available in the capital.

A fifth possible criticism against associative democracy is that it relies on the idea that individuals are capable of identifying what their own needs

110 *Luís Cordeiro-Rodrigues*

are; however, individuals do not know how to fulfil their own welfare needs, instead, there is a need for specialists to do this. It can be argued that individuals are indoctrinated into their cultures and they mistake their culturally constructed preferences for their needs. Hence, in this view, individuals are indoctrinated in their culture to a point where their conscious preferences and needs are false ones. In the case of LGBs within a homophobic group, they could think their need is to convert their sexual orientation to a more 'acceptable' one, but their need is, in fact, to take a healthy approach to their own sexuality. This model of associative democracy endorses a form of moderate universalism, which argues for the protection of basic needs and rights no matter what groups wish. So in associative democracy, the most basic needs of individuals are protected, independent of their preferences.

4 – Conclusion

To conclude, in this chapter I looked into a normative dilemma currently discussed with regards to multiculturalism. The normative dilemma is that giving rights to groups may empower leaders of these groups to discriminate against internal minorities. More precisely, I looked into how such group power can be instrumental to discriminating against LGB individuals within minorities. The solution offered in this chapter is that a model of associative democracy can be a fair approach to address heterosexism within minorities. This model, of course, would require a radical change on how state and group institutions would work.

Taking this on board, I would like to suggest some topics for further research. Associative democracy is a model that has been underexplored, especially with respect to multicultural theory. For this reason, even though the impact of multicultural policies on women, children and other vulnerable individuals within minorities is a topic that has been widely studied, it would be a stimulating new approach to rethink the status of those internal minorities from an associative democratic point of view. In other words, it would be an interesting future contribution to look at the problem of minorities within minorities, taking into consideration the claims made by associative democrats. Furthermore, it would be interesting to carry out further research on the impact of attributing special rights to minority groups such as transgender, swingers, intersex and sado-masochists. These are sexual minorities who have a distinct set of interests from LGBs and whose interests and normative challenges to multicultural theory may slightly differ from other internal minorities.

Note

1   The particulars of this model, besides following the rules just mentioned, should also be such that are negotiated with groups' norms. See, for instance, Monique Deveaux's (2006) model for more details.

Bibliography

Amin, A. (1996) 'Beyond Associative Democracy', *New Political Economy* 1(3): 309–333.

Bader, V. (1995) 'Citizenship and Exclusion: Radical Democracy, Community, and Justice. Or, what is Wrong with Communitarianism?' *Political Theory* 23(2): 211–246.

Bader, V. (1997) 'The Cultural Conditions of Transnational Citizenship on the Interpenetration of Political and Ethnic Cultures', *Political Theory* 25(6): 771–813.

Bader, V. (1998) 'Dilemmas of Ethnic Affirmative Action. Benign State-Neutrality or Relational Ethnic Neutrality?' *Citizenship Studies* 2(3): 435–473.

Bader, V. (1999) 'Religious Pluralism: Secularism or Priority for Democracy?' *Political Theory* 27(5): 597–633.

Bader, V. (2001a) 'Associative Democracy and the Incorporation of Minorities: Critical Remarks on Paul Hirst's Associative Democracy', *Critical Review of International Social and Political Philosophy* 4(1): 187–202.

Bader, V. (2001b) 'Problems and Prospects of Associative Democracy: Cohen and Rogers Revisited', *Critical Review of International Social and Political Philosophy* 4(1): 31–70.

Bader, V. (2003a) 'Religious Diversity and Democratic Institutional Pluralism', *Political Theory* 31(2): 265–294.

Bader, V. (2003b) 'Taking Religious Pluralism Seriously. Arguing for an Institutional Turn. Introduction', *Ethical Theory and Moral Practice* 6(1): 3–22.

Bader, V. (2005) 'Associative Democracy and Minorities within Minorities', in A. Eisenberg and J. Spinner-Halev (eds.) *Minorities within Minorities: Equality, Rights and Diversity*, Cambridge: Cambridge University Press.

Bader, V. (2007a) 'Building European Institutions: Beyond Strong Ties and Weak Commitments', in S. Benhabib, I. Shapiro and D. Petranovich (eds.) *Identities, Affiliations, and Allegiances*, Cambridge: Cambridge University Press.

Bader, V. (2007b) 'Defending Differentiated Policies of Multiculturalism', *National Identities* 9(3): 197–215.

Bader, V. (2007c) 'The governance of Islam in Europe: The Perils of Modelling', *Journal of Ethnic and Migration Studies* 33(6): 871–886.

Bader, V. (2007d) *Secularism or Democracy? Associational Governance of Religious Diversity*, Amsterdam: Amsterdam University Press.

Bader, V. (2008) 'Secularism, Post-Structuralism or Beyond? A Response to My Critics', *Krisis: Journal for Contemporary Philosophy* 2008(1): 42–52.

Bader, V. (2009) 'Legal Pluralism and Differentiated Morality: Shari'a in Ontario?' in R. Grillo et al. (eds.) *Legal Practice and Cultural Diversity* (Cultural Diversity and Law), Surrey: Ashgate Publishing.

Bader, V. (2010) 'Constitutionalizing Secularism, Alternative Secularisms or Liberal-Democratic Constitutionalism? A Critical Reading of Some Turkish, ECtHR and Indian Supreme Court Cases on "Secularism"', *Utrecht Law Review* 6(3): 8–35.

Bader, V. (2012a) 'Associative Democracy and the Incorporation of Minorities: Critical Remarks on Paul Hirst's Associative Democracy', in V. Bader and P. Hirst (eds.) *Associative Democracy: The Real Third Way*, London: Frank Cass.

Bader, V. (2012b) 'Introduction', in V. Bader and P. Hirst (eds.) *Associative Democracy: The Real Third Way*, London: Frank Cass.

112 Luís Cordeiro-Rodrigues

Bader, V. (2012c) 'Problems and Prospects of Associative Democracy: Cohen and Rogers Revisited', in V. Bader and P. Hirst (eds.) *Associative Democracy: The Real Third Way*, London: Frank Cass.

Bader, V. and Engelen, E. R. (2003) 'Taking Pluralism Seriously Arguing for an Institutional Turn in Political Philosophy', *Philosophy & Social Criticism* 29(4): 375–406.

Bader, V. and Hirst, P. (eds.) (2012) *Associative Democracy: The Real Third Way*, London: Frank Cass.

BBC News. (2012) *Charity Loses Gay Adoption Fight* [Online]. Available at http://www.bbc.co.uk/news/uk-england-leeds-20184133 (Accessed 2 September 2013).

Carter, C. (2013) 'The Brutality of "Corrective Rape"', *The New York Times* [Online]. 27 July, 2013. Available at http://www.nytimes.com/interactive/2013/07/26/opinion/26corrective-rape.html (Accessed 2 September 2013).

Cohen, J. and Rogers, J. (1992) 'Secondary Associations and Democratic Governance', *Politics & Society* 20(4): 393–472.

Cohen, J. and Rogers, J. (1993) 'Associative Democracy', in P. K. Bardhan and J. E. Roemer (eds.) *Market Socialism: the Current Debate*, Oxford: Oxford University Press.

Deveaux, M. (2006) *Gender and Justice in Multicultural Liberal States*, Oxford: Oxford University Press.

Elstub, S. (2008) *Towards a Deliberative and Associational Democracy*, Edinburgh: Edinburgh University Press.

European Union Agency for Fundamental Rights. (2009) *Homophobia and Discrimination on Grounds of Sexual Orientation and Gender Identity in the EU Member States: Part ii – the Social Situation*. Available at http://fra.europa.eu/en/publication/2011/homophobia-and-discrimination-grounds-sexual-orientation-and-gender-identity-eu (Accessed 25 August 2013).

Herdt, G. H. (1997) *Same Sex, Different Cultures: Exploring Gay and Lesbian Lives*, Colorado: Westview Press.

Hirst, P. (1988a) 'Associational Socialism in a Pluralist State', *Journal of Law and Society* 15: 139–150.

Hirst, P. (1988b) 'Representative Democracy and Its Limits', *The Political Quarterly* 59(2): 190–205.

Hirst, P. (1992) 'Comments on "Secondary Associations and Democratic Governance"', *Politics & Society* 20(4): 473–480.

Hirst, P. (1994) *Associative Democracy: New forms of Economic and Social Governance*, Amherst: University of Massachusetts Press.

Hirst, P. (1997) *From Statism to Pluralism: Democracy, Civil Society, and Global Politics*, London and New York: UCL Press.

Hirst, P. (1998) 'Ownership and Democracy', *The Political Quarterly* 69(4): 354–364.

Hirst, P. (1999a) 'Associationalist Welfare: A Reply to Marc Stears', *Economy and Society* 28(4): 590–597.

Hirst, P. (1999b) 'Has Globalisation Killed Social Democracy?' *The Political Quarterly* 70: 84–96.

Hirst, P. (2000) 'Statism, Pluralism and Social Control', *British Journal of Criminology* 40(2): 279–295.

Hirst, P. (2001) 'Can Associationalism come Back?' *Critical Review of International Social and Political Philosophy* 4(1): 15–30.

Associative democracy and sexual orientation 113

Hirst, P. (2002) 'Renewing Democracy through Associations', *The Political Quarterly* 73(4): 409–421.

Hirst, P. (2012) 'Can Associationalism Come Back?' in V. Bader and P. Hirst (eds.) *Associative Democracy: The Real Third Way*, London: Frank Cass.

Hirst, P. and Jones, P. (1987) 'The Critical Resources of Established Jurisprudence', *Journal of Law and Society* 14(1): 21–32.

Hirst, P. and Thompson, G. (2002) 'The Future of Globalization', *Cooperation and Conflict* 37(3): 247–265.

Huffington Post. (2012) *Growing up Gay and Amish* [Online]. Available at http://www.huffingtonpost.com/2012/10/05/growing-up-gay-and-amish_n_1942538.html (Accessed 2 September 2013).

HuffPost Live. (2012) *Sins of the Father* [Video]. Available at http://live.huffington post.com/r/segment/a-sons-quest-to/5061ca662b8c2a18ce0002cf (Accessed 2 September 2013).

IGLHRC. (2010) *Violence Against LBT People in Asia: Summary Report on Violence on the Basis of Sexual Orientation, Gender Identity and Gender Expression Against Non-Heteronormative Women in Asia* [Online]. Available at http://www.iglhrc.org/content/violence-against-lbt-people-asia (Accessed 2 September 2013).

IGLHRC. (2013) *Our Issues | IGLHRC: International Gay and Lesbian Human Rights Commission* [Online]. Available at http://www.iglhrc.org/content/our-issues (Accessed 2 September 2013).

Koppelman, A. and Wolff, T. B. (2009) *A Right to Discriminate? How the Case of Boy Scouts of America v. James Dale Warped the Law of Free Association*, New Haven and London: Yale University Press.

Kranz, R. and Cusick, T. (2005) *Gay Rights*, revised. ed., New York: Facts on File.

Kuddus, O. (2013a) 'It's Time to come Out as Gay, Muslim and Proud', *Gay Star News* [Online]. 24 October 2013. Available at http://www.gaystarnews.com/article/it%E2%80%99s-time-come-out-gay-muslim-and-proud241013 (Accessed 18 November 2013).

Kuddus, O. (2013b) *What Does Sharia Law Have to Offer Britain?* [Video]. Available at http://www.4thought.tv/themes/what-does-sharia-law-have-to-offer-britain/omar-kuddus (Accessed 18 November 2013).

Lau, H. (2004) 'Sexual Orientation: Testing the Universality of International Human Rights Law', *The University of Chicago Law Review* 71(4): 1689–1720.

Parijs, P. V. (1995) *Real Freedom for All: What (If Anything) Can Justify Capitalism?* Oxford Political Theory, Oxford and New York: Oxford University Press.

Rahman, M. A. (2002) 'The Politics of "Uncivil" Society in Egypt', *Review of African Political Economy* 29(91): 21–35.

Romo, R. (2012) 'Ecuadorian Clinics Allegedly Use Abuse to "Cure" Homosexuality', *CNN* [Online]. 25 January 2012. Available at http://www.cnn.com/2012/01/25/world/americas/ecuador-homosexual-abuse/index.html (Accessed 18 November 2013).

Stears, M. (1999) 'Needs, Welfare and the Limits of Associationalism', *Economy and Society* 28(4): 570–589.

Swaine, L. (2005) 'A Liberalism of Conscience', in A. Eisenberg and J. Spinner-Halev (eds.) *Minorities within Minorities: Equality, Rights and Diversity*, Cambridge: Cambridge University Press.

Taylor, C. (1994) 'The Politics of Recognition', in A. Gutmann (ed.) *Multiculturalism: Examining the Politics of Recognition*, Princeton: Princeton University Press.

114 *Luís Cordeiro-Rodrigues*

Viviano, J. (2013) 'Fired Lesbian Teacher Carla Hale Won't Get Job Back in Deal with Diocese', *The Columbus Dispatch* [Online]. 16August 2013. Available at http://www.dispatch.com/content/stories/public/2013/08/15/fired-watterson-teacher.html (Accessed 2 September 2013).

Wareham, H. C. (2011) *Survivor: MIT Grad Student Samuel Brinton Remembers 'Ex-Gay' Therapy* [Online] *LGBTQNATION* [Online]. Available at http://www.lgbtqnation.com/2011/08/survivor-mit-grad-student-samuel-brinton-remembers-ex-gay-therapy/ (Accessed 2 September 2013).

Westboro Baptist Church FAQ. (2013a) *Why Are You So Harsh?* [Online]. Available at http://www.godhatesfags.com/faq.html#Harsh (Accessed 2 August 2013).

Westboro Baptist Church FAQ. (2013b) *Why Do You Picket Funerals?* [Online]. Available at http://www.godhatesfags.com/faq.html#Funeral (Accessed 2 August 2013).

Westboro Baptist Church FAQ. (2013c) *Why Do You Preach Hate?* [Online]. Available at http://www.godhatesfags.com/faq.html#Hate (Accessed 2 August 2013).

Westboro Baptist Church FAQ. (2013d) *Why Do You Use the Word "Fag"?* [Online]. Available at http://www.godhatesfags.com/faq.html#Fag (Accessed 2 August 2013).

Westboro Baptist Church. (2013e) *Death Penalty for Fags* [Online]. Available at http://www.godhatesfags.com/fliers/20130403_SIGN-MOVIE-Death-Penalty-For-Fags.pdf (Accessed 20 November 2013).

Winston, K. (2012) 'Nate Phelps Condemns Westboro Baptist Church Plan to Picket Newtown Funerals', *Huffington Post* [Online]. 18 December 2012. Available at http://www.huffingtonpost.com/2012/12/18/nate-phelps-condemns-westboro-baptist-church-picket-newtown-funerals_n_2318916.html (Accessed 2 September 2013).

7 Utilitarianism, religious diversity and progressive pluralism

Eric Russert Kraemer

What has made the European family of nations an improving, instead of a stationary portion of mankind? Not any superior excellence in them, which, when it exists, exists as the effect, not as the cause; but their remarkable diversity of character and culture. Individuals, classes, nations, have been extremely unlike one another: they have struck out a great variety of paths, each leading to something valuable; and although at every period those who traveled in different paths have been intolerant of one another, and each would have thought it an excellent thing if all the rest could have been compelled to travel his road, their attempts to thwart each other's development have rarely had any permanent success, and each has in time endured to receive the good which the others have offered. Europe is . . . wholly indebted to this plurality of paths for its progressive and many-sided development.

(Mill 1859: 43)

Utilitarianism is an ethical standpoint that typically inspires either strong devotion or intense dislike among philosophers. While utilitarians differ widely on theoretical details, they tend to agree on what sorts of activities utilitarianism should require and what kinds of policies and behaviors it should prohibit. It is common for utilitarians to claim that their view strongly supports progressive policies. While its detractors think that utilitarianism leaves important moral considerations out of account, its supporters maintain that it clarifies, simplifies and unifies moral thinking. This is one good reason to apply utilitarian thinking to the issue of religious diversity, which raises numerous problems within the context of a pluralistic democracy. In this chapter I address how utilitarians might treat the issues raised in general by multiculturalism and by multicultural religious diversity in particular. I shall take as my starting point not an ideal world but the actual conditions we currently find around us, namely many instances of differently organized pluralistic cultures with significant religious disagreements and antagonisms. Given this starting point, I shall emphasize the many virtues a utilitarian perspective on multiculturalism affords, and argue that a utilitarian perspective on multiculturalism is an essential component for achieving significant moral progress.

116 Eric Russet Kraemer

The organization of this chapter is as follows. After briefly introducing the problem of religious diversity, I identify key points on which there is widespread agreement among utilitarian thinkers. I shall then briefly note commonly recognized weaknesses with the liberal multiculturalist viewpoint on religious diversity and then demonstrate how aspects of the utilitarian tradition can be employed to craft a defensible and progressive public policy on religious diversity which avoids these weaknesses. I shall further illustrate how a utilitarian strategy can be used to respond coherently to specific examples of current religiously based multicultural controversies. In order to defend the utilitarian perspective on these matters, I shall also discuss and respond to a powerful objection that critics of a utilitarian approach to multiculturalism are likely to advance. And, I shall conclude by posing a challenge to all who would ignore the relevance of a utilitarian perspective on multicultural and religious diversity issues.

The issue of religious diversity

Religion plays an important role in almost all cultures; some sociologists claim that it is a cultural universal (Brown 1991). While many progressive thinkers have been predicting its gradual demise since the Enlightenment and especially for several decades after the middle of the last century, the current situation shows no promise of making this prediction come true any time in the near future. Cultures which officially banned religious practices for much of the last century (such as the former Soviet Union and the People's Republic of China) have experienced a resurgence of religious practice once official government structures of repression changed (Pomerantzev 2012; *The Economist* 2014).

Further, religion continues to be a powerful force with which we all continue to reckon. While is important to admit that most of the truly horrific evils perpetrated in the last century had almost nothing to do with religion, and that most of them were perpetrated by those who called themselves atheists, the problem to be confronted in the present discussion is that the effects of religion in the very recent past have often not been positive. If anything, the first decade of the present century has provided ample examples of powerful religiously motivated activities (such as 9/11, the current depredations of Boku Haram in Western Africa and sectarian violence in the Middle East) that have had significant negative effects. Thus, it is not surprising that there continue to be many who are convinced that religion can only have negative or neutral effects on cultures and on individuals. But, a more carefully nuanced examination reveals that there are many who find powerful benefits from their religious practices, and there are important moral advances in some cultures, such as the results of the Civil Rights Movement in the United States, in which religion is plausibly cited as having played a crucial positive role in terms of providing the leadership and support needed to organize a massive nationwide campaign (Taylor Cl. 2015).

Utilitarianism and progressive pluralism   117

It should be emphasized that theists, atheists and agnostics have all strongly defended utilitarianism, and that the view has no necessary connection to any specific view regarding religion. While some early utilitarians, such as Jeremy Bentham, were convinced that religion was simply "mischievous" (Bentham 1822), the utilitarian thinker who most strongly influenced Bentham's own views, Rev. William Paley, a clergyman in the Church of England, found no contradiction between utilitarianism and traditional theism, and used basic theistic principles to defend utilitarianism against its detractors (Paley 1815). Thus, a consistent utilitarian should not assume without substantive argument that any religious belief or practice is necessarily evil according to agreed-upon utilitarian principles. But, what is utilitarianism?

Some utilitarian varieties and commonalities

The basic concept behind utilitarianism has been discussed by philosophers at least since Plato, when Crito and Socrates argued about whether the consequences of Socrates' escaping from Athens would be better or worse than him not escaping, staying in prison and drinking the hemlock (Plato 2005). The view, however, started receiving major attention during the eighteenth century when first religious writers Richard Cumberland (Cumberland 1672) and John Gay (Gay 1731), and then David Hume (Hume 1738) and William Paley (Paley 1815) recommended it. The first serious early nineteenth century defender of the view was Jeremy Bentham, who made it the cornerstone of his attempts to reform British society (Bentham 1789/1907). The term 'utilitarianism', however, was not popularized until John Stuart Mill did so in the mid-nineteenth century (Mill 1859, 1871). These early utilitarians were concerned with evaluating the overall consequences of possible actions that could be performed and with establishing legislation that would improve society as a whole by improving the consequences for members of the society.

But, what features constitute maximally good consequences? For Bentham it was pleasure and the avoidance of pain. Bentham made famous the slogan, "The Greatest Good for the Greatest Number" and devised a hedonic calculus for its calculation. (Bentham's Hedonistic Calculus considers the factors of intensity, durations, certainty, propinquity, fecundity, purity and extent.)

Bentham's view earned the scorn of William Whewell, who termed utilitarianism a philosophy only "fit for pigs", claiming that it was better to be Socrates dissatisfied than a pig satisfied. To avoid Whewell's criticism, Mill first endorsed the distinction between higher and lower pleasures, claiming that intellectual pleasures were more valuable than gross bodily pleasures, and then later argued for an even more complicated notion of happiness which he termed "happiness in the largest sense", which included not only higher pleasures but also significant elements of self-affirmation, including constructing one's own form of life (Mill 1861, Chapter 2; Mill 1859, Chapter 5). In the early twentieth century, G. E. Moore argued for a multi-faceted

118   *Eric Russet Kraemer*

account of the good, defending a view now referred to as Ideal Utilitarianism, in which not only pleasure but also knowledge, virtue and beauty were to be maximized and their opposites minimized (Moore 1903/1988). Later in the last century, many utilitarians began to emphasize maximizing preference satisfaction (Hare 1981; Singer 1993). So, there has been and continues to be disagreement among utilitarians regarding what is to be maximized.

There is also divergence among utilitarians regarding the basic unit of moral analysis. Some utilitarians argue that individual *acts* are the proper locus of moral evaluation, while other utilitarians instead claim that it is moral *rules* which need to be considered (Smart 1956; West 2003). Yet others urge that it is whole *systems* of rules that need to be evaluated and compared with each other (Brandt 1998). So there is also no agreement among utilitarians as to exactly what aspect of social behavior is to be maximized and which level of analysis is definitive for moral evaluation.

But, there are at least four important points of agreement among utilitarians that are worth emphasizing. First, the notion of maximizing some feature or features and comparing items with respect to this maximization is common to all. The official technical term for what is to be maximized, which utilitarians seem to agree upon, is "utility". Second, the notion that there is always more than one option to be compared, and that moral evaluation involves comparative evaluations with respect to some feature or features of the relevant level consequences. Third, nothing else in addition to these comparative features is required to determine the moral status of the action, rule or system in question. Thus, any appeal to standard moral concepts as rights, duties or virtues is taken as reducible to, or determined by, considerations of consequences. And, fourth, there is the further common idea that two or more options might well turn out to be at the same moral level in terms of producing equally maximally overall good consequences, and thus both would be equally morally acceptable.

This last point is an important one to underline in connection with considerations of multiculturalism, for it opens up the important possibility that different actions, rules or systems of behavior might well be morally equivalent. If so, then different moral practices in different cultures could be demonstrated to be morally on a par. If so, this would in turn entail that utilitarians need not be forced to choose between them, and that utilitarians could in fact consistently advocate for both alternatives as equally acceptable. Thus, utilitarians can be supportive of multicultural arrangements within a single political unity. We should now ask how the utilitarian perspective on multiculturalism might be different from the current, dominant view, namely liberal multiculturalism.

Liberal multiculturalism and its commonly perceived failings

This volume officially uses the term "multiculturalism" in a minimal sense to refer to two or more cultures inhabiting the same geographical area. (I

Utilitarianism and progressive pluralism   119

also assume the additional stipulation that the geographical area be part of a single political entity – to avoid problems created by examples such as competing nomadic groups in contested areas such as Darfur.) In the past two decades multiculturalism has frequently been understood as "liberal multiculturalism", a term that carries with it significant ideological commitments (Strong 2007). One common notion associated with liberal multiculturalism is that of "group-differentiated rights" or cultural accommodations that one group can demand against another in the name of cultural preservation. According to liberal multiculturalists, certain groups can demand special treatment to protect their cultural identities.

Arguments for these accommodations include Charles Taylor's argument that one's self-respect is deeply connected to the respect accorded one's social group, and Will Kymlicka's argument that since one's choices are determined by one's cultural identity, inequalities arising from minority culture membership are not chosen and needed to be addressed (Taylor 1992; Kymlicka 1995). There are related concerns from those such as Thomas Nagel and Ronald Dworkin, who embrace Luck Egalitarianism, the view that since it is a matter of luck into which culture one happens to be born, special adjustments and accommodations are needed to level the playing field for members of disadvantaged minority cultures (Arneson, 1989; Nagel 1991). (Even critics of luck egalitarianism, such as Anderson [1999], defend a justice-as-equality view, according to which societies should take special measures to end oppressive relationships in order to guarantee equal and free participation for all.)

Worries about such special accommodation approaches to multiculturalism include the fluidity of cultural membership concern, the worry that mere recognition diverts attention from more important goals such as redistribution, the egalitarian complaint that one is responsible for one's own cultural affiliations, and the problem of vulnerable internal minorities. For the utilitarian, however, the question is whether the policies associated with liberal multiculturalism can be justified as producing maximally good overall consequences. Unlike those in the liberal Rawlsian tradition who are concerned about lack of fairness, the main problems that utilitarians raise with liberal multiculturalism are rather the bad consequences of uncritical promotion of certain harmful minority culture practices, and the potential better use of resources for other purposes. While slavery, headhunting and foot-binding have all been culturally sanctioned, it is difficult to conceive of a contemporary multicultural society's endorsing these practices on behalf of preserving important traditions of one or another of its cultural elements. But, how can the liberal multiculturalist justify rejecting such harmful traditions? If these practices are an integral part of a particular culture, then their preservation is required if the most important goal of multiculturalism is to keep each culture wholly intact. On the other hand, eliminating such harmful practices is a simple matter for utilitarians, who point to the horrible consequences of allowing customs such as these to continue.

120 *Eric Russet Kraemer*

While utilitarians are open to the possibility that many or even most current practices in a given culture have potentially beneficial consequences for societies as a whole and for individual cultures in particular, even most religious practices, the dominant concern for the utilitarian is whether or not significantly better results can be achieved in other ways. For this purpose the utilitarian is not interested in trying to provide an *a priori* theoretical argument regarding the moral status of a particular practice but instead asks for data regarding the effects of certain practices both on the specifically accommodated cultures and on the community as a whole. Might there be other practices that would lead to much better overall results? If so, then these other practices are to be preferred. If not, and there are relatively positive overall outcomes, then utilitarians can be supportive, but only so long as the outcomes remain overall more positive than their absence would be. Let us now consider the major problem related to religious diversity, namely religiously inspired conflict.

Some reasons for religious conflict

Some religious are absolutist and some are not. It is this important difference that explains why religious diversity can apparently exist with relatively little or no friction in some environments but not in others. There are significant examples of non-absolutist religious diversity, such as those situations which existed during the Greek and Roman empires, in which religious discord was not much of an issue. Some religions, however, take as their mission the creation of a religiously uniform culture; this requires the conversion of the non-believer and the imposition of one standard of rules for believers and a very different standard of treatments for non-believers. Monotheistic religions following in the Abrahamic tradition have tended to have such a practice. Jews, Christians and Muslims have all conducted, and some are still conducting, "holy" wars in the name of defending a particular faith or sect. In the middle of the last century, conflicts in Cyprus between Greek Orthodox Christians and Turkish Muslims and in Northern Ireland between Catholic and Protestant Christians captured major attention. Problems have continued ever since in Israel between Jews and Muslims, in Egypt between Muslims and Copts, in Lebanon between Christians and Muslims, and throughout the Middle East between Sunnis and Shiites.

The recent assassination of the staff of the satirical magazine, *Charlie Hebdo*, in Paris in January, 2014 is a powerful example of such behavior. Such actions are clearly rejected by utilitarians, who explain their immorality by noting how any positive effects experienced by some minority members of French culture and other religious fundamentalists around the world were heavily outweighed by the negative effects experienced by the vast majority of the world's population who learned of the incident and were outraged. The utilitarian argues that it is obvious that there were many other actions open to the perpetrators that would have had much better

Utilitarianism and progressive pluralism 121

overall effects. Clearly such acts of religiously motivated violence are not permissible in a multicultural society, as no one can feel safe in a society in which members of one culture regularly inflict murder and mayhem on members of another in the name of religious righteousness.

On extreme cases there is widespread agreement. Other cases of social friction caused by religious diversity, however, are much less clear from the moral point of view. These cases stem from the fact that it is commonly interpreted that observant religious practice dictates many specific aspects of human interaction. These include requiring [1] specific modes of dress, [2] particular dietary restrictions, [3] strict religious ritual observances, [4] prescribed body modifications and restrictions – including scarifications, head shavings, colorings, and ear, lip and neck modifications, [5] proscribed medical treatments, [6] precise regulation of all sexual relations including marriage laws, [7] the enforcing of separate gender roles and [8] specific punishments for breaking religious norms. All of these items are often governed by explicit religious rules and sanctions. Women in many religious cultures are required to wear special clothing to preserve modesty; there are religious prohibitions on the eating of pork, beef, shellfish, etc.; the number and time of prayer sessions per day or week are also widely religiously regulated; Orthodox Jewish women are required to shave their heads when they marry; Seventh Day Adventists are prohibited from receiving blood transfusions; Catholics must marry other Catholics and raise their children as Catholics; in Mormonism, Islam and Catholicism women are not allowed to become priestesses; and, according to Islam, apostates are to be killed. And, while it should be granted that many of these differences do not lead to significant social discord, sometimes they do. It is also important to note that many of these restrictions are only imposed on women, not on men. Utilitarians can point to the powerful example of John Stuart Mill's efforts (supported by his wife, Harriet Taylor) to remove unnecessary restrictions on women (Mill 1869).

Religiously motivated conflict arises in those cases in which members of one cultural group of a multicultural society are strongly religiously encouraged and motivated to act in ways that members of another cultural group do not think appropriate. This leads to special demands by one group to be allowed by the common society to behave in ways that other groups deem not only inappropriate but wrong. These demands create social conflicts requiring resolution. We have seen how liberal multiculturalists respond – their strategy is to insist on according specific group-based accommodations or rights. As noted above, what is by no means clear is how such a response can adequately handle the wide variety of sources of cross-cultural religious conflict.

Further, it seems that liberal multiculturalists are forced into accepting a variant of ethical relativism regarding customs currently in practice; none can be eliminated for fear of destroying cultural identities. For utilitarians, however, there is the major moral concern that some customs in some

122   *Eric Russet Kraemer*

cultures are simply morally wrong, that their practice inflicts significant and useless harm on many members of a particular group and, as a result, should be curtailed.

In addition, there is a further worry that some cultures, in scrupulously following traditional religious ways in the face of the challenge of trying to maintain a separate cultural identity amidst a sea of other cultures, may not be acting consistently with their own best interests and fundamental principles. This could happen for a variety of reasons of which the traditionalists themselves may be unaware. But, the limited resources of liberal multiculturalism seem unable to justify a culture's making important changes in social practices for the good of their own community.

These three problems pose a formidable challenge. Can the utilitarian do better? I shall take it as evident that utilitarians can account for the immorality of religiously motivated killing of members of *other* cultures. Similarly the utilitarian would argue that the religiously motivated killings of members of one's *own* culture (so-called "honor killings", the public lapidating of adulteresses, the immolation of living widows on the funeral pyres of their dead husbands, etc.) are all instances of immoral practices, as there are obvious alternative procedures with better overall consequences for all concerned. As such, even if officially blessed by cultural religious support mechanisms, these practices still need to be politically sanctioned. But, what about the many other aspects of religious practice listed above? What can utilitarians say about less clear cases? Under what circumstances should specific practices be encouraged or discouraged?

And can this be done in a consistent and helpful way? Let us now consider what utilitarians can propose as a means to avoid religious conflicts and also as a means to improve the lives of everyone in a multicultural setting.

Religious multiculturalism: A progressive utilitarian approach

It is my contention that utilitarians are able to provide a five-fold progressive approach to multiculturalism that I will characterize as having five related virtues, namely of being Protective, Empirical, Experimental, Progressive and Sensitive or PEEPS, for short. And, what's more, these virtues mutually reinforce each other. Let us now consider each of these virtues in turn.

First, following its own historical roots, utilitarianism is concerned with protecting and nurturing those who are most in need of being protected from predation by those more powerful. Utilitarians famously fought in the nineteenth century to abolish child labor and obtain public sanitation and free public schooling for all, fighting to change then traditional mores in Great Britain for the betterment of society as a whole. So, one important, general criterion for utilitarians of all stripes is whether certain religious norms impose risks, burdens or painful conditions on individual members of a culture who have not freely chosen to have these travails inflicted upon them. In other words, are there current behaviors in a particular society from which certain of its members need protection? A number of powerful examples spring to mind. While certain practices, such as killing twins on birth as they bring bad luck, are among the most horrific; these practices do not export well to multicultural settings. So, we need to consider those disturbing practices that do tend to follow their cultural members.

Consider the disturbing case of what is neutrally referred to as female genital excision, a procedure widely practiced in Saharan and Sub-Saharan Africa. Defenders of the practice refer to it as female genital circumcision; its opponents call it female genital mutilation. The practice is extremely widespread in both Saharan and sub-Saharan Africa. Current data from the web notes that Egypt has the largest total number of circumcised females, at 27.2 million or 91% of its female population, while Somalia has the largest percentage of circumcised females at 98% (World Health Organization website 2015).

This practice, which involves cutting off the clitoris of young girls and sewing them shut, is typically given a religious blessing, a way of making girls clean and safe for marriage. The results of the procedure are horrific (Kopelman 1994). Utilitarians argue that since there seems to be no good reason in terms of good consequences for continuing this practice in the standard multicultural setting, and overwhelmingly powerful evidence of the powerful negative effects from this practice, that it should simply be eliminated. This is an example of Protection, of protecting young women from an abusive and harmful practice. It is not clear how liberal multiculturalists could consistently ban the practice. In fact, there continue to be those who argue that the practice should continue.

This leads to an interesting side issue, namely that of male circumcision. The practice of circumcision on Jewish and Muslim males is dictated by religious sanction. There are those who claim that it is, in fact, comparable in barbarity to female genital mutilation. But is it? The utilitarian approach to the evaluation of religiously controversial practices in addition to being protective is also Empirical. That is, utilitarians will say that although they know that certain practices have been seen as morally permissible for thousands of years, one still needs to ask what the evidence has to report now regarding the consequences of the practice. Thus, the utilitarian will maintain that we must investigate the matter and get the best evidence we can as to whether or not the practice of circumcision is *overall* more harmful than the practice of non-circumcision. If it turns out that there is excellent evidence that circumcision is in fact more harmful than not, then this would be in fact a good reason to pass legislation to protect young male babies accordingly and to punish clandestine male circumcisers.

The empirical aspect of the utilitarian perspective also is demonstrated on the vexed topic of medical vaccinations. While vaccinations are legally required in most multicultural societies, some argue on religious grounds that they should not have to have their children vaccinated against major diseases. The problem that this presents for the treatment of the diseases that vaccination policies are designed to prevent, according to those who favor vaccination, is that only complete vaccination of a population will eliminate the disease. Here again the utilitarian asks us to look at what the evidence has to say. If the evidence is overwhelmingly in favor of vaccination, as it currently seems to be, then the virtue of protection requires vaccination and overrides any contrary religious policy. Related reasoning is also used to justify rejecting the objections of Seventh Day Adventist parents to medically necessary blood transfusions for their children. Since children are not deemed able to make medically reasonable choices for themselves, parental preferences against transfusions would need to be overridden in the case of minors.

The third virtue of the utilitarian approach to multiculturalism is closely related to the second. Just as the utilitarian is empirical, which demands refraining from taking a dogmatic stance on any practice without having thoroughly investigated the evidence regarding its consequences, so too the utilitarian must continue her non-dogmatic stance in exhibiting a willingness to be Experimental. Here one can see an important positive role that multiple cultures can play in any society. Cultural differences, by definition, provide the means for informative experiments on different practices regarding the same sorts of issues all of us face. For example, some cultures insist on piercing small children's ears while others insist on waiting until a child is a teenager. Having different practices that can be monitored and studied provides a means for determining whether a particular practice, for which there is currently insufficient data to make a definite decision one way or the other, is either benign or harmful.

One worthy application of the virtue of "experimentality" is the comparison of two prominent multicultural societies with very different overall approaches to the exhibition of religion in the public domain: the United States and France. Having radically different religious histories, the two countries have evolved two opposing perspectives: American secularism and French laïcité. While both systems prohibit the government from enforcing a particular set of religious beliefs, American secularism allows and perhaps even encourages individuals to express their individual religious beliefs in public, whereas French laïcité prohibits any outward sign of religious affiliation as contrary to republican interests, as religion in France is a private matter. For utilitarians it would be important to determine which approach really maximizes utility with respect to religious diversity, and then suggest that one society changes accordingly.

What multiculturalism also provides is an opportunity for one culture to see how another culture does things differently. And, as no culture is naturally static, this then permits cultures to change to the observed customs and behaviors that they find more appealing. It has been argued that all cultures in the United States have benefitted enormously from helpful new customs brought by immigrant minority groups (Kolker 2011). But, of course, not

Utilitarianism and progressive pluralism   125

all change is for the good. Only when it is can we call it an advance. But, how is a change for the good to be measured? For the utilitarian there is a clear answer: in terms of its utility. If a new practice has higher utility than a competing traditional practice, that is a conclusive reason to change.

The fourth virtue of the utilitarian approach is the Progressive virtue. A powerful example of this as applied to the religious context is the major change with respect to the issue of same-sex marriage in the different mainstream Protestant communities in the past decade. While a decade ago only the most liberal groups embraced the value of gay marriage, it has been instructive to observe more and more mainline religious groups struggle with the issue and gradually come to see that a more progressive approach consistent with their basic religious views did in fact require acceptance of same-sex marriage.

Here again the arguments were not only made on the basis of doctrine but on the basis of the available evidence that those involved strongly desired and would in fact benefit from changing the former institution of marriage to include same-sex couples. While followers of Rawls and Kant may insist that the primary moral issue is one of fairness, the utilitarian will reply that fairness only matters morally if it has significant consequences that are socially apparent. The reason the perception of fairness is important is that it provides a secure sense that one is living in a society in which one can count on certain principles to be followed. Reliance on social stability is an important feature for evaluating the good of a particular form of social existence. In the case of gay marriage, the debate originally involved responding to the complaint that gay marriage would undermine heterosexual marriage, an alleged consequence that under scrutiny widely came to be perceived as illusory.

Finally, unlike other approaches to religious multiculturalism which accord cultures specific rights and which value tradition for its own sake, the utilitarian perspective is Sensitive to environmental and other changes within a culture and within the larger social context that affect the reasonability of maintaining certain religious customs. For example, the ultra-Orthodox Jewish ban on "work" on the Sabbath has been interpreted to mean not turning on and off electricity during this period. This leads regularly to unfortunate consequences. (As this chapter was being written it was reported that a fire killed seven children in Brooklyn, New York in March of 2015 due to a hot plate deliberately being left on over the Sabbath to avoid the work of having to turn it off.) The utilitarian would insist that the fact that electricity did not exist when the religious tradition was established should be taken into account as well as the changes in social behaviors since then, including available procedures for meeting basic human needs, and that religious policies may need to be modified accordingly. Utilitarians are not opposed to religious ritual *per se*, only to practices that do not fit well the current environmental conditions and thus bring about unnecessary suffering and hardship. The same religious functions could be maintained by

126 *Eric Russet Kraemer*

modifying the current religious interpretation of certain rules to accommodate technological and environmental changes.

Thus, we can see that these five related virtues – being protective, empirical, experimental, progressive and sensitive – make a powerful case for the utilitarian's perspective on multiculturalism being able to solve many of the problems that beset the liberal multiculturalist. According to the progressive utilitarian multiculturalist, there are indeed significant values in not only permitting but supporting certain aspects of multicultural life, as there is much to be learned from others and as there are many different forms of life that are roughly morally equivalent. Since maintaining cultural identity is an important preference for many, it is an important consequence to be taken into consideration. But, the progressive utilitarian multiculturalist continues, there are also concerns to be addressed. Not every cultural practice should be encouraged or permitted. Individual cultures within the multicultural setting should initially be trusted to make changes over time that are in the interest of their members; but, when a given culture is not sufficiently attentive to the harms it is either causing or allowing, the state should intervene in an appropriate and respectful manner, using impartial evidence, to prevent needless damage. But, every view has its critics, and utilitarianism is no exception. So, it is important that we address a traditional criticism to utilitarianism that its critics would take to be a central problem for the utilitarian multicultural perspective advanced in this chapter.

Is utilitarianism truly consistent with multiculturalism?

Some might wonder whether utilitarianism is inconsistent with multiculturalism, since it favors "the greatest good for the greatest number" (see Kymlicka 2002, Chapter 2). According to some critics, utilitarians should favor a policy of cultural imperialist hegemony that imposes the unique maximal utility set of requirements on all of the world's cultures, not permitting participation in other forms of life. One might imagine, for example, natural, behavioral and social scientists investigating human, social and environmental nature thoroughly and figuring out what form of life would, in fact, maximize utility in the long run for all concerned. Armed with this information, the critics continue, utilitarians should then militate for a single world culture following the outlines established by scientific consensus, in which all cultures are modified to reflect these ideal results.

But just what such a form of life might be like is not at all clear to everyone. While some might envision a version of a Marxist Workers' Paradise, others might imagine a back-to-nature communal existence, while still others might imagine all humans living in large but sustainable urban environments surrounded by significant wilderness. In any event, utilitarians are not committed to preferring *a priori* one form of cultural existence over another, but for following the best information that emerges as to what the best overall set of cultural specifications might be. While such a claim might be

Utilitarianism and progressive pluralism   127

logically consistent with the utilitarian perspective, there are good reasons to doubt that utilitarians would ever have to take this possibility seriously.

First, given the significant variation in human preferences for the many different activities in which humans engage and from which they gather significant enjoyment, the claim that there is in fact only one maximal way of being a cultural being seems woefully under-motivated. If humans were less flexible and less adaptable, if their tastes and abilities were more restricted, if there were many fewer ways in which they could apparently not only survive but flourish, then it would be easier to imagine a single maximal cultural way of being. But, the fact that humans have been able to adapt to a remarkably diverse set of natural environments and to produce wildly varied sets of cultural behaviors makes this possibility seem quite remote indeed.

A further complicating factor stems from the concern regarding human fallibility, a point on which Mill insists. This theme questions whether we should ever be confident that we have enough information to identify such a maximal social model, even though we do seem to have practical certainty in some matters, such as female genital mutilation and vaccinations.

A third complicating consideration, again from Mill, is the importance of recognizing significant individualistic differences in preferences that would impede any project of training to limit human options. The form of social life, such as that envisioned by Aldus Huxley in *Brave New World*, in which the ideal culture consists of five different social groups with prescribed roles and activities would not necessarily be one that utilitarians would endorse, in spite of what some critics might claim (Huxley 1932).

A further complicating factor is that even if it could be established that a particular way of being as a culture was ideal now, there is no reason to suppose that there will not be significant changes in the future, both cultural and environmental, that would cause a rethinking of what should count as ideal. And, were not a variety of cultural models in existence upon which to test these changes, it would not be clear how to continue to provide maximal utility in a particular cultural setting as important changes occur. This problem is analogous to that of mono-cultural practices in agriculture, which have been demonstrated to expose a whole aspect of production or the environment to the risk of devastation if a particular pest/disease comes on the scene. Thus, it can be argued that maintaining the valuable diversity provided by multiculturalism is an important safeguard for all. This is one reason why utilitarians should bemoan the disappearance of particular language communities and the cultures associated with them, as each culture represents a significant period of human experience in which important empirical discoveries might have been made that could provide significant benefit to all.

Finally, it may also be the case that important differences in environment and in local gene pools strongly favor requiring different cultural adaptations in which different professions and cultural arrangements are to be

128 *Eric Russet Kraemer*

preferred as better fitting particular individuals in those environments. Further, there are noteworthy harms to be considered in totally obliterating any group's cultural heritage and thus depriving its members of a valuable sense of tradition and identity. Thus, the assumption that utilitarians must favor a single culture for all is not supported.

There are other standard worries that utilitarians face. Can one really measure happiness or preference satisfaction or whatever it is that is to be maximized? How can we compare positive and negative elements? Doesn't utilitarianism support persecuting a tiny minority for the advantage of the overwhelming majority? Are immoral actions that no one ever discovers really not morally bad? Isn't there more to morality than maximizing consequences, such as basic human rights, virtues, doing one's duty or being fair even if the consequences aren't maximized, etc.? All of these customary objections have equally compelling utilitarian responses, but reasons of space prevent an in-depth discussion of them here. It is to be hoped that the present discussion will suggest likely utilitarian replies to the reader. So now let us conclude.

Conclusion

In this chapter I have outlined a progressive utilitarian perspective on multiculturalism. Inspired by John Stuart Mill's argument for the advantages of different cultures in different nations, I have expanded on Mill's original insights to argue for similar advantages to having different cultures within the same society. Although Mill was concerned to promote the importance of developing and maintaining one's individuality against the conformist pressures of society, similar concerns support the importance of strong multiculturalism within a single society. While some are able to sustain their individuality in opposition to social norms, others require strong connections to traditional groups in order to define their identity and find meaning. Robust utilitarian multiculturalism supports both those who favor individual development as well as those who prefer group connection. Further, the approach outlined in this chapter also provides mechanisms for determining both which practices need to be changed and for improving cultural practices.

These two critical criteria should be used to measure all other perspectives on multiculturalism. This leads to a final challenge.

Any culture which claims to have figured out exactly how to live in all situations is in serious trouble because the conditions of the world are constantly changing. Any culture which clings tightly to tradition to solve future challenges is likely to be doomed. Only a progressive approach to one's own culture and to learning from other cultures offers us hope to withstand future developments. In order to be progressive, we must continue to be sensitive regarding what needs to be done and protective of those most in need of our protection; but we must also be empirical and experimental

Utilitarianism and progressive pluralism   129

if we are to devise better strategies. One way to achieve such an approach is to embrace the progressive utilitarian perspective. Can other perspectives do as well, or better? It is hard to imagine how any alternative view which did not consider the consequences of social customs could be regarded as a serious competitor.

Bibliography

Anderson, E. (1999) 'What Is the Point of Equality', *Ethics* 109(2): 287–337.

Arneson, R. (1989) 'Equality and Equal Opportunity for Welfare', *Philosophical Studies* 56: 77–93.

Bentham, J. (1789/1907) *An Introduction to the Principles of Morals and Legislation*, Oxford: Clarendon Press.

Bentham, J. (1822/2003) *The Influence of Natural Religion on the Temporal Happiness of Mankind*, Amherst, NY: Prometheus Books.

Brandt, R. (1998) *A Theory of the Good and the Right*, Amherst, NY: Prometheus Books.

Brown, D. (1991) *Human Universals*, New York: McGraw Hill.

Cumberland, R. (1672/1978) *De Legibus Naturae Disquisitio Philosophica*, London; trans. by John Maxwell, *A Treatise of the Laws of Nature*, reprinted New York: Garland.

Economist. (2014) 'Cracks in the Atheist Edifice', *The Economist*, 11 January 2014. Available at http://www.economist.com/news/briefing/21629218-rapid-spread-christianity-forcing-official-rethink-religion-cracks

Feldman, F. (1997) *Utilitarianism, Hedonism and Desert*, Cambridge: Cambridge University Press.

Gay, J. (1731) *A Dissertation Concerning the Fundamental Principle and Immediate Criterion of Virtue*, in Frances King, *An Essay on the Origin of Evil*, London.

Hare, R. M. (1981) *Moral Thinking: Its Levels, Method, and Point*, Oxford: Oxford University Press.

Hume, D. (1738/1978) *A Treatise of Human Nature*, L. A. Selby-Bigge (ed.), Oxford: Oxford University Press.

Huxley, A. (1932) *Brave New World*, New York: Harper and Brothers.

Kolker, C. (2011) *The Immigrant Advantage*, New York: Free Press.

Kopelman, L. M. (1994) 'Female Circumcision/Genital Mutilation and Ethical Relativism', *Second Opinion* 20(2): 55–71.

Kymlicka, W. (1995) *Multicultural Citizenship: A Liberal Theory of Minority Rights*, Oxford: Oxford University Press.

Kymlicka, W. (2002) *Contemporary Political Philosophy: An Introduction*, Oxford: Oxford University Press.

Mill, J. S. (1859) *On Liberty*, London: Longman, Roberts and Green.

Mill, J. S. (1871) *Utilitarianism*, Roger Crisp (ed.), Oxford: Oxford University Press.

Mill, J. S. (with H. Taylor) (1869) *The Subjection of Women*, London: Longman, Greens and Co.

Moore, G. E. (1903/1988) *Principia Ethica*, Amherst, New York: Prometheus Books.

Nagel, T. (1991) *Equality and Partiality*, New York: Oxford University Press.

Paley, W. (1815/2002) *The Principles of Moral and Political Philosophy*, Boston: West and Richardson [8th American Edition].

130 *Eric Russet Kraemer*

Plato. (2005) 'The Crito', in E. Hamilton and H. Cairns (ed.) *The Collected Dialogues of Plato*, Princeton, NJ: Princeton University Press.

Pomerantzev, P. (2012) 'Putin's God Squad: The Orthodox Church and Russian Politics', *Newsweek*, 9 October 2012. Available at http://www.newzealand.mid.ru/religion-in-russia.htm

Ronald, Dworkin, R. (1981) 'What Is Equality? Part 2: Equality of Resources', *Philosophy and Public Affairs* 10: 283–345.

Singer, P. (1993) *Practical Ethics*, Cambridge: Cambridge University Press.

Smart, J. J. C. (1956) 'Extreme and Restricted Utilitarianism', *The Philosophical Quarterly* I: 344–354.

Strong, S. (2007) *Justice, Gender, and the Politics of Multiculturalism*, Cambridge: Cambridge University Press.

Taylor, Charles. (1992) 'The Politics of Recognition', in A. Guttmann (ed.) *Multiculturalism: Examining the Politics of Recognition*, Princeton: Princeton University Press.

Taylor, Clarence. (2015) 'African American Religious Leadership and the Civil Rights Movement', *The Gilder Lehrman Institute of American History*. Available at http://www.gilderlehrman.org/history-by-era/civil-rights-movement/essays/african-american-religious-leadership-and-civil-rights-m (Accessed 20 April 2015).

West, H. (2003) *An Introduction to Mill's Utilitarian Ethics*, London: Cambridge University Press.

World Health Organization. (2015) World Health Organization Website. Available at http://www.who.int/reproductivehealth/topics/fgm/prevalence/en/ (Accessed 20 April 2015).

Section 3

Eastern philosophy approaches to multiculturalism

8 Multiculturalism, Indian philosophy, and conflicts over cuisine

Lisa Kemmerer

The International Food Fair is always a popular event at Montana State University Billings (MSUB), where I work. The dining hall is crowded with booths smelling of spices from Saudi Arabia and China, tended by international students eager to share their favorite foods with their newfound friends. For the cooks and those doling out food, there is perhaps "an imagined community implied in the act of eating food 'from home' while in exile, in the embodied knowledge that others are eating the same food" (Sutton 2001: 84). For locals, it is a time when meat-and-potato-eating ranch-raised students sample spicy rice dishes, tidy egg rolls, and other cultural, culinary delicacies prepared diligently by fellow students. The International Food Fair is a multicultural moment at our little university – one of precious few such moments in Billings, Montana – a time of promoting and sharing multiple cultural traditions.

The United States came into being and continues to take shape through the introduction of people from diverse cultures from around the world. Cuisine is central to culture, and the United States is a nation rich with food possibilities. Every city of any size offers cuisine from China, Thailand, Mexico, Mongolia, and India, while larger cities offer a host of other international culinary options. Additionally, international food fairs are fairly common. In the United States it is somewhat commonplace to celebrate diversity and promote multiculturalism through food.

This is also true at Montana State University, a campus that takes pride in being accessible to diverse peoples. (Our motto is "Access and Excellence.") Yet I notice that certain types of cultural dishes are conspicuously absent at our international food fair. For example, Korean students never offer *boshintang*; Japanese students do not offer *sanma aisu*; Philippian students never bring *balut*; and Chinese students fail to offer a dish that translates as "dragon, tiger, phoenix big braise". If the food fair is about sharing cultures, celebrating diversity, and promoting multiculturalism, why are these particular delicacies and mainstays so profoundly absent at every MSUB International Food Fair?

To answer this question, we only need to examine these dishes more carefully. *Boshintang* is a Korean soup made with dog meat. *Sanma aisu* is fish

134 Lisa Kemmerer

ice cream. *Balut* is a boiled duck or chicken embryo four days before it would have hatched. "Dragon, tiger, phoenix big braise" is a mix of flesh from snakes, cats (usually domestic), and pheasants. These dishes are not exactly the sorts of foods one finds at the Billings corner grocery store. Indeed, locals are likely to be disgusted and outraged by a dish featuring snake flesh or leg-of-cat.

We might expect the ranching state of Montana – a state with more than twice as many cattle as people and a state where vegetarians and vegans often complain that they are marginalized[1] – to be more open to such meaty meals ("All Cattle"; "Montana Population"). But these dishes would be met by the vast majority of MSUB students, as elsewhere in North America, with horror, disgust, and revulsion. Apparently, local sentiments about eating cats and snakes prevent international students from sharing these cultural delicacies at multicultural events. But is not the point of multiculturalism to let go of prejudices, of normative practices, and be part of something larger than local traditions? Does not multiculturalism – sharing and promoting the splendors of multiple cultural traditions – *require* that chick embryos and dog ribs be brought to the table and that the majority welcome these cultural delicacies?

For human beings, "food preferences and taboos, are deeply social" (Alkon 2013: 664). Cultures – clothes, dance, sports, language, art, religion, music, cuisine – tend to be extremely important to human beings, and nothing is quite as personal as what we eat. "Food – what is chosen from available possibilities, how it is presented, how it is eaten, with whom and when, and how much time is allotted to cooking and eating – is one of the means by which a society creates itself and acts out its aims and fantasies" (Visser 1987: 12). Few (if any) cultural differences create the intense reactions created by food, and this is as true in Montana as it is in South Carolina or South Africa: wear your sari, speak German, dance the drum dance – but if you are eating with mainstream America, best not to bring dog meat or a fetal chicken to the communal table (Kymlicka and Donaldson). In *Sociology on the Menu: An Invitation to the Study of Food and Society*, Alan Beardsworth and Teresa Keil write, "When humans eat, they eat with the mind as much as with the mouth" (1997: 53). In short, cultural tensions are rife in foodways, and if not always the main course, they are at least a side dish at every multicultural meal.

The power of food is evidenced in the centrality of food to "broad-ranging social movements" (Alkon 2013: 675). For example, in the Southern United States, white supremacy was mirrored and maintained in entrenched Southern foodways that were as difficult to change as it was essential that they be changed if the South was to experience anything remotely like equality. New Deal programs "identified 'southern diet' and 'southern cookery' – two distinctly different views of the region's food – as both the South's greatest problem and most beloved treasure" (Ferris 2012: 7). Food and food-sharing are sullied with the weight of prejudice and privilege around the globe. Food is "unequally available based on hierarchies of race, class,

Indian philosophy, and conflicts over cuisine 135

gender", nationality, and so on (Alkon 2013: 667). This is nowhere more evident than with regard to meat, which is commonly associated with wealth and good health, as well as with manly strength (Adams 2003: 36). Consumption of dairy – a food choice that many people in other nations associate with the United States – is on the rise: cow's milk has become a "metaphor for individual and national power and wealth" (Wiley 2011: 1).

Multiculturalism would seem positioned to encourage communities to swing wide that refrigerator door so we can gather around the community table to appreciate the cultural, culinary splendors of our neighbors. Multiculturalism would seem poised to encourage us to open our minds and our mouths, to set aside our prejudices, and bring on that *boshintang, sanma aisu, balut*, and "dragon, tiger, phoenix big braise" at the community table.

In light of the cultural complexity and cultural significance of foods, we ought not to assume, but to carefully assess what stand multiculturalism ought to take with regard to food planning for community meals. A brief examination of foundational Indian philosophy offers insights as to why it might make sense to *reject* certain food categories at community meals. This, in turn, invites a wider examination of religious ethics and food proscriptions. A survey of contemporary animal agricultural practices offers further insights as to how religious ethics ought to be reflected in the contemporary world – and the voices of a few contemporary Hindus provide examples. After briefly touching on physiology and racism, common practices at MSUB exemplify the need for a strong and somewhat unexpected influence from multiculturalism with regard to community meals.

Dietary restrictions and culture

Most traditional Hindus do not consume meat – and they have not for centuries – consistent with foundational Indian philosophical teachings such as *ahimsa*, karma, and reincarnation. Indian philosophy continues to shape Indian culture, especially for those within India's dominant religion, Hinduism. How are *ahimsa*, karma, and reincarnation central to Indian cuisine?

Ahimsa

Ahimsa, which literally means "not to harm" or "noninjury", carries an injunction for "non-injury toward all living beings" (Jacobson 1994: 287). *Ahimsa* is "the first and foremost ethical principle of every Hindu", who is thereby called to abstain "from causing hurt or harm to all beings" (Subramuniyaswami 1993: 195). *Ahimsa* "is not simply a matter of refraining from actual, physical harm. *Ahimsa* is the absence of even a desire to do harm to any living being, in thought, word, or deed" (Long 2009: 97). While the Hindu worldview holds that people "have no special privilege or authority over other creatures", human beings "do have more obligations and duties", including *ahimsa* (Dwivedi 2000: 6). The cardinal Hindu virtue

136   *Lisa Kemmerer*

is "compassion for all" (Subramuniyaswami 1993: 183), and Hindus are encouraged to practice nonviolence toward "the community of all beings" (Kinsley 1995: 65).

The Hindu moral obligation for *ahimsa* is exemplified in the *Mahabharata*, when Yudhishthira (a moral hero) finds himself in a great desert where he is befriended by a small dog. All of his beloved human companions die for want of water, while the dog survives. When the God Indra pulls up in his chariot to rescue Yudhishthira from the desert, Yudhishthira first inquires as to the whereabouts of his lost human companions. He is told that they have "gone before" (*Mahabharata* 1973: 365). Lord Indra encourages Yudhishthira to join his fallen companions, but Yudhishthira is concerned about the dog:

> "Lord of the Past and Present," said Yudhishthira, "this little dog who is my last companion must also go."
> "No," said Indra. "You cannot enter heaven with a dog at your heels. . . ."
> "He is devoted to me and looks to me for protection. Left alone he would die here."
> "There is no place for dogs in heaven. . . . It cannot be."
> Yudhishthira frowned. "It cannot be otherwise."
> "Don't you understand: *You have won heaven!* Immortality and prosperity and happiness in all directions are yours. Only leave that animal and come with me; that will not be cruel."
> (Mahabharata 1973: 365–366)

With regard to *ahimsa*, Yudhishthira's reply, and Indra's attempts to barter with the dog's life, are nothing short of profound:

> "I do not turn away my dog; I turn away you. I will not surrender a faithful dog to you. . . ."
> "But I can't take him! I'll put him to sleep; there will be no pain. No one will know."
> "Lord of Heaven," said Yudhishthira, "you have my permission to go."
> "Your splendor will fill the three worlds if you will but enter my car alone," said Indra. "You have left everyone else – why not this worthless dog?"
> "I am decided," answered Yudhishthira.
> (Mahabharata 1973: 365–366)

Yudhishthira will not sacrifice the dog's life, even painlessly – *even for eternal bliss*. Here Hindus see a moral and spiritual champion, Yudhishthira, the hero-son of the god of moral and cosmic law, turn away the powerful Indra – simultaneously rejecting a life in paradise with his loved ones – in light of his spiritual/moral responsibility to a stray dog.

As the *Mahabharata* continues to unfold, the stray dog transforms into Yudhishthira's father, none other than Dharma (the god of moral and eternal law), who praises Yudhishthira for his steadfast moral commitment to the dog – even against the will of a powerful god, even if he must sacrifice his own eternal happiness. While many might view Indra's advice to ditch the dog and run for heaven common sense – justifiable self-interest – Hindu moral law, rooted in *ahimsa*, does not.

Reincarnation

Reincarnation (transmigration) is the belief that, after death, the imperishable *atman* (perhaps best translated as "soul") takes lodging in another body. Indian philosophy holds that time has no beginning, which means that reincarnation has been in play for eons. Across incalculable ages, each *atman* has moved from birth to birth, from body to body, dwelling in billions of species. Each *atman* has been a Namdapha flying squirrel and an Andaman spiny shrew, one day a capped leaf monkey, the next an Indus River Dolphin. In this way reincarnation creates bonds between every living being, and diminishes the human tendency to view human beings as separate and distinct from other creatures, or from one another. Every animal, whether primate or rodent or human, has been reincarnated as our mother, brother, or best friend at some point across the incalculable eons. For Hindus (and other Indian religions), our present manifestation is merely "an infinitesimal part of a much larger picture that encompasses all of life" (Kinsley 1995: 64).

Karma

Karma means "action". Karma is an unavoidable force, like gravity – but karma is a force of justice whereby "every act carries with it an inevitable result" (Embree 1972: 51). In the Hindu worldview, reincarnation (the nature of one's next life) rests on karma. We are the rulers of our fate; we reap precisely what we sow. Daily actions determine our karma and our future fate.

In the Hindu worldview all living beings are in moral relationship with one another (Curtin 1995: 71). Hindu texts expounding Hindu philosophy and practice (*Shastras*) note that in seeking to cut the bonds of karma, one should do what is "good for all creatures" (O'Flaherty 1988: 124). Indian philosophy teaches that when we harm others, we ultimately harm ourselves: The "pain a human being causes other living beings . . . will have to be suffered by that human being later, either in this life or in a later rebirth" (Jacobson 1994: 289). Therefore, those aspiring to relatively pain-free future existences must avoid even accidental harm or killing (Basham 1989: 59).

Ahimsa, reincarnation, karma, and diet

Why and how do *ahimsa*, reincarnation, and karma affect the Hindu diet? The *Mahabharata* calls attention to Indian philosophy and dietary choice

138   Lisa Kemmerer

through Bhishma, one of the most respected heroes in this much-loved epic, as he extols nonviolence (*ahimsa*) and renounces the eating of flesh:

> 25. Nonviolence is the highest dharma [duty], . . .
> by this dharma [one's duty] is done
> 26. Meat is not born of grass, wood, or rock.
> Meat arises from killing a living being.
> Thus, in the enjoyment of meat there is fault . . .
> 29. If there were no meat-eaters,
> there would be no killers.
> A meat-eating man is a killer indeed,
> causing death for the purpose of food.
> 30. If meat were considered not to be food,
> there would be no violence.
> Violence is done to animals
> for the sake of the meat-eater only.
> 31. Because the life of violent ones
> is shortened as well (due to their deeds),
> the one who wishes long life for himself
> should refuse meat. . . .
> 32. Those fierce ones who do violence to life
> . . . are to be feared by beings as beasts of prey.
> (Chapple 1996: 118–119)

The *Mahabharata* also states that the "one who kills beings for the sake of food is the lowest sort of person, a maker of great sin" (Chapple 1996: 120). In light of reincarnation and karma, we harm ourselves when we eat others. The *Manu Smriti* (*Laws of Manu*), one of the oldest and most important Hindu law texts, warns that one "who kills an animal for meat will die of a violent death as many times as there are hairs on that killed animal" (Dwivedi 2000: 7). In light of reincarnation, many Hindus view "wanton killing of animals [as] little better than murder, and meat eating [as] little better than cannibalism" (Basham 1989: 58). In the Hindu worldview, eating hens or cows is "like eating the flesh of one's own son" (Chapple 1996: 114).

Indian philosophy teaches that one cannot eat meat and live a peaceful, harmonious life (Subramuniyaswami 1993: 201). The *Manu Smriti* refers to a vegetarian as a "friend of all living beings" (Chapple 1996: 113). Even though the consumer never touches the living animal, from the Indian point of view, a flesh eater's hands are stained with blood: "the meat eater's desire for meat drives another to kill and provide that meat. The act of the butcher begins with the desire of the consumer" (Subramuniyaswami 1993: 201). Consequently, anyone who buys "flesh performs *himsa* (violence) by his wealth; he who eats flesh does so by enjoying its taste; the killer does *himsa* by actually tying and killing the animal" (Subramuniyaswami 1993: 205).

Indian philosophy, and conflicts over cuisine 139

For traditional Hindus, avoidance of meat and eggs is a religious commitment. *Ahimsa*, reincarnation, and karma lead Hindus to avoid eating anymals[2] (any animal other than my own species) and eggs. Avoiding animal products is "a way to live with a minimum of hurt to other beings, for to consume meat, fish, fowl or eggs is to participate indirectly in acts of cruelty and violence" (Subramuniyaswami 1993: 201). Indeed, Hindus have tended to be lacto-vegetarian for centuries (although coastal communities, in particular, also consume a fair amount of fish); avoidance of meat remains standard practice for millions of Hindus as "a function of inherited cultural practice" (Yadav and Kumar 2006).[3] Cows in particular would never be killed or consumed in a Hindu community because they are revered; they are associated with the beloved God, Krishna. Meaty McDonalds built its first vegetarian franchise in New Delhi in order to avoid what would surely be viewed as culinary cruelties – best to offer what someone in the area chooses to eat (*CBSNEWS* 2012).

In spite of hundreds of years of British influence followed by decades of influence from the United States, Indian philosophy and religion remain visible in the Hindu tendency toward a lacto-vegetarian diet. For traditional Hindus, this diet is not mere preference, religious requirement rooted deep in an ancient, shared culture. With regard to diet, "religion and community matter" (Yadav and Kumar 2006). Avoidance of all flesh is "*dharma*" or duty – a requirement – for traditional Hindus (Dwivedi 2000: 7).

Religions and the global table

Among religions born in India (Hindu, Buddhist, and Jain traditions), teachings of compassion and simplicity are frequently expressed in dietary proscriptions against the consumption of animal products, but such teachings are universal in the world's dominant religious traditions. In fact, every major religion encourages a diet free of bloodshed and suffering. This should not be surprising given that the world's major religions are each rooted in a morality of compassion and care, especially toward those comparatively weak and helpless (Kemmerer 2012: 282).

Judaism, for example, carries "a profound moral commitment to respect" anymals (Cohn-Sherbok 2006: 90). Well-respected Jewish authors encourage readers to be merciful and kind to all that God has created (*Little Sefer Hasidim*) (Schochet 1984: 246). In the words of Rabbi Sherira Gaon (10th century), anymals were created so that "good should be done to them" (Kalechofsky 2006: 95). The "Hebrew phrase *tsa'ar ba'alei chayim* provides a biblical mandate not to cause 'pain to any living creature'" (Schwartz 2001: 15). Judaism teaches that "God condemns and harshly punishes cruelty to animals" (Regenstein 1991: 21). The *Shulchan Aruch* (*Code of Jewish Law*) is explicit about our obligation not to harm anymals: "It is forbidden, according to the law of the Torah, to inflict pain upon any living creature. On the contrary, it is our duty to relieve the pain of any creature" (Ganzfried

140   *Lisa Kemmerer*

1961: 84; Schwartz 2001: 19; Cohn-Sherbok 2006: 83). Humans, made in the image of God, are to reflect divine compassion (Schochet 1984: 144). The Tanakh teaches: "As God is compassionate, . . . so you should be compassionate" (Schwartz 2001: 16). Perhaps most telling, God creates a vegan world in Genesis (Gen. 2:15–16; Gen. 1:29–31). Not surprisingly, Genesis 2:15–16 records that people are permitted to eat of every tree but one – a vegan diet. Similarly, Genesis 1:29 ordains a vegan diet: "I give you every seed-bearing plant that is upon the face of all the earth, and every tree that has seed-bearing fruit. They will be yours for food".

Christians share the Jewish creation story of Genesis, and therefore worship a God who created a vegan world, a world in which "no creature was to feed on another" (Hyland 1988: 21). Jesus, the quintessential moral exemplar, lived a life devoted to the service of weak and imperfect beings. His overall message speaks of compassion and service of the strong for the weak, of the high for the lowly. The Gospels portray Jesus as engaging in self-sacrificing service to "the least of these" (Mat. 25:40). Christians are intended to stand as "witness to Christ's love, compassion, and peace" (Kaufman 2004: 48). Christian sensitivity to suffering measures fidelity to a compassionate Creator and is understood to originate in the munificence of divine love that connects each of us with the Almighty (Allen 1971: 214). Those who argue that love must first and foremost be directed toward humanity may as well argue that Christian love should first and foremost be directed toward Caucasians, Europeans, or the wealthy. If love is not expansive, it is not Christian love.

Islam shares the Judeo-Christian belief in a benevolent, all-powerful creator. "Islamic teachings have gone to great lengths to instill a sense of love, respect and compassion for animals" (Masri 45). Allah created the universe with the "breath of compassion" (Bakhtiar 1987: 16–17), and notes that any "act of cruelty toward animals is strongly forbidden" (Siddiq 2003: 455). Anymal rights are rooted in one no less than the creator, who "desires no injustice to His creatures" (Qur'an 3:105–110). In the world of Islam, "each creature has its rights accordingly", provided by Allah (Nasr 97), who "desires no injustice to His creatures" (Qur'an 3:105–110). Muslims are expected to treat this world, and all that has been created, with love: "a true Muslim is one who honors, sustains, and protects the lives of creatures of God and does not kill them for her own food" (Foltz 2005: 111). In the Islamic world, a vegan diet is ideal, so that anymals are "allowed to live their natural lives" without cruel exploitation, and without "having their throats slit" (Masri 2007: 56). Since the earliest days of Islam, there have been Muslims who "abstained from meat for spiritual reasons" (Foltz 2005: 109).

Among Chinese religious traditions, tenderness and altruism, kindness and benevolence are central to Confucian morality, and compassion is the ultimate virtue (Tu 1985: 81–84). In Confucian traditions, "sensitivity to animals is not only ethically suitable but also carries religious authority" (Taylor 2006: 294). Daoism also provides a "universalistic ethic" of compassion that extends "not only to all humanity, but to the wider domain of all living things" (Kirkland 2001: 284). Sacred writings encourage people to be compassionate, nurturing, caring, and selfless "for the sake of all beings" (Kohn 2004: 68). Daoist precepts protect anymals and promote "compassion, empathy, and kindness" (Kohn 2004: 71). Daoist precepts usually contain five foundational precepts, the first of which is usually an injunction not to kill, including warnings against "eating meat" (Kohn 2004: 67–136). Key texts for the Daoist clergy teach: "Do not kill or harm anything that lives in order to satisfy your own appetites [22a]. Always behave with compassion and grace to all, even insects and worms" (Kohn 2004: 255–256). Because dairy products are largely absent across China, many "vegetarians" are actually free of all anymal products with the possible exception of eggs. Monastery meals consist "largely of rice, wheat, and barley, combined with various vegetables and tofu. In Daoist religious literature, meat is not even mentioned among the five main food groups" (Kohn 2004: 51).

For Buddhists, no creature lies beyond spiritual concern (Martin 1985: 99), and "*ahimsa*, or noninjury, is an ethical goal" (Shinn 2000: 219). "Indeed, Buddhists see this orientation to the suffering of others as a sine qua non of ethical life" (Waldau 2002: 138). Buddhist practice is "built on the vast conception of universal love and compassion for all living beings" (Rahula 1959: 46) and requires "compassionate protection of all living beings" (Mizuno 1995: 132). The *Sutta Nipata* states plainly: Buddhists may not kill, cause to kill, or incite others to kill. They may "not injure any being, either strong or weak, in the world" (*Dhammika Sutta* [Snp 2.14]; Fausböll 26). A Tibetan Buddhist monk claims compassion as the root of Buddhist teachings and law (Tashi 2008). Indeed, compassion is "one of the indispensable conditions for deliverance" (Kushner 1981: 148–149). Across time, "many Buddhists have felt that meat-eating of any kind is out of harmony with the spirit of the Law of Righteousness, and have been vegetarians" (De Bary 1972: 91). Buddhist philosophy teaches that, just as surely as one who throws dirt into the wind will have dust in their eyes, a flesh-eater piles up negative karma (Kemmerer 2012: 107).

Judaism, Christianity, Islam, Daoism, and Buddhism teach an ethic of compassion and attentiveness to the need of those who are at our mercy, encouraging people to eat in a way that does not cause suffering. (Plants are not sentient and therefore cannot suffer, and so grains, tubers, leaves, fruits, and nuts are not proscribed.) While religious requirements for a vegan diet are less evident among mainstream Jews, Christians, and Muslims than among Hindus, these foundational moral teachings are evidenced in thriving contemporary organizations such as the Christian Vegetarian Association, Jewish Vegetarian Society, and Islamicconcern.com.

Those committed to *ahimsa*, compassion, or love in any of the world's dominant religious traditions forego flesh. For millions of people, including traditional Hindus, flesh is off the menu – *proscribed as a matter of religious ethics, as a matter of culture*. Additionally, eggs are proscribed for Hindus.

142 *Lisa Kemmerer*

Indian philosophy, Hindu dietary proscriptions, and religious ethics more broadly have dropped a fly in the multicultural soup. Multiculturalism – sharing and promoting cultural traditions – would seem poised to encourage people to open their minds and their mouths to meaty meals of every kind from around the globe. But the Hindu tradition shows us why serving meat or eggs is serving a dish of exclusion. To choose to offer dishes at community feasts that a particular group of people will not be able to share exemplifies cultural ignorance and exclusivity. Why are we so oblivious to multicultural needs at the community table?

The soup thickens: *Ahimsa*, dairy, and multiculturalism

Indian philosophy has provided a springboard for exploring religious dietary ethics. *Ahimsa*, karma, and reincarnation are just one piece of a broader phenomenon: a religious ethic that runs across traditions, discouraging humanity from harming other creatures, and encouraging compassion. Religious ethics encourage a vegetarian diet. This means that, counterintuitively, multiculturalism should *not* ask that we eat cat meat and chick embryos, but rather that we provide only vegetarian fare at community meals.

We are gaining clarity into the phenomenon of food proscriptions, multiculturalism, and community meals, but there is yet more to digest. Are flesh and eggs the only products that we will need to remove from the community table?

Proper application of Hindu teachings such as *ahimsa* (as well as teachings such as Christian love and Islamic anymal rights) requires that we understand how anymal products are produced. And this requires that we examine contemporary anymal agriculture. Only then can we know whether or not cheddar cheese and blueberry ice cream satisfy the requirements of *ahimsa*, compassion, and anymal rights. The Hindu tradition provides an excellent springboard and backdrop for exploring anymal agriculture.

Cows are cherished and protected among Hindus because they are vulnerable to human exploitation, and protecting cows is therefore an expression of *ahimsa* that is "symbolic of reverence and respect for all forms of life" (Kinsley 1995: 65). Cows also exemplify munificence and mother's love. Harming such vulnerable, motherly beings is particularly offensive to Hindus. Therefore, how cattle are treated in the process of creating dairy products is pertinent to any sincere Hindu who consumes lemon yogurt or cream cheese.

Developed before the advent of factory farming, United States federal laws are narrow in their reach because they were formed before the advent of the cruelest of contemporary practices. More importantly, federal laws do not regulate the treatment of animals kept for meat, eggs, or milk. In order to avoid impinging on the enterprises of ranchers and farmers,

Indian philosophy, and conflicts over cuisine   143

customary animal agriculture practices are exempt from animal cruelty statutes. Almost any industry practice is legal.

> In the United States, farming and animal welfare are governed by only two federal laws: the Humane Methods of Slaughter Act (HMSA), enacted in 1958, and the Twenty-Eight Hour Law, enacted in 1877. Perhaps the most famous federal animal-protection law and certainly the most ambitious attempt Congress has made to protect animals is the Animal Welfare Act (AWA). But the AWA does not apply to farm animals except when they are used for "research, testing, and teaching" – essentially making it blind to ninety-eight percent of all animals killed each year and inapplicable to farming and animal welfare.
>
> (Matheny and Leahy 2007: 334)

Current U.S. laws offer a tiny bit of regulation for the slaughter of farmed anymals through the HMSA. Additionally, farmed anymals must be given a break if they are transported for more than 28 hours at a time. This leaves all that happens on the farm untouched, and the AWA does not provide any protection for farmed animals who are exploited for food – including dairy products. Those expecting laws to require compassion (or even common decency) in the treatment of farmed animals will find no such laws in the United States.

Economics drives U.S. animal agriculture. But other businesses do not revolve around the lives of massive numbers of anymals. In the industry of animal agriculture, individual anymals are viewed as expendable – birthed to be killed in adolescence. Those running animal agriculture businesses weigh the costs of essential veterinary care, housing, and feed against returns – profits – which are the ultimate purpose and guiding principle for Big Ag (Bakan 2004: 36–37; Matheny and Leahy 2007: 329). Consequently, the term "animal welfare," used "in conjunction with current industry guidelines is inappropriate . . . in many cases the guidelines fail to provide what an average American would consider basic animal care" (Farm Sanctuary 2005: 71). This is true for all types of anymal agriculture in the United States.

The extraordinary suffering that is common among farmed animals in the United States shapes the lives of cows and calves who are exploited in the dairy industry. Cows must be impregnated each year so they will give birth and lactate. They carry their young for ten months, but at birth their calves are snatched from their watchful eyes. Cows – like most mothers – try desperately to protect and keep newborns, but are powerless against the humans who own them and control their lives (Kemmerer 2011: 174). In the United States dairy industry, cows are dehorned and tails are docked without anesthesia. They can be motivated with electric prods, tied perpetually in stalls, and slaughtered without stunning (Farm Sanctuary 2005: 4). What would Krishna think of such insensitivity to a mother cow?

144   *Lisa Kemmerer*

Most fundamentally, "dairy" cows endure mechanized milking for ten out of twelve months every year (and for the first year, this includes the first seven months of a nine-month pregnancy). Cows naturally produce just over two tons of milk per year, but with Bovine Growth Hormone (BGH/BST) cows provide as much as thirty tons of milk annually, enough for *ten* calves. As a result of this excess, one-in-five factory farmed "dairy" cows secretes pus from her udders (which invariably mixes with her milk) (Kemmerer 2011: 174; Kemmerer 2012: 293). Cows are so exhausted by the process of repeated calving, the loss of their calves, and intense milking, that they are often "spent" and sent to slaughter after four or five years of perpetual birth and lactation, although cows can live upwards of twenty years. Their aged flesh is used for soup, burgers, or processed foods. Most cows are pregnant when slaughtered (Kemmerer 2011: 174; Kemmerer 2012: 293). Those practicing *ahimsa* will not purchase products that stem from such cruelty.

Anyone who buys dairy products also supports and enables the veal industry: the veal industry exists because of the strength of the dairy industry (Kemmerer 2011: 174). Calves born of cows who are exploited by the dairy industry can be removed from their mothers before they even touch the ground. They are

> typically tethered by the neck or confined in individual stalls, or both; the stalls are so small that the calves cannot turn around during their entire sixteen to eighteen week lives. Immobilizing calves reduces labor and housing costs and prevents muscle development, making the resulting meat a pale color, preferred by some consumers.
>
> (Matheny and Leahy 2007: 332)

Every year one million calves suffer and die for veal. Cows exploited for dairy suffer longer than cattle exploited for beef, and in many ways their suffering is more acute.[4] Hindus in the United States who wish to practice *ahimsa*, and who make dietary choices with an eye to reincarnation and karma, must choose vegan.

Indeed, informed Hindus turn away from dairy. Mahatma Gandhi was raised lacto-vegetarian (Shinn 2000: 219; Gandhi 2002: 12). He taught that spiritual progress requires us to "cease to kill our fellow creatures for the satisfaction of our bodily wants" (Roberts 2006: 119). Consistent with Hindu philosophy of karma and reincarnation, Gandhi viewed killing animals for food as ultimately killing "ourselves, our body and soul" (Roberts 2006: 124). On learning of "the tortures to which cows and buffaloes were subjected by their keepers", Gandhi stopped consuming milk from these sources (Gandhi 1993: 272–273, 328).

Anuradha Sawhney, a contemporary Hindu, states that only through *ahimsa*, by not harming other beings, can we acquire "good karma" (Sawhney 2011). She notes that "being compassionate towards animals comes easy because I am a Hindu and a vegan" (Sawhney 2011).

Dr. Alka Arora, an Indian-American feminist scholar who grew up in a Hindu home, notes that most Hindu vegetarians avoid meat because they view meat-eating as violent, but they tend to view the consumption of milk products not only as harmless, but as noble. She goes on to say that Hindus revere cows as "mother-like", sharing their milk with a needy world, but that Hindus must recognize the extent of the suffering now experienced by both cows and calves in the process of milk production: "our beloved 'mother cow' is repeatedly raped, separated from her calves, confined in small spaces, and eventually killed for meat. There is immense, intrinsic suffering in the production of milk – and the dairy industry is inseparable from the meat industry" (Arora 2015, pers. comm.). Arora concludes that contemporary milk production methods indicate "that Hindus should adhere to a vegan diet rather than a vegetarian diet" (Arora 2015, pers. comm.).

Hinduism offers a sound philosophical framework – *ahimsa*, karma, and reincarnation – for their traditional foods. The idea of *ahimsa* is echoed in each of the world's great religions, and as information about anymal agriculture becomes better known, the consumption of dairy will be as problematic as the consumption of flesh. For many ethical and religious vegans it already is. Exploring anymal agriculture demonstrates that those committed to any religious ethic of compassion must forgo not only flesh and eggs, but also dairy. *All* anymal products are saturated with suffering. Consequently, those providing multicultural meals – those intending to offer foods to be shared by *all*, including devout Hindus, Muslims, and Christians, will plan vegan meals.

The nail in the coffin: Lactose intolerance

Religious proscriptions against cruelty are not the only concern with regard to multiculturalism and dairy at community meals – there are also physiological concerns. Anthropologist Marvin Harris divides communities into "'lactophiles' and 'lactophobes'" (Harris 1985: 130–131); hatred or love of cow's milk is "a profound delineator of cultural difference" (Wiley 2011: 11). Lactophiles are definitely in the minority, and are localized among those of northern European descent, pastoralists of West and East Africa, as well as among Middle Eastern and Central Asian populations, where dairy has been consumed for long periods of time (Harris 1985: 130–153). Outside of these areas, dairy products are somewhat rare due to lactose intolerance, a condition in which the body cannot digest dairy products, including 40 million Americans. Ninety percent of the Asian American community and ninety percent of the Black or African-American community are lactose intolerant (Harper 2012; Statistic Brain Research Institute 2015). Due to entrenched racism, the assumption in the United States is generally that "most people have a Euro-Anglo-Saxon relationship to food" and can digest dairy products (Harper 2012).

146 *Lisa Kemmerer*

For those with lactose intolerance, diets devoid of dairy are not a moral proscription, but rather a physiological necessity: consuming dairy products causes diarrhea, abdominal cramps, bloating, gas, nausea, and sometimes vomiting (*Mayo Clinic* 2015b). For the majority of humanity, a dairy-free diet is a matter of basic wellbeing. In contrast, there appears to be no group of people physiologically incapable of eating plant products – indeed, consuming plants and plant products is essential to human health. Indian philosophy – the idea of *ahimsa* – can inform multiculturalism: to care about others is to serve what they can eat. This requires a vegan menu at any multicultural meal.

Meanwhile, back at the ranch . . . multiculturalism in Montana?

Montana State University Billings is fortunate to attract international students from India, students that are very likely to be practicing *ahimsa* with an eye to karma and reincarnation, and who are likely accustomed to a strict lacto-vegetarian diet. For these students, hamburgers are not only proscribed, but extremely offensive. Moreover, there are roughly two million Hindus in the United States, suggesting that *local* students are also likely to be Hindu, with dietary practices that proscribe flesh – especially cow's flesh (OntarioTolerance.org 2015).

MSUB also welcomes people from a handful of other nations, at least some of whom must be committed to a fundamental religious ethic that requires compassion, whether Buddhist, Christian, Daoist, Muslim, or Jewish. Should not multiculturalism take these common religious proscriptions into consideration when planning community meals?

Yes, but instead MSUB kicks off the school year with both a hamburger grill *and* an ice cream social. At least some students are likely to be excluded from these events on cultural grounds – more specially, due to religious ethics. Building a community event around food choices that are likely to exclude ethnic minorities is offensive – and racist. In light of Hindu ethics and religious ethics more broadly, if community meals are to be inclusive, they must be vegan.

Conclusion

Multiculturalism is about acceptance, about sharing different ways, about dropping prejudice to try something different so that we do not offend those whose ways are different from our own. Multiculturalism encourages people to create a supportive, inclusive environment rather than alienate those who do not share mainstream cultural traditions. Yet food proscriptions in the United States tend to prevent foods such as *boshintang*, *sanma aisu*, *balut*, and "dragon, tiger, phoenix big braise" from showing up at International Food Fairs around the country, although such feasts are billed as multicultural events. At first bite, it seemed that multiculturalism ought to

Indian philosophy, and conflicts over cuisine   147

encourage the larger community to move beyond food prejudices that prevent cultural food sharing – that fridge doors and mouths ought to swing wide to accommodate dishes from around the world, carefully prepared and proudly presented – flesh of dog, fish ice cream, and fetal chicks. But examining foundational principles from Indian philosophy, universal religious ideals, contemporary animal agriculture practices in the United States, and lactose intolerance proves otherwise.

Indian philosophy provides a window into religious dietary ethics more broadly, all of which require compassion toward all living beings. A review of standard anymal agricultural practices in the United States reveals an extremely cruel industry – especially with regard to dairy products. This highlights the importance of rethinking meal plans at international events out of respect for religious ethics, which require compassion, which precludes the consumption not only of flesh, but of all anymal products. As it turns out, if we wish to be inclusive and avoid offense, we must discourage *boshintang, sanma aisu, balut*, and "dragon, tiger, phoenix big braise" at the community table, as well as vanilla yogurt, egg salad sandwiches, and hamburgers. Counterintuitively, those interested in fostering multiculturalism must *restrict* food possibilities at community meals as a matter of cultural sensitivity. In the spirit of Beardsworth and Keil, we must plan and execute community meals "with the mind as much as with the mouth" (1997: 53). When we understand religious ideals such as *ahimsa*, we understand why, if we wish to welcome all to the table – which would seem fundamental for any multicultural meal – community meals must be vegan.

Ahimsa *and multiculturalism amid a meaty majority*

There are now roughly two million Hindus in the United States – a significant cultural minority (OntarioTolerance.org 2015). They are vastly outnumbered by omnivores in a nation "where meat is consumed at more than three times the global average" (Daniel et al. 2015). In the United States, meals are not generally considered complete without flesh; whether in Baltimore or Billings, meat dishes are to be expected (unless specifically indicated). Those gathering at the community table might also expect to find themselves seated across from a Hindu who does not eat meat – especially meat from cows. At any community meal in the United States, as in many other wealthy nations, Hindus are likely to be confronted with meat eaters sitting across from them – *himsa* (violence), often against revered cows. What stand should multiculturalism take with regard to this uncomfortable yet common predicament?

Multiculturalism calls us to respect diverse cultural traditions. This requires, at a minimum, that we *avoid excluding and offending minorities.* At the community table, multiculturalism ought to stand as a force against serving foods – even normative foods such as meat and eggs – that are *proscribed for and offensive to others, such as Hindus.* Offering eggs and

148 *Lisa Kemmerer*

flesh – especially the flesh of cows – at a community meal is culturally insensitive in light of Indian philosophy and Hindu dietary proscriptions. What people do in their own homes, or when they visit the homes of others, is a separate matter. The question here is, why bring foods to the community table that are proscribed for minority populations – especially given the plethora of wonderful alternatives, including staples such as corn, rice, oats, and potatoes.[5]

Notes

1 Not only are there no vegan restaurants in Billings, there are no vegetarian restaurants, and finding a vegan meal at many restaurants can be challenging. Only in the last few years have restaurants started to be familiar with the term "vegan", although this does not mean that your meal will actually be vegan when it arrives. Whenever my credit union or any other local business offers a get-together, it is usually a hamburger barbeque. Generally speaking, people either eat meat or they do not show up. These practices exclude vegans and vegetarians, and there are also ample examples of overt hostility. For example, when I mentioned at church that I was sad during thanksgiving because of the slaughter and the suffering, a member of the congregation said that he would eat some extra meat for me. Although a progressive church, no one called him on his behavior. My vegan and vegetarian friends often mention similar instances of hostility and rejection. In Montana (as elsewhere in the country), meat-eating is a protected norm often expressed in defensiveness.

2 "Anymal" (a contraction of "any" and "animal", pronounced like "any" and "mal"), refers to *all* animals who do not happen to be the same species as the speaker/author. This means that if a signing chimpanzee signs "anymal", human beings will be included in this reference, and the chimpanzee will not. In the case of this article, the speaker/author is a human being, so "anymal" refers to any animal who is not a human being. Avoiding "non" and "other", anymal is neither dualistic nor speciesist.

3 Generally speaking, Hindus eat dairy products but not eggs, although coastal communities tend to eat fish. (See Harris 1985; Wiley 2011; Yadav and Sanjay 2006.)

4 Morally, it makes no sense to choose to be a vegetarian who consumes *more* dairy to replace flesh products. *To reduce suffering, we must cut back or eliminate all animal products.*

5 It is important to note that, in any instance where diet is not a choice, there is no moral requirement to avoid animal products – or any other products. Affordable, available food options are essential to choice, and choice is essential to ethics.

References

AAANativeArts.com. (2015) 'Foods Native Americans Consider Taboo', *Native American Indian Tribes of the U.S.* Available at http://www.aaanativearts.com/foods-native-americans-consider-taboo#axzz3foDKw6Mj (Accessed 13 July 2015).

Adams, C. J. (2003) *The Pornography of Meat*, New York: Continuum.

Alkon, A. H. (2013) 'The Socio-Nature of Local Organic Food', *Antipode* 45(3).

Allen, C. J. (1971) *Broadman Bible Commentary*, vol. XXII, Nashville: Broadman Press.

Arora, A. (2015) Personal email. 11 August.

Bakan, J. (2004) *The Corporation: The Pathological Pursuit of Profit and Power*, New York: Free Press.

Bakhtiar, L. (1987) *Sufi: Expressions of the Mystic Quest*, New York: Thames and Hudson.

Basham, A. L. (1989) *The Origins and Development of Classical Hinduism*, Oxford: Oxford University Press.

Beardsworth, A. and Keil, T. (1997) *Sociology on the Menu: An Invitation to the Study of Food and Society*, London: Routledge.

Burtt, E. A. (ed.) (1955) *The Teachings of the Compassionate Buddha: Early Discourses, the Dhammapada, and Later Basic Writings*, New York: New American Library.

The Cattle Range. (2015) 'All Cattle and Calves: Map of Cattle Distribution'. Available at http://www.cattlerange.com/cattle-graphs/all-cattle-numbers.html (Accessed 22 August 2015).

CBSNEWS (2012) 'McDonald's to Beef Up in India with Meatless Menu', 5 September 2012. Available at http://www.cbsnews.com/news/mcdonalds-to-beef-up-in-india-with-meatless-menu/ (Accessed 17 June 2015).

Centers for Disease Control and Prevention. (2015) 'Leading Causes of Death'. Available at http://www.cdc.gov/nchs/fastats/leading-causes-of-death.htm (Accessed 23 August 2015).

Chapple, C. K. (1996) 'Ahimsa in the *Mahabharata*: A Story, a Philosophical Perspective, and an Admonishment', *Journal of Vaishnava Studies*.

Chapple, C. K. (1997) 'Animals and Environment in the Buddhist Birth Stories', in M. E. Tucker and D. R. Williams (eds.) *Buddhism and Ecology: The Interconnection of Dharma and Deeds*, Cambridge: Harvard University Press.

Cohn-Sherbok, D. (2006) 'Hope for the Animal Kingdom', in P. Waldau and K. Patton (eds.) *A Communion of Subjects: Animals in Religion, Science, and Ethics*, New York: Columbia University Press.

Curtin, D. (1994) 'Dogen, Deep Ecology, and the Ecological Self', *Environmental Ethics* 16.

Curtin, D. – (1995) 'Making Peace with the Earth: Indigenous Agriculture and the Green Revolution', *Environmental Ethics* 17.

Daniel, C. R., Cross, A. J., Koebnick, C. and Sinha, R. (2015) 'Trends in Meat Consumption in the United States', *PMC: US National Library of Medicine*. Available at *National Institutes of Health.* http://www.ncbi.nlm.nih.gov/pmc/articles/PMC3045642/ (Accessed 22 August 2015).

de Bary, W. T. (ed.) (1972) *The Buddhist Tradition in India, China, and Japan*, New York: Vintage.

Dwivedi, O. P. (2000) 'Dharmic Ecology', in C. K. Chapple and M. E. Tucker (eds.) *Hinduism and Ecology: The Intersection of Earth, Sky, and Water*, Cambridge: Harvard University Press.

Embree, A. T. (ed.) (1972) *The Hindu Tradition: Readings in Oriental Thought*, New York: Vintage.

Embree, A. T. (1988) *Sources of Indian Tradition: From the Beginning to 1800*, New York: Columbia University Press.

150 Lisa Kemmerer

Farm Sanctuary. (2005) 'Farm Animal Welfare: An Assessment of Product Labeling Claims, Industry Quality Assurance Guidelines and Third Party Certification Standards', *A Farm Sanctuary Report*. Available at http://www.fda.gov/OHRMS/dockets/dockets/06p0394/06p-0394-cp00001–15-Tab-13-Farm-Animal-Welfare-01-vol1.pdf (Accessed 13 July 2015).

Fausböll, V. (trans.) (1881) "MettaSutta" and "Uragasutta" in "Urugavagga." *The Sutta-Nipâta, The Sacred Books of the East, Vol. 10*. Oxford, UK: Clarendon Press.

Ferris, M. C. (2012) ' "The Deepest Reality of Life": Southern Sociology, the WPA, and Food in the New South', *Southern Cultures* XVIII(2).

Foltz, R. C. (2005) *Animals in Islamic Tradition and Muslim Cultures*, Oxford: Oneworld.

Gandhi, M. K. (1993) *An Autobiography: The Story of My Experiments with Truth*, Boston: Beacon.

Gandhi, M. K. (2002) *The Essential Gandhi: An Anthology of His Writings on His Life, Work, and Ideas*, Louis Fischer (ed.), New York: Vintage.

Ganzfried, R. S. (1961) *Code of Jewish Law*, bk. 4, ch. 191, New York: Hebrew Publishing.

Harper, B. (2012) 'Secret Buddhist Reveal – Breeze Harper', *Buddhist Peace Fellowship: Cultivating Compassionate Action*. Available at http://www.buddhistpeacefellowship.org/secret-buddhist-reveal-video (Accessed 23 August 2015).

Harris, M. (1985) *Good to Eat: Riddles of Food and Culture*, Prospect Heights, IL: Waveland Press.

Holy Bible. (1998) *New Revised Standard Version*, New York: American Bible Society.

Hyland, J. R. (1988) *The Slaughter of Terrified Beasts: A Biblical Basis for the Humane Treatment of Animals*, Sarasota: Viatoris Ministries.

Jacobson, K. (1994) 'The Institutionalization of the Ethics of "Non-Injury" toward All "Beings" in Ancient India', *Environmental Ethics* 16.

Kalechofsky, R. (2006) 'Hierarchy, Kinship, and Responsibility', in P. Waldau and K. Patton (eds) *A Communion of Subjects: Animals in Religion, Science, and Ethics*, New York: Columbia University Press.

Kaufman, S. R. and Braun, N. (2004) *Good News for All Creation: Vegetarianism as Christian Stewardship*, Cleveland, OH: Vegetarian Advocates Press.

Kemmerer, L. (2006) 'Verbal Activism: "Anymals" ', *Society and Animals* 14(1), May: 9–14. Available at http://www.animalsandsociety.org/assets/library/593_sa1413.pdf

Kemmerer, L. (2011) *Sister Species: Women, Animals, and Social Justice*, Urbana-Champaign: University of Illinois.

Kemmerer, L. (2012) *Animals and World Religions*, Oxford: Oxford University Press.

Kinsley, D. (1989) *The Goddesses' Mirror: Visions of the Divine from East and West*, Albany: State University of New York.

Kinsley, D. (1995) *Ecology and Religion: Ecological Spirituality in Cross-Cultural Perspective*, Englewood Cliffs: Prentice-Hall.

Kirkland, R. (2001) ' "Responsible Non-Action" in a Natural World: Perspectives from the Neiye, Zhuangzi, and Daode Jing', in N. J. Girardot et al. (eds.) *Daoism and Ecology: Ways within a Cosmic Landscape*, Cambridge, MA: Harvard University Press.

Kohn, L. (ed.) (2000) *Daoism Handbook*, Leiden: Brill.

Kohn, L. (2004) *Cosmos and Community: The Ethical Dimensions of Daoism*, Cambridge, MA: Three Pines.

Kushner, T. (1981) 'Interpretations of Life and Prohibitions Against Killing', *Environmental Ethics* 3.

Kymlicka, W. and Donaldson, S. (2014) 'Animal Rights, Multiculturalism, and the Left', *Journal of Social Philosophy* 45(1): 116–135.

Long, J. D. (2009) *Jainism: An Introduction*, New York: I. B. Tauris.

Mahabharata. (1973) trans. W. Buck, Berkeley: University of California.

Martin, R. (1985) 'Thoughts on the Jatakas', *The Path of Compassion: Writings on Socially*.

Masri, B. A. (2007) *Animal Welfare in Islam*, Leicestershire, UK: Islamic Foundation.

Matheny, G. and Leahy, C. (2007) 'Farm-animal Welfare, Legislation, and Trade', *Law and Contemporary Problems*.

Mayo Clinic (2015a) 'Causes: Diseases and Conditions: Lactose Intolerance'. Available at http://www.mayoclinic.org/diseases-conditions/lactose-intolerance/basics/causes/con-20027906 (Accessed 2 July 2015).

Mayo Clinic (2015b) 'Symptoms: Diseases and Conditions: Lactose Intolerance'. Available at http://www.mayoclinic.org/diseases-conditions/lactose-intolerance/basics/causes/con-20027906 (Accessed 2 July 2015).

Mizuno, K. (1995) *Basic Buddhist Concepts*, Tokyo: Kosei.

Nasr, S. H. (2003) 'Islam, the Contemporary Islamic World, and the Environmental Crisis', in R. C. Foltz et al. (eds.) *Islam and Ecology: A Bestowed Trust*, Cambridge, MA: Harvard University Press.

O'Flaherty, W. D. (ed.) (1975) *Hindu Myths: A Sourcebook*, London: Penguin.

O'Flaherty, W. D. (ed.) (1981) *The Rig Veda*, New York: Penguin.

O'Flaherty, W. D. (ed.) (1988) *Textual Sources for the Study of Hinduism*, Chicago: University of Chicago.

Ontario Tolerance.org. (2015) 'Hinduism: How Many Hindus Are There in the U.S. and the Rest of the World?' Available at http://www.religioustolerance.org/hinduism5.htm (Accessed 2 July 2015).

ProCon.Org. (2012) 'US and International Meat Consumption Chart'. Available at http://vegetarian.procon.org/view.resource.php?resourceID=004716 (Accessed 17 June 2015).

Rachels, J. (2015) *The Elements of Moral Philosophy*, 8th edn, New York: McGraw Hill.

Rahula, W. (1959) *What the Buddha Taught*, New York: Grove Weidenfeld.

Regenstein, L. G. (1991) *Replenish the Earth*, New York: Crossroad.

Roberts, H. (2006) *The Vegetarian Philosophy of India: Hindu, Buddhist, and Jain Sacred Teachings*, New York: Anjeli.

Sawhney, A. (2011) 'A Fight for Justice', in *Sister Species: Women, Animals, and Social Justice*, Urbana-Champaign: University of Illinois.

Schipper, K. (2001) 'Daoist Ecology: The Inner Transformation. A Study of the Precepts of the Early Daoist Ecclesia', in N. J. Girardot et al. (eds.) *Daoism and Ecology: Ways Within a Cosmic Landscape*, Cambridge, MA: Harvard University Press.

Schochet, E. J. (1984) *Animal Life in Jewish Tradition: Attitudes and Relationships*, New York: KTAV.

Schwartz, R. H. (2001) *Judaism and Vegetarianism*, New York: Lantern.

152 Lisa Kemmerer

Shinn, L. D. (2000) 'The Inner Logic of Gandhian Ecology', in C. K. Chapple and M. E. Tucker (eds.) *Hinduism and Ecology: The Intersection of Earth, Sky, and Water*, Cambridge: Harvard University Press.

Siddiq, M. Y. (2003) 'An Ecological Journey in Muslim Bengal', in R. C. Foltz et al. (eds.) *Islam and Ecology: A Bestowed Trust*, Cambridge, MA: Harvard University Press.

Statistic Brain Research Institute. (2015) 'Lactose Intolerant Statistic'. Available at http://www.statisticbrain.com/lactose-intolerance-statistics/ (Accessed 23 August 2015).

Subramuniyaswami, S. S. (1993) *Dancing with Siva: Hinduism's Contemporary Catechism*, Concord: Himalayan Academy.

Sutton, David. (2001) *Remembrance of Repasts: An Anthropology of Food and Memory (Materializing Culture)*, New York: Bloomsbury.

Tashi, K. P. (2008) 'Importance of Life Protection: A Tibetan Buddhist View', *The Government of Tibet in Exile*. Available at http://www.tibet.com/Eco/eco5.html (Accessed 8 May 2008).

Taylor, R. L. (2006) 'Of Animals and Humans', in P. Waldau and K. Patton (eds.) *A Communion of Subjects: Animals in Religion, Science, and Ethics*, New York: Columbia University Press.

Tu, W. (1985) *Confucian Thought: Selfhood as Creative Transformation*, Albany: State University of New York Press.

Visser, M. (1987) *Much Depends on Dinner: The Extraordinary History and Mythology, Allure and Obsessions, Perils and Taboos of an Ordinary Meal*, New York: Grove.

Waldau, P. (2002) *The Specter of Speciesism: Buddhist and Christian Views of Animals*, New York: Oxford.

Weise, E. 'Sixty Percent of Adults Can't Digest Milk', *USA Today: Technology: Science and Space*. Available at http://usatoday30.usatoday.com/tech/science/2009–08–30-lactose-intolerance_N.htm (Accessed 23 August 2015).

Wiley, A. S. (2011) 'Milk for "Growth": Global and Local Meanings of Milk Consumption in China, India, and the United States', Food *& Foodways: History & Culture of Human Nourishment* XIX(1/2): 11–33.

World Population Review. (2015) 'Montana Population 2015'. Available at http://worldpopulationreview.com/states/montana-population/ (Accessed 22 August 2015).

Yadav, Y. and Kumar, S. (2006) 'The Food Habits of a Nation', *The Hindu*. 4 August 2006. Available at http://www.thehindu.com/todays-paper/the-food-habits-of-a-nation/article3089973.ece (Accessed 9 August 2015).

9 A Daoist stance on multiculturalism?

The case of Zhang Taiyan

Lin Ma

In recent years, European countries have given up explicit multicultural policies and come to favour assimilation. This claim is substantiated by Angela Merkel's affirmation that multiculturalism has failed. However, the demographic fact of multiculturalism remains. Scholars feel obliged to reflect upon the basic presumptions and principles of multiculturalism and to seek fresh alternatives as well as theoretical reconstruction.

One of the purposes of this chapter is to elucidate elements of a Daoist stance regarding guiding ideas about equality and investigate how these ideas can be applied to political theory and in particular to the relation between different ethnic groups. This is to be achieved via an examination of Zhang Taiyan's (章太炎, 1869–1936) mid-term Daoist political philosophy, which is shaped by his interpretation of Laozi (老子, circa 571–471 BCE) and Zhuangzi's (莊子, circa 369–286 BCE) texts and development of their thinking. Zhang Taiyan, also known as Zhang Binglin (章炳麟), is one of the most prominent philosophers and erudite scholars of his time, as well as an intellectual leader of the Xinhai (辛亥) revolution in 1911 that brought an end to China's last dynasty and established the Republic of China.

This chapter falls into four sections. In the first section, I discuss Zhang Taiyan's understanding of equality through his study of the *Zhuangzi*. On the one hand, Zhang emphasizes that equality refers to the pre-originary state of the myriad things before any naming practices. Instead of taking equality as some final objective to be achieved, Zhang regards it as the original truth of the world. On the other hand, he does not evade addressing the varying divergences among things. Differences are the actual ways of being of things. So long as one does not enforce any superficial "equality" by trying to obliterate differences, but instead accepts differences without imposing a fixed general criterion, the equality of things shows forth in all their differences.

In the second section, I examine Zhang Taiyan's nationalistic position on the relation between the to-be-established "Republic of China" and the other four major ethnic groups. Despite his self-claimed allegiance to the Daoist philosophy, Zhang's proposals, in favouring strong assimilation, remain in contiguity with a traditional Confucian legacy that maintained a hierarchy in evaluating other cultures. His definition of the "Chinese people" is also essentialistic and goes against the Daoist grain.

154 *Lin Ma*

In the third section, I investigate Zhang Taiyan's unique theory of the state, which, in contrast with the spirit of previous proposals in the second section, shows clear signs of his appropriation of the Daoist idea of the "nothing". According to him, the state should modestly keep to a lower weak place as an empty container, which constantly receives and lets go the flow of water, and yet does not assume power and possesses nothing. These ideas also bear out in Zhang's more concrete suggestions concerning the political system of the Republic of China.

In the fourth section, I explore the discordance in Zhang Taiyan's thinking despite his privileging of Laozi and Zhuangzi's ideas. It seems that Zhang has, no matter unintentionally or deliberately, restricted drawing upon Daoist philosophical resources solely to its application to the political system of the Republic of China as supposedly a single-nationality state where ethnodiversity is not valued. In the conclusion, I make suggestions concerning what both Western and Chinese theorists can learn from Daoism on the basis of the Daoist notion of equality.

I. Zhang Taiyan's understanding of equality via Zhuangzi

Zhang Taiyan's study of the *Zhuangzi* focused in particular on chapter two, "The Sorting that Evens Things Out" (*Qiwulun* 齊物論) (Graham 1981: 48). He wrote *A Commentary on the Qiwulun* in 1910 and produced a revised edition in 1914–15 (Zhang 1986).[1] According to Zhang, *qi* (齊) has the implication of "treating things in accordance with what they are" (Zhang 1986: 3, 61). The very first sentence of his exegesis of the title goes:

> The *Qiwu* is a discourse on equality (*pingdeng* 平等). If one delves into its actual signification, one would find that it means not only that one should treat all sentient beings with equality without making differentiations regarding superiority and inferiority. "It is only when one is detached from speech, detached from words, and detached from the mind taking objects as its causal conditions" (離言說相，離名字相，離心緣相) that one can see that things are always equal, and this coincides with the signification of the *Qiwu*.[2]
>
> (Zhang 1986: 48–49)

One can see that Zhang's idea of equality via Zhuangzi is rather radical. The *Qiwulun* opens with the state of losing one's self and ends with the idea of transformation of things, as embodied in the famous butterfly story, thus abolishing the stark opposition between thisness and thatness, and between affirmation and negation. All the things share pre-originary equality despite their great divergence. Furthermore, one needs to treat words, names and mind from the perspective of the pre-originary equality of things.

Now we take a look at Zhuangzi's text: an imaginary conversation between Ziqi of Nanguo and Yancheng Ziyou. Ziqi claims that he has lost

A Daoist stance on multiculturalism? 155

his own self in that his body is like withered wood and his heart dead ashes. He tells the latter that he (Ziyou) has only heard the pipes of men but not the pipes of earth and the pipes of heaven:

> The no-thing (*dakuai* 大塊) blows out breath, by name the "wind." Better if it were never to start up, for whenever it does ten thousand hollow places burst out howling, . . .
>
> Ziyou further asks, "The pipes of earth, these are the various hollows; the pipes of men, these are rows of tubes. Let me ask about the pipe(s) of heaven."
>
> Ziqi replies, "Blowing on the ten thousand things that are never the same (*cuiwan butong* 吹萬不同), so that each can be itself – all take what they want for themselves, but who does the sounding?"
>
> (Graham 1981: 48–49)

Zhang explains that the *Qiwu* is based upon an examination of names and forms and their union in mind. The wind is a metaphor for different kinds of cognition of things in the mind. The ten thousand hollow places burst out howling and yet their sounds are all different. These are the pipes of earth. This parallels the fact that there are different names and discourses in the world that voice different views, just as a domestic hen and a wild magpie sing in different ways in expressing themselves, and just as even floating dust makes different shapes and rises up to the heaven (Zhang 1986: 65).

Zhang considers the "pipes of heaven" as a metaphor for the seeds in the storehouse consciousness (*cangshi* 藏识, Chinese translation of *alaya* consciousness). These seeds not only generate names and discourses, but also are the essence of forms. Hence Zhuangzi says, "Blowing on the ten thousand things that are never the same". Nevertheless, from another perspective, the hollow places into which the pipes of heaven blow are not uneven, since all the blowing and howling can be traced back to the essence of forms. "So that each can be itself" means that proceeding from the storehouse consciousness there are produced the faculty of mind (*yigen* 意根, Chinese translation of Sadindriya, which is one of the six sense organs in Buddhist philosophy). By holding onto the faculty of mind, the self comes into being.

As we know, when he was in jail from 1903–06, Zhang engrossed himself in studies of Buddhist scriptures, specifically those of the "Consciousness-Only Yogācāra School" (唯識瑜伽行派). But his reading of the *Laozi* and the *Zhuangzi* started much earlier in his life. He held that the *Qiwulun* in particular articulated well and embraced the insight of the Buddhist wisdom, rather than the other way around. All the same, occasionally his efforts of trying to fit Zhuangzi's phrases into the model of Buddhist terminology seem to have hampered rather than helped his elucidations. In any case, we have to be assured that Zhang has superb mastery of the profound implications of *Zhuangzi*'s ideas as elaborated in traditional commentaries.

156 Lin Ma

The *Qiwulun* is opened with the situation where Ziqi is said to have lost his self. Cheng Xuanying (成玄英, active during 627–649) thus commented,

> Ziqi . . . has brilliantly grasped the spirit of naturalness. He becomes disjointed from his figure and distances himself from intelligence; both his body and mind are banished, and both things and selves are forgotten.
>
> (Guo 1985: 43)

In light of Cheng's description, when Ziqi loses his self, nothing persists any more. It is as if he has become a hollow space that holds to nothing. Everything becomes transient and fluid. In such a spirit that is emptied of everything, he is able to hear the pipes of heaven. Ziqi starts his description of the pipes of earth with reference to a wind that comes out of an invisible no-thing. As Guo Xiang (郭象 252–312) defines it, "*Dakuai* is no-thing (*wuwu* 無物). It belches forth breath, so is there any thing?" (Guo 1985: 43). This no-thing does not have any sound of its own and does not depend on other things, nor on one's self. Nevertheless it makes possible the sounding of the pipes of earth as well as the pipes of men by blowing into the ten thousand hollow places and rows of tubes. This no-thing is in fact the pipe(s) of heaven.

The ten thousand hollow places have different shapes and produce enormously divergent types of sound. In this respect, they seem to be uneven (*buqi* 不齊). However, in view of the fact that each of them has produced its own music within the limit of its own capacity, it cannot be said that they are uneven. We can still modify the translation as: "Blowing on the ten thousand things evenly [or that are different]". It fits with our common sense that the wind always blows evenly, instead of unevenly, on everything without regard of their difference in shape or their status according to human valuations. Zhang thus comments on this point,

> Trying to even out what are not even/same (*qiqi buqi* 齊其不齊) is the shallow and obstinate practice of the inferior scholars; Achieving evenness/equality while leaving things uneven/unlike (*buqi erqi* 不齊而齊) is the superb discourse of the superior philosophers.
>
> (Zhang 1986: 61)

One should not be restrained by words, names and mind, and thus fail to perceive the pre-originary evenness of things. Neither should one in the least try to force a fake equality on things. Instead, one should return to hollowness (*xu* 虛), just as the pipe of heaven that is no-thing and that belches forth breath without any partiality, and just as the mind of Ziqi that has emptied his own self, and let things remain uneven according to their own capacity. Only in this way can one realize real evenness of things.

It seems that the *Qiwulun* offers Zhang a unique notion of equality that transcends the Western ideal of equality as abstract and utopian egalitarianism, which was imported into China around that time. It is beyond the

A Daoist stance on multiculturalism? 157

antinomy between sameness and difference, and, more importantly, it annuls the presumably abysmal gap between humans and other sentient beings. As Zhang remarked in another work:

> What modern people call equality (*pingdeng* 平等) refers to the equality between human beings. Thus they leave human beings and birds, beasts, grass and trees unequal. The notion of equality in Buddhism equalizes human beings with birds and beasts. Zhuangzi goes one step further in equalizing [human beings] with things. Even so he does not remain contented. He takes the tendency to making judgments concerning rightness and wrongness (*shifei* 是非) to be a sign of inequality. One can only achieve equality after one gets rid of such tendency. Just before his death, Zhuangzi says, "Using criteria that are unequal in order to obtain equality, such presumed equality is not equal." This is a footnote to his notion of equality.
>
> (Zhang 1987: 64–65)

It seems that Zhuangzi's notion of equality deals not only with sentient beings in the life world, but also with names such as good and evil, right and wrong. One has to remain vigilant of the fact that one's criteria of values are constrained by one's prejudice; therefore one cannot stick to a fixed value system in weighing things. However, this does not mean that there can be neither rightness nor wrongness, but that one should proceed from the actual situation of a particular thing, and treat things as what they are. Zhang cited the *Laozi* to further explicate this point: chapter 64 of the *Laozi* says, "To help the myriad things to be natural and to refrain from daring to act"; chapter 49 goes,

> The sage has no constant mind,
> He takes the mind of the people as his own mind.
> Those who are good I treat as good.
> Those who are not good I also treat as good.
> In so doing I gain in goodness.[3]

Zhang commented that Laozi meant to say that one should not bring in one's preconceptions concerning good and evil, right and wrong, and on this basis impose an apparently true but yet fake equality. Rather, one should acknowledge the dissimilarity between things, be alert of the limitation of one's own value judgments, proceed from the natural characteristics of things, and comport oneself in constant correspondence with the actual situation, just as the hinge of a door keeps on opening and closing according to need. This is what Zhuangzi describes as "open[ing] things up to the light of heaven", and as using "Illumination" (Graham 1981: 52).

The implication of these Zhuangzian ideas for political thinking is that all the states, nationalities, communities and individuals have their right of existence and of free development. One cannot resort solely to one's own

158   *Lin Ma*

criteria to draw final conclusions in evaluating other cultures. Toward the end of his opening commentary on the title of the *Qiwulun*, Zhang mentions in particular the story about Yao's asking Shun (both being legendary ancient sage kings) whether he could launch a war against three supposedly backward states. The story goes,
Formerly Yao asked Shun:

"I wish to smite Zong, Kuai and Xu-ao. Why is it that I am not at ease on
  the south-facing throne?"
Shun replied, "These three states survive among the weeds. Why be uneasy?
  Formerly ten suns rose side by side and the myriad things were all illu-
  minated, and not to mention the fact that virtue is much more greater
  than suns."

(Watson 1968: 45; Graham 1981: 58)

Zhang in his exegeses cited from Guo Xiang's comments, "[This story] refers to the great sages in order to reveal the principle of equality/evenness (*qiyi* 齊一)"; "where one feels at ease, there is no meanness. Hence, the weeds are the wonderful dwelling-places for the three kings".[4] Different states are located in different environment. One cannot impose one's own criteria to draw the conclusion that the states that took their dwelling-places among weeds are uncivilized. Worse than that, one cannot use this as an excuse to smite them and try to adapt them to the "civilization" of the middle country. To do this can be compared to feeding a seagull with a luxurious banquet, and entertaining a bird with magnificent music, Zhang said (Zhang 1986: 100).

Different states have divergent (literally "uneven" *buqi* 不齊) customs; what is called civilization and what is called barbarism ascribe value to different things. However, they all remain at ease with their own customs and do not bring in hindrance to one another, just as the ten suns do not affect one another. Virtue is supposed to be greater than the sun, so a virtuous king such as Yao should have no problem in allowing the coexistence of the three states. This is real equality. This can be considered a Daoist version of multiculturalism. The will of trying to civilize them arises from a prejudice that considers them as uneven with the middle country. In the foregoing I have offered an analysis along the line of most commentaries.

Zhang seemed to take himself as a steadfast devotee to Zhuangzi's ideas. However, his discussions concerning how to build up a new nation-state of China and how to deal with the major minorities who decided to join the country show signs of traditional Sino-centrism and the will of trying to equalize what are unequal, the reverse of Zhuangzi's insight.[5]

II. Zhang's nationalistic position on the relation between the "Republic of China" and other cultures

Zhang's proposal for a single-nationality new China is based upon his standard concerning how to define the extension of what has been generally

A Daoist stance on multiculturalism? 159

called the Chinese people. He put forward this standard against such scholars as Kang Youwei, Liang Qichao (梁启超, 1873–1929), and Yang Du (楊度, 1875–1931), who advocated that after thousands of years of living together, various ethnic groups (*minzu* 民族) in China had been as a matter of fact integrated, including in particular the five major ethnic groups, namely Han, Man, Meng, Hui and Zang. They suggested titling such an integrated big nationality the "Nationality of China (*zhonghua minzu* 中華民族)". The second word *hua* in *zhonghua minzu* is related to *huaxia* (華夏), a traditional reference to the people in the middle country. These scholars emphasized *hua*'s cultural connotation and argued that the minorities who had adopted Han's culture and customs were also part of the "Nationality of China". This view was also called definition by culture instead of blood lineage. Liang called this idea "big nationalism" and opposed it to "small nationalism", which concerned itself only with the Han (Liang 1989: 75–76).

Against this trend, Zhang defended a position of what was called "small nationalism". In "An Explanation of 'The Republic of China (*zhonghua minguo* 中華民國)'" written in 1907, he traced the complicated history of how the very large *huaxia* (which he considered to be just another name for the Han) nationality came to be shaped (Zhang 1985a). According to his detailed historical research, the word *hua* came from Mount Hua; *xia* came from River Xia. *Hua* was originally used as the name of the country, while *xia* was properly speaking the name of the people of such an ethnic group who lived in the middle country (Zhang's word is *zhongzu* 种族, which normally translates "race". From this one can already see his emphasis on blood lineage). Zhang's last point is reflected in the fixed expression "Keeping *yi* and *xia* separate" (*yixia zhifang* 夷夏之防), where *yi* designates the people who live outside the middle country. The name for the Han nationality came from the Western Han dynasty (202–9 BCE), which occupied the same geographical area as the country of Hua. Hence, Hua, Xia and Han overlap and share the same meaning. Hence, Zhang argues, the ethnic name Han contains a reference to the country Hua, and Hua, as highlighted in the name of the to-be-established new nation-state, that is, *zhonghua minguo*, carries the implication that the Han people are to be the citizens of this nation-state (1985a: 252–253).

The background against which Zhang emphasized the geographical connotation of Hua in using it in the name of the new nation-state was Yang Du's distinction between *zhongguo* (中國, literally "the middle country/kingdom") and *zhonghua* (中華). In his text, Zhang several times referred to Yang in terms of an adherent to the Gold-and-Iron-Doctrine,[6] who contended that *zhongguo* had primarily been used as a geographical notion in order to distinguish between areas close and far, while *zhonghua*, where *hua* was set against *yi*, had been used to judge the superiority and inferiority of cultures. Hence, *hua* was neither the name for the country, nor that of a certain race. Rather, it was the name for a culture; it indicated cultural unification. *Zhonghua minzu* (the "Nationality of China") was the epithet

160 *Lin Ma*

for the people of all the ethnic groups living in China who have become unified after a long period of integration.[7] In contrast, Zhang adhered to a narrow view of China as a three-fold union in terms of geography, tradition/culture, and (Han) nationality/race. He stressed in particular the importance of blood lineage in defining the Han:

> When we talk about race (*zhongzu* 种族), it is not that we are overdoing it, but we have to restrict it to those most of whom share the same blood lineage. This is because the sharing of culture started with sharing the same lineage. Only on the condition that this [standard] is unshakable can the people of other nationalities come under the umbrella of our government, and can [culture] be transferred and adopted. If two groups of people of different lineages oppose to one another, even if we want to assimilate the other group, there is no way for that.[8]

Proceeding from such "small nationalism", Zhang presented his vision of the relationship between the Han and the four other major nationalities (or ethnic groups). Recall one of the ingredients of his definition of nationality is location. Zhang defined the current geographical boundary of China in view of that from the Western Han dynasty, and declared that the regions outside it, namely Mongolia, Xinjiang, Tibet (and North-East China), were not part of China. Hence, the people of these nationalities, Meng, Hui, Zang (and Man), should have the freedom to choose whether they want to establish their own independent nation-states. If they choose to do so, then China can establish a sort of union with them as independent nation-states. If they are unwilling to be separate from China, then they have to be assimilated into the Chinese culture. Zhang's preference for the idea of a single-nationality state was influenced by modern Western theories. As he states:

> Since the 19th century, nationalism appeared among numerous states. Its legacy still remains and its influence extends far. To put its purport in a nutshell: the people of the same nationality in a number of countries sought integration; while the people of different nationalities in the same country sought separation.
>
> (Zhang 1985b)

In a way, Zhang's proposal that a number of single-nationality states be established does not necessarily entail a prejudice against other nationalities. Insofar as Zhang considered that other nationalities should have the right to build up their own autonomous states, it seems that he was placing them on the same par as the Han, so that equality could be maintained. However, Zhang did not devote much thought to this possibility. Perhaps it was partially because for him the political right of self-determination on the part of other nationalities at that time was actually only justifiable in theory, but yet unfeasible in practice in view of the under-development of those regions. Hence, in his "An Explanation of 'The Republic of China' ", which is to be a state composed mainly of the Han, he devoted lengthy discussions to the ways in which the people of these other nationalities could be successfully absorbed into China.

Zhang evaluated the possibility of assimilation in several respects:[9] with respect to language, there are more Han people in Xinjiang than in other outer regions, and the members of the Hui are more intelligent than the Mongolians; therefore it is relatively easier to integrate them into the Chinese culture. Although the Mongolians are retarded in intelligence, they have begun to learn the Chinese language because of frequent trade with the Han. The Tibetan people are most remote from contact with the Han. In addition, they have built up their own distinctive religion and civilization, and their language derives from a completely different linguistic system. For this reason, it requires the most efforts to adapt the Tibetans in terms of language and writing.

With respect to livelihood, the form of agriculture in the Hui area does not differ from the Han custom, and the people there live in houses and build city walls in the same way as the Han. In Tibet, by contrast, high mountains and deep valleys form obstacles for access. There are no vast places for pasture, and its land is so far from fertile that only highland barley can grow. The Tibetans live in shabby wooden houses, which are better than tents. In Mongolia, Gobi extends overall; even in flat land there are huge areas of deserts. For the sake of their pastoral life, the Mongolian people have to live in tents. Although their king and aristocrats live in proper houses, the commoners do not have such an advantage. Therefore, the most efforts are needed in order to adapt the Mongolians in terms of livelihood.

With respect to laws and administration, in the Qing dynasty the central government often dispatched Manchu officials to Tibet to assist although theocracy reigns there. This practice can continue in the future by sending Han officials instead. The Mongolians have their chief, and their laws differ greatly from the middle country. However, for those tribes that submit and pledge allegiance to the Han government, it is not impossible to dispatch Han officials there. Only the Hui people were a possible problem in this aspect. The Manchu government has mistreated them ruthlessly, banishing them in spite of their innocence, totally unlike the situation where it regarded the Mongolians as brothers and paid respect to the religion of the Tibetans.[10] Since the Manchu government treated the Hui as trash, the Hui harboured deep resentment against the Manchus, and by extension also against Han officials. Unrest easily started with them. Hence, according to Zhang, the most effort with respect to laws and administration has to be invested with the Hui. If one wants to assimilate the Hui, one can send officials and set up schools there, and yet leave their laws unchanged for the time being. After twenty years or so, the Hui region would become almost the same as the Inner land (Zhang 1985a: 257).

162 *Lin Ma*

Regarding the Manchus, one can observe two aspects in Zhang's thinking. On the one hand, he exhibited strong sentiments of repulsion against the Manchus in saying that they originated in raccoon dog, a sort of animal (Zhang 2012: 18). They have a different language, teaching and lifestyle. One cannot consider them as a part of the *huaxia*. As an alien nationality, they are not entitled to assuming governorship over the Han. Although they worship Kongzi and follow the teaching of Confucianism, that is in essence a political strategy for the sake of their monarchical dominance in China. In addition, although most of them have mastery of the Chinese language and adopt Chinese customs, it cannot be said that they have been assimilated with the Han in view of the fact that they rule over the Han, whose population (400 million) far exceeds that of the Manchus (5 million). Hence, it is absolutely necessary to overthrow the Manchu monarchical government.

In this respect, Zhang was opposed to Kang Youwei, who deemed that the Manchu monarchy could be allowed to continue its reign provided that the emperor engaged himself in reformation and modernization. Kang invoked historical documents as well in attempting to prove that the Manchus have descended from the same ancestor as the Han, and that therefore one could not regard them as alien.

One the other hand, Zhang disagreed with the radical view that the Han should exterminate the over five million Manchus because they are beasts. He held that as long as the Manchus surrender their governorship and return to their place of origin in the northeastern area, the Han government could treat it in the same way as it would Japan and Thailand. Suppose that the Han take revenge and try to kill the Manchus, then the descendents of the Manchus would take their turn to kill the Han, and then there could be no end to such rounds of revenge. In addition, the Han officials appointed by the Manchu government were comparable with them in terms of degree of ruthlessness. So it is unfair to take revenge only on the Manchus (1985d: 262–263).

III. Zhang's Daoist notion of the state

In the previous section, we saw that Zhang was strongly in favour of a single-nationality state for various reasons, the most fundamental one being his vision of the new China as a three-fold union in terms of geography, tradition/culture and (Han) nationality/race. He attached special importance to blood lineage in defining (Han) nationality/race. These ideas are under the sway of modern Western nationalism, and also show close affinities to the Confucian heritage that Zhang himself had severely attacked. However, in his other political writings, Zhang voiced a view of state that was properly Daoist.

In "On State", composed in 1907, the same year as he wrote "An Explanation of 'The Republic of China'", Zhang outlined a political theory that prioritized the individual over the state. According to him, "each of the individual entities consists in a compound of a plurality of things, and has

A Daoist stance on multiculturalism? 163

by itself no substantial being (*shiyou* 實有)" (Zhang 1985c: 457). A human being is composed of numerous cells that are in constant movement between life and death. Similarly, a state is composed of people and by itself has no substance. The relation between people and state is comparable to that between yarn and cloth. Yarns crisscross one another and bring forth cloth. In a similar way, via dynamic connections with one another, individuals give shape to a state. Relative to the state, individuals have real existence, whereas no organizations, no matter a village, an army, a herd or a state, possess real substance or existence. This resembles the fact that when a piece of cloth disintegrates, the yarns may still remain, but there is no longer the cloth. Hence, it seems that, for Zhang, the state is dependent upon people, rather than the other way around. In this connection, Zhang charges other contemporary scholars of letting the state dominate the people in treating the state as the host and the people as the guest (Zhang 1985c: 458).

Zhang employs yet another metaphor to illustrate his point. A riverbed may remain unchanged for thousands of years, while the water drops that run through the riverbed are in constant change. In this sense, one may say that the riverbed is the host while water drops are the guests. However, if one examines the riverbed closely, one can see that there are banks on the left and right, mud and sands beneath and hollow space in the middle. Although banks, mud and sands bring forth the riverbed, they are in themselves just earth, and so cannot be referred to as the riverbed itself. What one can refer to as the riverbed is only the hollow space in between. Therefore, the "host" is actually hollow and has no real existence.

By comparison, one can observe the hollowness of the riverbed, but not that of the state. Apart from people, what one can observe in terms of a state are not more than fields, mountains and lakes. But these cannot possibly be referred to as what constitute "the state". Zhang concludes that the state has barely more than a name. Much as the hollow riverbed, the state is a hollow space consisting in people who are in constant change (Zhang 1985c: 458–459). Here we can already sense the inconsistency of Zhang's political philosophy when we recall that he took recourse to geographical boundaries as well as blood lineage in demarcating the sphere and the nationalities of China and on this basis advocated a Han-centered national state. In today's China, the 55 nationalities other than Han live all over China; they have become much less restricted to those regions Zhang mentioned.

Proceding from such a Daoist view of the state, Zhang advocated a weak central government. According to him, the political chaos in the 1910s was caused by the dense concentration of power on a strong central government. Because president and premier assumed abundant power, every warlord would like to compete in order to get the post. Hence, the central government should have very limited power to such an extent that it becomes like a "weak female [*xupin* 虛牝]" (Zhang 1999: 163–164). There is even no need for a central parliament. Only so can there be no power struggle. Zhang was well-known for supporting the system of "Joint-Province Autonomies

164   *Lin Ma*

(*lianshen zizhi* 联省自治)" in the 1920s. It seems that he was only considering the Han provinces.

According to Zhang, each province should establish its own autonomous government and draw up its own constitution. Both civil and military officials, soldiers and policemen should be natives, and officials at all levels should be selected by public vote. Then these provinces can be joined together to form a government, which is almost symbolic, on the basis of their own autonomies.

In terms of laws and regulations, Zhang held that one should *not* blindly follow Western countries; instead, one had to make decisions in view of traditional customs, practices and people's preferences. These formed the "compasses and set squares (*guiju* 规矩)" of the ten thousand things.

> The sage goes along with the 'compasses and set squares' of the ten thousand things. Hence [Laozi] says that [the sage] does not dare to be the first under the heaven. . . . What is crucial is to abolish one's personal wits, annul disparities, and to consult the people in order to conform to most of them.
>
> (Zhang 2007: 50)

Zhang often stressed the primal importance of listening to the opinion of people when one wants to make changes in policy. For example, he was opposed to shifting to the solar calendar in place of the traditional lunar calendar at that time. The reason for his opposition was not that the solar calendar was not good, but that the way in which this decision was made did not conform to the rule. It was finalized by the committee of consultation, whereas Zhang insisted that, in view of the fact that the Chinese people had long been accustomed to the lunar calendar, such an important decision had to be made on the basis of their opinion (Zhang 1977: 539, 547).

On the whole, Zhang found it inappropriate to impose a Western political system on China. According to him, the system of democratic constitution originated in France and received modification in the United States, and China should create yet a third-genre system of democratic constitution. There could be no universally applicable political system. The rules and regulations should suit people's preferences (Zhang: 537).

IV. Discordance in Zhang's thinking

When it comes to the political issues related solely to the Han people, Zhang has consistently abided by Laozi's idea of *wuwei* (無為, no coercive action) and placed people in the central place, rather than the state, which for him was non-substantial and did not have real existence. However, when it comes to the relation between the Han and other nationalities who would remain part of China, he unreservedly believed in the power of the Han central government to assimilate other people in terms of almost every aspect:

A Daoist stance on multiculturalism? 165

language, customs, livelihood, laws and regulations. He did not entertain the idea whether the people (who he took to have priority and right in making policy changes) of other nationalities should also have a say in whether they were willing to change their lives and even identities in such a radical way. Proceeding from Zhang's proposal for "Joint-Province Autonomies", one wonders why the people of other nationalities are not allowed to have similar autonomies in drawing up their own constitutions, having their own armies and selecting their own officials.

Zhang disputed the universal validity of the Western political system and criteria of civilization. Recall the story about Yao who entertained the plan to demolish the barbaric states. As a matter of fact, this story could have served as a best example illustrating how one could treat other cultures outside the middle country. Nevertheless, Zhang seemed to relate this story to the issue of the relation between Han China and Western countries alone. He argued that different states have different values, and a presumably civilized state should not try to smite other states in the name of their alleged barbarism. It is a pity that, in undoubtedly assuming Sino-centrism and holding prejudice against other people's languages and customs, Zhang seemed to have forgotten what he had learned from Zhuangzi's notion of equality when he turned to deal with the issue of other cultures in Han China.

Zhang subscribed to the Zhuangzian insight of "achieving evenness/equality while leaving things uneven/unlike (*buqi erqi*)". However, he failed to bring this insight to bear on the *mutual* relation between different ethnic groups within the "Republic of China". He presented a model of complete absorption conceived *unilaterally* from the Han people. It is not the case that other ethnic groups can choose assimilation if they remain part of China, but that they have no choice but to become assimilated by the Han.

It seems to be remarkable that Zhang attempted to maintain equality in granting Meng, Hui, Zang (and Man) the right to decide whether they would like to have their own independent state or remain part of China, assuming that they have a fixed dwelling place. However, he had only talked about the four major nationalities; there are in total 55 nationalities in China other than the Han, and these people were dispersed over all of China. What to do with them? Should the people of Meng, Hui, Zang and Man who live in the inner land be deported if they choose to be independent? Should abandoning one's language, customs and social system be absolute conditions for remaining part of China? Zhang has failed to address such questions.

Despite Zhang's resorting to blood lineage as the most crucial criterion for distinguishing the Han, the thousands of years of interaction between *xia* and *yi* has made it impossible to identify completely pure Han blood lineage uncontaminated by *yi*. The influence of tribal people on the custom of the middle country was recorded as early as in the *Commentary of Zuo* (左傳), a classic of history covering the years from 722 to 468 BCE: the people in the now Henan province were seen to have their hair unbound

166 Lin Ma

as the *yi* people did. In addition, as an erudite scholar, could Zhang totally deny traces of vocabulary and expressions from other tongues in the Han language? The point here is that a purely blood criterion for dealing with ethnic problems in China is not possible. The blood criterion, we can see, serves political, nationalistic purposes.

Of course, one of the causes for the bankruptcy of Western multicultural policy has been attributed to a sort of *laissez faire* policy regarding minority ethnic groups, in particular the Muslim people. Some scholars may discern similarities between such liberal multiculturalism and the Daoist non-interference or *wuwei* and for this reason may wonder what lesson one can get from Daoism. In this connection, we should not identify *wuwei* with *laissez faire* or mere tolerance or disengagement. *Wuwei* is, as Zhang once defined it, "To help the myriad things to be natural and to refrain from daring to act" (Zhang 1995: 15).

It is clear that, first, *wuwei* is the opposite of the policy of total assimilation, which is a strong form of interference. Second, *wuwei* does not mean doing nothing, but conforming to things' own naturalness or inner rhythm rather than imposing external standards upon things. *Wuwei* is non-compulsive action, just as Zhuangzi describes in the *Qiwulun*, the wind blows over thousands of hollow places evenly, and yet leaves it to the hollow places themselves to produce their individual tunes. All these tunes together, uneven when compared one by one in a close study, nevertheless constitute a magnificent (and even) symphony.

A metaphor from Zhang's "On State" can well be used to illustrate how different ethnic groups can be embraced in one state. Zhang came upon this metaphor when talking about the boundary of a state. First he put forward the thesis that there is no taking for granted that all things have determinate extensions. The ten thousand things are in truth all connected and mutually adaptable. It is only when protection is needed that a tree takes on bark, a worm takes on a shell, and human beings and animals take on skin (Zhang 1985c: 459). Hence, boundaries arise as a negative strategy, rather than something fundamental.

Similarly, the boundary of a state is demarcated for the purpose of protecting the land. But it is not an inborn necessity that there should be boundaries. For example, the scenes on the two sides of a river appear to be distinct; however, there is no problem for both scenes to be contained in the same river (as a reflection) (Zhang 1985c: 460). Hence, originally it is not the case that things cannot embrace or adapt to one another. Zhang has previously compared the state to the riverbed; here we can take the river to be a state that embraces different ethnic groups, which can be compared to distinct scenes on the sides of the river. Although one can say that their distinctiveness might still remain (*buqi*), they are all evenly (*qi*) reflected in the same river.

If Zhang would really admit that the state should be hollow and non-coercive, then it seems that he had to drop his conception of the Republic of

A Daoist stance on multiculturalism? 167

China as a single-nationality Han state and consider the idea of China as a state that can embrace a great plurality of nationalities, 56 in total. Proceeding from the Daoist stance, the state should deal with different ethnic groups evenly without exerting a strong policy of unilateral assimilation on what have come to be called minority groups.

VI. Concluding remarks

Some scholars on multiculturalism expect that Confucianism is able to provide an alternative discourse on this issue. This is not the main topic of the present chapter. But we can see from our discussion that traditional Confucian policies are unavoidably based upon the distinction between *yi* and *xia*, in other words, a distinction between civilization and barbarism. Even if some authors argue that the other ethnic groups were treated as younger brothers under the patronage of the Han government, who were like elder brothers, and pledge the value of harmony and fusion (He 2005). However, such values undoubtedly presuppose maintenance of the Han leadership as well as the hierarchical evaluations of other ethnic groups.

As we know, the modern Western political ideal of a nation-state formed one of the intellectual sources for Zhang Taiyan's idea of a single-nationality new China. One wonders whether the current Chinese government, as well as such authors as Baogang He, who write on "minority rights with Chinese characteristics", are also under the sway of Western theories imported via Marxism. For example, the 55 nationalities except the Han were just not given a blanket epithet "minority ethnic groups" (*shaoshu minzu* 少数民族) before the establishment of the People's Republic of China in 1949. It is worth reflecting whether such terms as majority versus minority, despite their Western origin, have retained and even exacerbated the distinction of *yi* and *xia*. In my view, the distinction of majority versus minority contains the explicit appeal to the commonly held principle that the minority should conform to the majority, and seems to have served as a stronger basis for the policy of unilateral assimilation and homogenization. During the Qing dynasty, Meng, Zang, Man and Han were all official languages, but in the new China only Han is the official language.

Hence, the present author suggests that Confucianism may not be able to offer what these scholars seek. Above all, we need to have a perspicuous analysis concerning what had actually been at play behind the abortion of Western multicultural policy. Has the *laissez faire* tendency of liberal multiculturalism quietly encouraged the differentiation and distancing of different groups? Has this further led to general ignorance and even prejudice against "minorities", which is veiled behind aloofness? Instead of rashly trying to find ready alternatives in a supposedly different intellectual tradition, liberal multiculturalism need to first problematize and think through some of its basic notions and assumptions.

168 *Lin Ma*

On the other hand, we have to understand Zhang Taiyan's subscription to the ideal of a single-nationality state in relation to his times, when China was frequently invaded by Western powers and its chief task was to struggle to keep sovereignty. Hence, he may have conceived such a vision of the new China out of his concern to invigorate nationalism in order to combat Western countries. This standpoint actually corresponded to the Gold-and-Iron Doctrine. Nevertheless, even in these extreme and extraordinary circumstances, Zhang has made utmost efforts to draw upon Daoist sources for his political thinking on the state and its organization.

I consider that both Western and Chinese theorists on multiculturalism can learn from Daoism on three points, all based upon the Daoist insight of "evening out things" or *buqi erqi*: first, one should give up starting reasoning from one's own standpoint from the presumably dominating majority (unfortunately most theorists seem to come from the majority group in their countries), and to treat other cultures as a certain object to be evaluated, tolerated, absorbed or to be kept at distance. It is better to avoid using such determinations as majority versus minority, which are misleading and entail unequal evaluations. As Zhang Taiyan rightly pointed out via Zhuangzi, the tendency to make judgments concerning *shifei* (right or wrong) was a sign of inequality. Second, one needs to realize that there are no strict boundaries between things, and by extension, between various ethnic groups, and in particular those who have been living together or side-by-side and so have *mutually* affected one another. Third, if policies have to be drawn up concerning relations between different ethnic groups in the same state, one should guard against promulgating *unilateral* regulations from the standpoint of the central government constituted in the main by, presumably, representatives from the "majority".

Notes

1 In this chapter, unless otherwise noted, English translations from original Chinese texts are all mine.
2 Zhang's citation comes from the *Discourse on the Awakening of Faith in the Mahāyāna* 《大乘起信論》. Here I follow Murthy's rendition of this citation (Viren Murthy, *The Political Philosophy of Zhang Taiyan: The Resistance of Consciousness*, Leiden/Boston: Brill, 2011, p. 210).
3 See Zhang (1995: 5–17, 14–15). English translations of the *Laozi* are from Lau (1963: 95, 71); translation modified. Zhang also cited chapter 49 (Zhang 1986: 17).
4 Zhang (1986: 39, 99–100); also see Guo (1985).
5 To my knowledge, despite a few works devoted to Zhang Taiyan's political philosophy, his relevant discussions in this aspect, which are to be presented in the following section, have hardly been revealed nor commented upon.
6 The Gold-and-Iron-Doctrine is the idea that China should seek to become economically wealthy (gold) and diplomatically strong (iron-cannon).
7 See Zhang (1985a: 253); also cf. Yang (1986).
8 Zhang (1985a: 255). Zhang did not make a clear distinction between race and nationality.

A Daoist stance on multiculturalism? 169

9 What follows is a summary of Zhang's suggestions in Zhang (1985a: 257). Some of his statements are disconcerting and even racist according to current criteria.
10 In this connection, He (2005) seems to have given a naïve picture of the "multi-culturalism" policy by the Manchu government.

References

Graham, A. C. (1981) *Chuang-Tzu: The Inner Chapters*, Indianapolis: Hackett Publishing Company.

Guo, Q. (ed.) (1985) *Collected Exegeses of the Zhuangzi* 《莊子集釋》, Beijing: Zhonghua shuju 中華書局.

He, B. (2005) 'Minority Rights with Chinese Characteristics', in W. Kymlicka and B. He (eds.) *Multiculturalism in Asia*, New York: Oxford University Press, 56–79.

Lau, C. D. (1963) *Tao Te Ching*, Hong Kong: The Chinese University Press.

Liang, Q. (ed.) (1989) *Collected Works from the Ice-Drinker's Studio* 《飲冰室合集》 2, Beijing: Zhonghua shuju 中華書局.

Watson, B. (1968) *The Complete Works of Chuang Tzu*, New York: Columbia University Press.

Yang, D. (1986) *Collected Works by Yang Du* 《楊度集》, Changsha: Hunan renmin chubanshe 湖南人民出版社.

Zhang, T. (1977) *Selected Writings on Politics* 《章太炎政論选集》, Beijing: Zhonghua shuju 中華書局.

Zhang, T. (1985a) 'An Explanation of "The Republic of China" 中華民國解', *Complete Works by Zhang Taiyan* 《章太炎全集》, 4, Shanghai: Shanghai renmin chubanshe 上海人民出版社: 252–262.

Zhang, T. (1985b) 'A Discussion on a Short History of Politics 《社會通诠》商兑', *Complete Works by Zhang Taiyan* 《章太炎全集》, 4, Shanghai: Shanghai renmin chubanshe 上海人民出版社: 322–337.

Zhang, T. (1985c) 'On state 國家論', *Complete Works by Zhang Taiyan* 《章太炎全集》, 4, Shanghai: Shanghai renmin chubanshe 上海人民出版社, 457–466.

Zhang, T. (1985d) 'On Repelling the Manchus 排滿平議', *Complete Works by Zhang Taiyan* 《章太炎全集》, 4, Shanghai: Shanghai renmin chubanshe 上海人民出版社: 262–270.

Zhang, T. (1986) 'A Commentary on the Qiwulun 《齊物論釋》', *Complete Works by Zhang Taiyan* 《章太炎全集》, 6, Shanghai: Shanghai renmin chubanshe 上海人民出版社, 1–58; revised version: 59–124.

Zhang, T. (1987) *Introduction to the National Learning* 《國學概論》, Q. Cao (ed.), Chengdu: Bashu shushe 巴蜀書社.

Zhang, T. (1995) 'On the Relation between Buddhism and Religion, Philosophy and Reality 論佛法與宗教、哲學以及現實之關係', *Selected Works by Zhang Taiyan and Yang Du* 《章太炎集、楊度集》, Beijing: Zhongguo shehui kexue chubanshe 中國社會科學出版社.

Zhang, T. (1999) 'On Joint-Province Autonomies and Placing the Central Government in a Hollow Place 聯省自治虚置政府議', *Zhang Taiyan's Essays on Learning and Culture* 《章太炎學術文化隨筆》, Beijing: Zhongguo qingnian chubanshe 中國青年出版社.

Zhang, T. (2007) 'Lectures on the National Heritage 《國故論衡》', *Selected Readings from Zhang Taiyan* 《精读章太炎》, Xiamen: Lujiang chubanshe 鷺江出版社.

Zhang, T. (2012) *Qiushu* 《訄书》, Shanghai: Zhongxi shuju 中西書局.

10 Islamic multiculturalism

Coexistence overcoming "Kufr" in Tayeb Saleh's *Season of Migration to the North* and Hanan El-Sheik's *Beirut Blues*

George Sadaka

> O mankind! We have created you from a male and a female, and made you into nations and tribes, that you may know one another.
>
> (Quran 49: 13)

Since its foundation, Islam has always been an experience of multiculturalism operating upon the conglomeration of different cultures, races, and ethnicities by the dogma and praxis of a universal religion. By multiculturalism I mean the coexistence of Muslim and non-Muslim cultures in the same geographical space. The Quran supports, at varying degrees, the aforementioned definition of multiculturalism as it numerates and names pre-Islamic nations that have always coexisted with Islam:

> Verily, those who believe [the Muslims] and those who are Jews and Christians and Sabians, whoever believes in Allah and the Last Day and does righteous good deeds shall have their reward with their Lord, on them shall be no fear, nor shall they grieve.
>
> (Quran 2: 63)

Throughout history, Islamic multiculturalism has been challenged by intricate interventions and interruptions caused by politics (geopolitics, ethno-politics, political economy) and sectarianism. The Quran reads: "and if your Lord had so willed, he could surely have made mankind one *Ummah* [nation or community], but they will not cease to disagree" (Quran 11: 118). Therefore, if Islam involves a call for Muslims to be unified in one *Ummah*, Muslims need to experience multiculturalism within Islam itself at first because the *Ummah* does not preclude differences in culture, language, race, and other classifications of alterity. In this essay, multiculturalism is appropriated within a bipartite of intra-cultural and cross-cultural encounters. My overarching argument is that multiculturalism is not *kufr* (apostasy) in Islam by virtue of the fact that when real-life (extra-textual) events do not seem to be working in a multicultural fashion, creative imagination (the pitfalls of which are discussed in this essay) rushes to transpire and transfigure multiculturalism.

Islamic multiculturalism 171

The Islamic concept of *kufr* stands as one stone block in the path of multiculturalism. In *Al-Munjid Dictionary*, *kufr* is defined as a derivative of *kafar* (verb), which means "covering, veiling, hiding, and cloaking" an idea, a belief, or any truth of any kind (1956: 691). A *kafir*, therefore, is the one who hides or the one who does not express a certain shared conventionalized truth. A second definition reads: "disbelief in God" regardless of religious sect, which means that a Christian, a Jew, a Muslim or any other who does not believe in God (the Judeo-Christian Jehovah and the Islamic Allah) is a *kafir*. This being said, Islam does not and cannot monopolize the usage of the words "*kufr*" and "*kafir*" to apply to non-Muslims because every non-Christian may be a *kafir* to Christianity just as every non-Jew may be a *kafir* to Judaism. In Islamic discourse, *takfirism* is the act of labeling a human as a *kafir* or a cultural activity as a *kufr*. These two words may be seen as primary causes behind the failure of multiculturalism within Islamic cultures. Tolerance and intolerance are encouraged, at varying degrees, by the Quran and Islamic tradition, so my essay quotes the *Quran* in considering the *raison d'être* of the two models of tolerance and intolerance towards *kuffar*. In my selection of two twentieth-century Arabic novels: *Season of Migration to the North* (1969) by the Sudanese novelist Tayyeb Saleh and *Beirut Blues* (1992) by the Lebanese writer Hanan El-Sheikh, Islam is practiced within an intransigent polarity of "us" versus "other". It is also practiced within a resilient attitude of reconcilable and peaceful worlds of Muslims and non-Muslims.

In this essay, I use "intra-cultural" to expound the experience of multiculturalism at the internal (Muslim-Muslim) level, and I use "cross-cultural" to construe the experience of multiculturalism at the external (Muslim-Christian) level. *Season of Migration to the North* dramatizes the conflict of multiculturalism in the encounters between Sudanese and British people (labeled in the novel as Muslims and Christians/infidels respectively). *Beirut Blues* dramatizes the challenges of multiculturalism in the encounters between Lebanese Muslims and Christians during the Lebanese Civil War. The two novels cleave geographically but coalesce generically. In both novels, Islam is delineated as encouraging both cultural tolerance and cultural *takfirism*. My contention is that the two novels valorize and encourage the exemplary of tolerance and multiculturalism (within clear dogmatic and practical parameters of Islam) as they construct inhibited and exhibited forms of cultural mutual exclusiveness, anthropomorphic metonymies, and other age-old inherited fallacies as obsolete and deplorable. Remarkably, the authors, Saleh and Sheikh, seem to propound the idea of the incompatibility of Islam with intolerance. They do not whitewash Islam (and neither do I). Yet, their novels dramatize the malaise of fanaticism, which has its roots in popular versions of Islam.

As my title suggests, *takfirism* in the two novels is one problematic that derails Islamic multiculturalism. The novels may be seen as working towards rerouting MENA people, more through common sense than

172 George Sadaka

through Islamic theology, to embrace multicultural attitudes in order to be on a par with contemporary cosmopolitanism and pluralism. For this purpose, real and imaginary erotic encounters are often employed individualistically for the sake of redefining and reinventing multiculturalism. Erotic attraction to a "different other" may be one good model for multiculturalism, but Mustapha in *SMN* (*SMN* is short for *Season of Migration to the* North) and Asmahan in *Beirut Blues* exemplify one bad illustration of it. The solution that I suggest through the novels lies in the Islamic/Quranic belief in coexistence. In other words, the solution lies not in making love but in living love. My argument is superintended within the boundaries of novels, dealing with them as literary texts that dramatize fictional events in a fictional framework. Nevertheless, as literary texts, novels produce (and become) discourse, which involves mimetic representations of extra-textual experience. Fiction is imaginative in the sense that, unlike history, sociology, and anthropology, it does not treat events as if they have happened in the extra-textual world. On the other hand, fiction enables the study of discourse, and it may be seen not merely as expressive of worldly realities, but also as constitutive of these realities in the sense that the literary experience (the text) accompanies real-life experience (the world) and may act as a platform for the world. Therefore, the imaginative encounters of the Muslim Mustapha and Asmahan with Christian characters tread where real-life, non-fictional, or extra-textual experience dares not to tread. For this reason, it is important to take the study of multiculturalism seriously in novels and in literature as a whole.

Quranic Islam vs. popular Islam at the intra-cultural level

The Quran addresses the *kuffar* in a chapter named "Surat Al-Kafirun", which Muslims believe to be Allah's word to Muhammad to treat the *kuffar* with indifference:

> Say O Disbelievers.
> I worship not that which you worship,
> Nor will you worship that which I worship.
> And I shall not worship that which you are worshipping,
> Nor will you worship that which I worship.
> To you be your religion, and to me my religion.
> (Quran 109)

Although this *sura* addresses Muhammad, all Muslims may identify with it paradigmatically. We notice a clear call not to interfere with other peoples' (non-Muslims) creeds or religions. On the other hand, Muslim readers of the Quran may also be inspired by other verses that may be read as

Islamic multiculturalism 173

encouraging violence against non-Muslims. To cite a very brief example, Surat Al-Taubah reads:

> then kill the Mushrikin [those who worship Allah side by side with other gods] wherever you find them, and capture them and besiege them, and lie in wait for them in each and every ambush. . . . Fight against them so that Allah will punish them by your hands and disgrace them and give you victory over them and heal the breasts of a believing people.
>
> (Quran 9: 14)

This verse may often be read out of context and in a superimpositional manner – especially if Christians (who are otherwise considered in the Quran as *Nasara* or *Ahl Al-Kitab*; literally the people of the Book [Bible]) are considered "Mushrikin". Noticeably, Surat Al-Taubah is one of the most militant *suras* in the Quran, but it should not be alienated from its original historical context where the Prophet was involved in a series of battles against the "Mushrikin", who no longer exist today. So, if the word "Mushrikin" is read as expansive enough to encompass Christians (because Christians worship Jesus Christ as the Word of God, the second hypostasis of the Holy Trinity of God, and as the Son of God), then we are face to face with a serious problem between selective innovative Muslim *takfirism* and Christianity. It is noteworthy to mention that the Quran constructs Christians as the closest group of people to the Muslims: "and you will find the nearest in love to the Muslims those who say: 'we are Christians.' That is because amongst them are priests and monks, and they are not proud" (Quran 5: 82). The word love in here is used as *wudd*, which means "abundant in love" (Al-Munjid Dictionary 1956: 893). In *Tafsir Ibn Kathir*, which is the interpretation of the Quran written by the Imam Ibn Kathir in 1370, the latter argues that the aforementioned Quranic verse was dictated to Muhammad after the incident of the conversion of the Abyssinian Christian king Al-Najashi and his tribe to Islam between 610 and 629. Ibn Kathir adds that although this verse has a specific historical context, it is not depleted of meaning and it is always relevant to all readers at all times until doom's day: "the *Nasara* who follow Christ and the method of his Bible have deep love for the religion of Islam and for all the Muslims because of the abundance of tenderness and clemency in their hearts as followers of Christ" (Kathir 1984: 143). This being said, the Quran constructs all Christians at all times as the "nearest in love to the Muslims".

The Quran contains other verses that may be less tolerant with Christians and other non-Muslims: "and whoever seeks a religion other than Islam, it will never be accepted of him, and in Hereafter he will be one of the losers" (Quran 3: 85). Non-Muslims may be recognized by Muslims as "losers" in religion or in the afterlife, not losers in humanity, in this life, and in anything else outside religion. It is useful to recognize the fact that the choice of

174 *George Sadaka*

tolerant and intolerant verses from the Quran depends on their chronological historical ordering:

> There are two contradictory verses concerning the same fact. For example, this is the case concerning the correct attitude toward non-Muslims, especially Jews and Christians. In the Koran there are some verses counseling tolerance toward them, and others counseling holy war and constant struggle. The experts on abrogation devote detailed analyses to the contradictory verses and come to the conclusion that the last revealed verses are the ones that should be taken into account, and therefore it is necessary to situate the verses in time.
>
> (Mernissi 1993: 165)

It is not the scope of this essay to argue for or against abrogation because the Quran is one body of revelation compiled in one book and approached by Muslims as the living word of Allah. The Quran is read as a one and final book of Allah that is accessible to Muslim and non-Muslim readers alike. It is this dimension that I emphasize in my essay, and it is this principle that governs my overarching argument. Multiculturalism is often a contentious topic in Islam due to the presence of many verses in the Quran that may be used to oppose multiculturalism, just as there are many other verses that may be used to propose multiculturalism. My essay succinctly discusses the two poles of this antinomy because such a topic is too wide to be entirely and conclusively addressed in one essay. Reaching a comprehensive agreement on the topic of multiculturalism from a *fiqhi* perspective (*fiqhi* is an adjective for *fiqh*, which means Islamic jurisprudence) is the prerogative of Islamic scholars and clerics belonging to the different sects of Islam. For this reason, I confine my argument to the discussion of multiculturalism as constructed and as appraised in two novels that dramatize the drawbacks and the difficulties of life for some Muslims who steer away from the multicultural aspect of their religion.

Moving to the discussion of popular versions of Islam at the intra-cultural level in the two novels, Muslim members of the same society and culture are at conflict with one another within a traditional dichotomy of liberal and conservative Islam. Muslims and Christians are also at loggerheads with one another at the cross-cultural level. To illustrate, Christians in *SMN* are considered by some illiterate villagers who may have never encountered a Christian in their lives as "uncircumcised infidels" (Saleh 2008: 3). It is female circumcision that is meant in this passage. One old villager, a certain Bint Majzoub, says, "The infidel women aren't so knowledgeable about this business as our village girls. . . . They are uncircumcised and treat the whole business like having a drink of water" (Saleh 2008: 64). Bint Majzoub is erroneously made to believe that female circumcision is one of the conditions of Islam. She is also made to believe that an uncircumcised woman is deprived of all the pleasures and sensations of sexual intercourse. As a

Islamic multiculturalism 175

matter of fact, circumcised women have less sexual pleasures – or even no pleasures at all. Could this be one reason why Mustapha Sa'eed sought exuberant erotic escapades with uncircumcised women? Nawal El-Saadawi observes that female circumcision "was well known and widespread in some areas of the world before the Islamic era" (1980: 39). Female circumcision is only one residue of pre-Islamic popular practices that, when amalgamated with Islam, results in a popular Islam which is not a universal Islam (Nasr 1980). Another ancient villager, Wad Rayyes, replies to Bint Majzoub:

> What Islam are you talking about? [. . .] It's your Islam and Hajj Ahmed's Islam, because you can't tell what's good for you from what's bad. The Nigerians, the Egyptians, and the Arabs of Syria, aren't they Moslems like us? But they're people who know what's what and leave their women as God created them. As for us, we dock them like you do animals.
>
> (Saleh 2008: 64)

I argue that Saleh and Sheikh share a didactic dramatization of fanatic and intolerant characters within popular Islam in these novels for the purpose of deploring their model through the novel bulwark so that readers may learn a good lesson from a bad example.

In *Beirut Blues*, whose narrative timeline is the Lebanese Civil War (1975–1990), one Iranian-centered popular version of Islam (the Lebanese Hizbullah) is superimposed on some Lebanese Shia' Muslims, which makes Asmahan say:

> This is my city and I don't recognize it. I'm a stranger here . . . there are Iranian signs on the shop fronts, on the walls, posters of men of religion, of leaders I don't know. I no longer understand the language people use. I knew it is Arabic but it has become a series of riddles . . . how can I recognize a city which tolerates fanatics.
>
> (Al-Sheikh 1996: 208)

In *Beirut Blues*, Hizbullah is accused of increasing intra-cultural conflicts by adding a Muslim-Muslim conflict to the already existing Muslim-Christian conflict, which stands out as yet another challenge facing multiculturalism in the Arab world that is already cleaved by creeds. In brief, we learn through these novels that the experience of multiculturalism in the MENA region is challenged by popular practices occurring erroneously in the name of Islam.

Popular cross-sexual encounters as subverting the Islamic experience of cross-cultural encounters

Erotic or cross-sexual intersections have been practiced (or imagined) by some Muslims as one trajectory that leads to a vibrant experience of

176   *George Sadaka*

multiculturalism. However, this trajectory is unrealistic and unworkable because it can neither be proliferated as a Muslim version of multicultural-ism nor can it be treated as a useful model for cross-cultural encounters. Popular Islam has always been problematic and provocative to textual or *fiqhi* Islam. In fact, the Quran points out clearly a distinction between Islam as a religion and Muslims as followers of Islam in the sense that the close-ness of any Muslim to Islam is measured by deeds rather than by designa-tions: "Allah burdens not a person beyond his scope. He gets reward for that (good) which he has earned, and he is punished for that (evil) which he has earned" (Quran 2: 286). Being a Muslim does not immediately imply that the person always behaves as a Muslim or that the person is all Islam (anthropomorphism). Especially when practiced within an erotic frame, anthropomorphism may be the greatest enemy to multiculturalism. To illus-trate, Mustapha in *SMN* considers his British wife Jean Morris as an anthro-pomorphic representation of London – the capital of the British Empire and the metropolitan "centre" of colonial power to which the rest of empire is a "periphery" (Aschroft et al. 1989: 11) as an act of topping and overcoming the 'enemy' in such a way that Jean Morris becomes not only the colonial British Empire but the entire European Christendom:

> My bedroom became a theatre of war; my bed a patch of hell. When I grasped her it was like grasping at clouds, like bedding a shooting-star, like mounting the back of a Prussian military march. [. . .] The city was transformed into an extraordinary woman, with her symbols and her mysterious calls, towards whom I drove my camels till their entrails ached and I myself almost died of yearning for her. My bedroom was a spring-well of sorrow, the germ of a fatal disease. The infection had stricken these women a thousand years ago.
>
> (Saleh 2008: 27)

In a colonial context, for a non-white, non-western, non-Christian African to marry a white western Christian woman is as impossible as "grasping at clouds" and "bedding a shooting-star". The bedroom becomes the only theatre of war because Mustapha avenges colonialism melodramatically and unrealistically in bed. Just like a theatre, his bed becomes a place for performance. The script of Mustapha's performance is written by others and played by him. It is written "a thousand years ago" by the history of wars between Islam and Christendom. Allegorically speaking, every intolerant Arab or Muslim may become as unreal in hatred and intoler-ance as Mustapha. The latter repentantly realizes his "unreality", and he cathartically conveys his story to the narrator, who builds on it as one malignant trajectory that ought to be avoided by Arabs and Muslims. The narrator then makes the worst out of Mustapha's story to present readers with an exemplary of the worst that the world would be if Muslims reject multiculturalism or if they live it the way that Mustapha does. The only

Islamic multiculturalism 177

power that Mustapha can desperately practice over the English people and culture lies in his masculinity, so he uses this sole element of "power" as a means of revenge. Mustapha dedicates his life to such a pathetic and pathological endeavor: "I will liberate Africa with my penis" (Saleh 2008: 95). England makes Mustapha feel culturally and ethnically emasculated, so he needs to reconstruct a certain "masculine" national/ethnic/religious pride by practicing a physical chauvinistic erotic masculinity over British women. Even before Edward Said wrote his notorious *Orientalism* (1979), which regards the orient as a supine woman facing an exuberantly male occident, Tayeb Saleh's novel illustrates the pitfalls of oriental men resorting to their masculinities as tools of power to be used against the west (through its women). Mustapha's sole solace comes through making Britain pay for colonizing Sudan and through making all Europe (the "North") pay for its past battles against the Muslims by making British/ European girls pay for this in his bed (Geesey 1997). In this novel, we move with Mustapha from the context of British the Empire in the early twentieth century to the context of the Middle Ages and the encounters between Christendom and the "saracens".

The Prussia that Mustapha conjures up during the mental operation of his revenge is a nation that had no existence at the time of the narration of *SMN*. History is so muddled up in his mind that he selects Prussia to be a remnant and a reminder of the bygone Holy Roman Empire, which is one of the traditional European defense walls against Islamic invasions. The mere presence of the word "Prussia" in Mustapha's mind attests to his delusion. Mustapha exhumes Prussia in order to punish it with his own body, and then he sends it back to the perdition of books of history. Saleh seems to convey that the whole idea of an imaginary enemy or an imaginary war is elusive and destructive to the self and to the other. Mustapha's didactic example could be one invaluable lesson for some Muslim fundamentalists who, like Mustapha, live in traditionally non-Muslim lands. The three decades that Mustapha spends in England are lived phantasmagorically, as if he were in a desert riding his camel and meeting the Christian enemy in a religious war. The narrator portrays Mustapha's superimposition as a burlesque in which the Arabian and the North African sands conjure up and resurrect from the sandy mists of time the golden age of the battles between Islam and Christianity (when conquering Muslims established Islam within a geographically vast "land of Islam"). Mustapha also transplants scenes of bygone battles that occurred between Muslims and Christians in the past onto the British landscape: "for a moment, I imagined to myself the Arab soldiers' first meeting with Spain: like me at this instant sitting opposite Isabella Seymour, a southern thirst being dissipated in the mountain passes of history in the north" (Saleh 2008: 34). Spain is conflated with England because Spain is the former land of Andalusia. If England is a colonial pride, Spain/Andalusia is an imaginative postcolonial pride for the formerly colonized/oppressed Muslim Sudanese people – or at least it is singularly so to

178 George Sadaka

Mustapha. Mustapha sees all Europe lumped together with England. He mentions Prussia, Spain, Vienna, and Flanders as one molten mold and one target, the enemy (the *kuffar*). This "lumping together" is portrayed as a calamitous and an erroneous stance to be adapted in a postcolonial, post-modern, multicultural, and cosmopolitan world that is ideally governed by political correctness in discourse as well as in behavior.

In *Beirut Blues*, Asmahan experiences cross-sexual encounters not to destroy the "other" like Mustapha does, but to reconstruct, with words of love and desire, a multicultural experience that is denied to her in that part of the world. Spain becomes, anthropomorphically, the Spaniard who is about to save Asmahan from Beirut. Asmahan says, "All the same I threw myself at a Spaniard and tried to make him like me enough to kidnap me and keep me at his country estate. The idea of settling there for good had slowly taken hold of me" (Al-Sheikh 1996: 35–36). Her kidnapping seems to be a parody of the mythical story of the abduction of Europa. Notice that Europa is Phoenician in origin and Lebanon is, originally, Phoenicia. Can we make an interesting argument out of the slightly farfetched link between the bull that attracted Europa and the notorious bull-fighting culture of the Spaniard that attracts Asmahan? The exotic does turn into the erotic, as Asmahan expresses in her letter:

> All he did was wrap a blanket around me, then bend over me, breathing heavily and reaching out to touch my face. I opened my eyes and smiled at him and let him put his lips on mine. The only sensation I got was the smell of wine and cigar, but I submitted to his lips and kissed him back and let him put his tongue in my mouth.
>
> (Al-Sheikh 1996: 49)

Asmahan constructs an imaginative affair with a Spaniard, and Mustapha imagines the British women with whom he fornicates as Spanish women in Andalusia. The erotic encounters with the Spanish or with what is imagined as Spanish are supposed to be shocking to Muslims eyes, ears, and readership. Erotic encounters with Christians may be seen as strong statements against the miseries and frustrations of the enclaves of enmity in Beirut and in Wad Hamid (the modest village in *SMN*). In the above quotation, Asmahan is not scandalized, as a Muslim, by the "smell of wine" that emanates out of the kissing mouth, breath, and lips of the Christian Spaniard. She "submits" to his lips. Submission to Allah's religion is one synonym for Islam (*Istislam* is submission in Arabic; notice how close it is to the word Islam). Asmahan intentionally makes her semi-idolatrous submission to the wine-reeking kisses of the Spaniard a bold cultural statement. In fact, Asmahan invents this imaginative cross-cultural encounter with the Spaniard while she hides from war in a shelter under a certain building in west Beirut. She writes her letters while struggling not only for physical survival but also for mental survival in her staunch Muslim milieu. In her discourse and letters, she craves multicultural life as if she were craving the body of a man. Therefore, she opens up to imaginative cross-sexual encounters out of her frustration with bloody domestic cultural encounters. Asmahan's virtual multiculturalism may itself be a virtue in hard times of war. Her letters act as prison dreams, which draw the attention of a war-destroyed nation to imaginative terrains of love and freedom celebrated in a multicultural atmosphere (that Lebanon used to be before the war). As a novelist, Sheikh is not capacitated to find solutions to the world; nevertheless, the erotic encounters of her novel may be seen as a statement against the frustrations of reality. If war-segmented peoples can hardly experience a peaceful coexistence, a certain sublimation of "co-sex-istence" may serve as one outlet.

The topos of cross-sexual encounters I discuss here has precedence in earlier Islamic texts. Grand texts like *The Arabian Nights* and Firdawsi's *The Shahnama*, for example, dramatize the disasters of employing sexuality as a bridge between cultures and as a vehicle of movement towards the "different other". *The Shahnama*, written in the ninth century for the sake of re-inventing Iran's pre-Islamic past, carries perhaps the most evident allegorical dimension, which is transfigured through the consideration of Rostam, the mighty Persian king and warrior, anthropomorphically as Shi'a Iran, and Tahmineh, a princess from Samangan (modern-day Afghanistan), as Sunni Turkic neighboring lands. This tale is a mixture of pre-Islamic myth with Islamic and nationalistic politics. So, the asynchronous reading of Rostam as representing the Shi'a Iran and Tahmineh as representing the Sunni Turkic nations is a superimposition that is intended by Firdawsi for didactic purposes. Firdawsi was commissioned to write this epic to help "imagine [Iran] as a unique Islamic community with a distinct history and a particular strand of heroism to enable it both to accept its Islamic character and to forget its defeat at the hands of the Arabs three centuries earlier" (Damrosch and Pike 2009: 508). Firdawsi writes this epic with clear political and allegorical dimensions. Sohrab is the fruit of the erotic encounter between Rostam and Tahmineh. The murder of Sohrab at the hands of Rostam is the peak of tragedy that may be read as didactically denouncing inter-marriages among enemies. *The Shahnama* dramatically deplores cross-sexual encounters as a durable model for peace and multicultural coexistence. To briefly illustrate this stance, Rostam enters the land of Samangan searching for his horse Rakhsh, which was stolen upon the king's orders to drag Rustom into Samangan. The king's daughter, Tahmineh, seduces Rostam and promises to return his horse if he agrees to have sex with her:

> It's first because I do so long for you,
> That I've slain reason for my passion's sake.
> And next, perhaps the Maker of the World
> Will place a son from you within my womb.
> Perhaps he'll be like you in manliness

180   George Sadaka

And strength, a child of Saturn and the Sun.
And third, that I may bring your horse to you.
                    (Damrosch and Pike 2009: 511)

Epic exaggeration serves as a doxology that lauds the masculinity of Rostam/Iran vis-à-vis the yearning and passionate Tahmineh/Samangan, who craves breeding a new generation of strength and valor if she, symbolizing her land, bears the seed from such an impetuous warrior as Rostam. The line of Rostam comes from "Saturn and the Sun", and it passes on to his son Sohrab, who lives in Samangan. But the peerless Rostam cannot be replicated in Samangan through his son. Therefore, Rostam kills his son unknowingly, thus consummating fate and preventing the growth of a duplicate hero in Turkic lands.

The Thousand and One Nights, known to the West as *The Arabian Nights*, is another Islamic text that depicts the pitfalls of cross-sexual encounters. The tragedy of Shahrayar slaughtering a thousand women happens before the intervention of the wise and charming Shahrazad, which begins with Sharhayar's wife having an adulterous affair with a black slave named Sa'ad al-Din Mas'ud. Over and above the fact that he is a slave and she is a queen, Mas'ud is a virile black man who gives the queen unrivaled pleasures. To illustrate, this is how Shahrayar witnesses his wife's infidelity:

> The private gate opened, and there emerged as usual the wife of king Shahrayar, walking among twenty slave-girls. They made their way under the trees until they stood below the palace window where the two kings sat. Then they took off their women's clothes, and suddenly there were ten slaves, who mounted the ten girls and made love to them. As for the lady, she called, "Mas'ud, Mas'ud," and a black slave jumped from the tree to the ground, came to her, and said, "What do you want, you slut? Here is Sa'ad al-Din Mas'ud." She laughed and fell on her back, while the slave mounted her and like the others did his business with her.
>   (Damrosch and Pike 2009: 412)

Shahrayar's wife expresses her dissatisfaction with her free white husband, who does not seem to give her the pleasure that the black slave can offer. She is even pleased to be treated as a commoner and to be called a slut. As queen, all her wishes may come true, except for the wish of sexual pleasure, which she seeks with Mas'ud. Allegorically speaking, Mas'ud may be seen as the "inferior other", who is deified by women (for his erotic appeal) but demonized by men (for being a black slave). The queen's death punishment would not have been lessened had Mas'ud not been a black slave. Nevertheless, the idea and image of a queen falling in love with a black slave may be taken as an audacious statement against imbedded frustrations within courtly life in specific and cultural life in general. Noticeably, Saleh dramatizes the same deification versus demonization conundrum with Mustapha: "How

Islamic multiculturalism   181

strange! How ironic! Just because a man has been created on the Equator some mad people regard him as a slave, others as a god" (Saleh 2008: 85).

Back to the novels, the employment of libidinal attraction is one way of experiencing coexistence in a multicultural fashion, but it is not the best and only way. If the real world seems to be going against multiculturalism, multiculturalism has to be established by the hook or by the crook of imagination. One of the biggest problems portrayed in the two novels lies in the lack of yearning for multicultural existence/coexistence. The weltanschauung dimension of *Beirut Blues* transfigures with the fact that Asmahan's private problem with staunch Muslims becomes a public problem that is at the core of multiculturalism and its obstacles and obstructions. Asmahan's Beirut, therefore, "lies at the core of some of the world's most crucial issues" (Accad 2002: 86). *SMN* is also "caught in the turbulence that is at the heart of the contradictions it reflects" (Makdidi 1992: 808). In these novels, Wad Hamid and Beirut are treated as textual microcosms of the macrocosmic challenges of multiculturalism in a world of multiple countenances, cultures, creeds, and canons.

Antithetically, the narrator in *SMN* balances himself against Mustapha to elucidate the idea that the multicultural model which the Sudanese (or Arabs in general) need to follow should have nothing to do with Mustapha's cross-sexual encounters. Erotic attraction to a "different other" may be one good model for multiculturalism, but Mustapha exemplifies one bad illustration of it. Thanks to the presence of Mustapha's bad example in the life and text of the narrator, the latter propounds an alternative model, which rectifies the deplorable exemplum of Mustapha. The narrator says:

> while I, lying under this beautiful compassionate sky, feel that we are all brothers; he who drinks and he who prays and he who steals and he who commits adultery and he who fights and he who kills. The source is the same. No one knows what goes on in the mind of the Divine. Perhaps He doesn't care. Perhaps He is not angry.
>
> (Saleh 2008: 85)

In this quotation, the narrator regards all humans as "brothers" in humanity because the source of all their desires, differences, and aspirations is one and the same: human nature. This quotation is in line with the Quran, which reads: "There is no compulsion in religion" and "And had your Lord willed, those on earth [the entire world population] would have believed [in Islam]" (Quran 2: 256 and 10: 99).

It is useful to consider Fredric Jameson's argument concerning the allegorical dimensions of non-western literature:

> Third-world texts, even those which are seemingly private and invested with a properly libidinal dynamic-necessarily project a political dimension in the form of national allegory: *the story of the private individual*

182   George Sadaka

destiny is always an allegory of the embattled situation of the public third-world culture and society. [. . .] [I]n third-world texts . . . the relationship between the libidinal and the political components of individual and social experience is radically different from what obtains in the west and what shapes our own cultural forms.

(1986: 69 and 71)

C. L. Innes criticizes Jameson's sweeping generalization that "all" third-world texts are to be read as national allegories (Joseph and Wilson 2006: 178).

Nevertheless, the usefulness of Jameson's observation is undeniable. The two novels of my selection teem with "libidinal" encounters that may resonate with "political" experience, and this is a fact that neither Mustapha nor Asmahan denies. Mustapha refers to England as "the world of Jean Morris" (Saleh 2008: 23). Moreover, when Mustapha relates the story of his encounter with Ann Hammond, he says:

In her eyes I was a symbol of all her hankerings. I am South that yearns for the North and the ice. Ann Hammond spent her childhood at a convent school. Her aunt was the wife of a Member of Parliament. In my bed I transformed her into a harlot. My bedroom was a graveyard.

(Saleh 2008: 24)

One can hardly resist the allegorical reading of this quotation – especially that Mustapha sets himself as the "South" or Africa vis-à-vis the Euro-Colonial/Imperial North. The convent-school childhood of Ann attests to her Christian upbringing. Her familial connection to a British MP attests to her social eminence (culture and politics). When he transforms her into a harlot in his bed, he sees beyond and passes through Ann into her background, which is subjugated to the carnal control of his Muslim African body. Why would he do so? Mustapha acts in a contra-multicultural manner and he makes his retaliation appear as defensive rather than offensive in the sense that he blames the North for abusing, enslaving, and hating the South despite the fact that the North has given him the best that the world can offer: doctoral education, British nationality, and proper assimilation, which rendered him indistinguishably British. Mustapha's experience is inappropriate as a Muslim version of multiculturalism; it is more appropriately an anti-colonial response to the failures of colonialism at maintaining genuine hybridity in colonial cultures. My contention is that Edward Said has read this novel very well because it seems to have inspired him to write his famous *Orientalism*, in which he considers western colonial powers as having male dominance over an otherwise feminine supine Orient.

In *Beirut Blues*, Asmahan attends a Christian wedding in the Christian sector of the city, and she celebrates her freedom as a woman away from the constraints of her Muslim milieu by "leav[ing] the wedding party in the middle of the night hand in hand with a Christian man . . . leaning against him or lying back on the stony ground happy to feel him breathing close up against [her]" (Al-Sheikh 1996: 49). Asmahan does not regard Simon only as a man, but also as a Christian who lives in a Christian sector and who, in the darkness of mid-night, escapes with her to the wilderness in order to experience the pleasures of sex with the "enemy". Asmahan's statement is bold and cliché, yet powerful, a call to "make love not war" in times of war to help transform war encounters into love encounters.

Asmahan represents mild multiculturalism, whereas Mustapha represents malevolent multiculturalism, which trespasses against all notions and norms of the social contract and the harm principle. Multiculturalism is propounded in the two selected novels as one solution to the problem of contending cultures. In *Beirut Blues*, it can be explained through Asmahan's affairs with two types of men. With Simon, the Christian who lives in East Beirut, she promulgates a model of cultural openness which entails a deep desire for the "different other". With Nasser, the Muslim Palestinian warrior who lives in West Beirut, she promulgates the model of closed-mindedness and the rejection of multiculturalism. This is how Asmahan describes her bipolar sexual encounters with Simon in a bipolar city like Beirut:

> My meetings with Simon gave me a feeling of warmth and excitement, snatching me out of the city as it surged back and forth between uproar and fragrant calm. . . . Our eyes shone and our breathing grew faster whenever we were close to one another. I waited until we lay down naked on the sofa. Then the drugged sensation and the love took over, and the feeling that I wanted to have my pleasure whatever happened. It is only when we got up and dressed that I knew I didn't love him.
> (Al-Sheikh 1996: 41)

Sex with a Christian becomes a defense mechanism, a strategy for survival, and a bold statement of defiance against the war. The classical theory of the *eros/thanatos* dichotomy reigns supreme in the above quotation. Sigmund Freud argues that "the instinct itself could be pressed into the service of *Eros*, in that the organism was destroying some other thing, whether animate or inanimate, instead of destroying its own self" (Freud 2010: 63). The human organism, which is threatened by death and annihilation in the external world, seeks life and regeneration in the internal world, which operates upon the pleasure principle as an alternative to the pain principle of war and death. As the city surges "back and forth" in war and demolition (*thanatos*), Asmahan and Simon seek to forget or to assuage this surging with yet another similar surging: love-making (*Eros*).

Conclusion: Living love instead of making love

Expressions of love-living (the non-libidinal form of love) from an Islamic standpoint can be amply condensed in the Quranic epigram that overshadows

184 *George Sadaka*

my argument. It specifies that Allah created humans in different nations so that they may "know one another". Inspired by this verse, Muslim scholars, like Ali Bin Abi Taleb and Ibn Arabi, promulgate the idea that knowledge of the "other" may have to follow knowledge of the "self". In addition, Ali Bin Abi Taleb, the second most important man in Islam, is believed to have said this proverb, which is very famous in Islamic jurisdiction and in Sufism: "he who knows himself also knows his God" (Ibn Arabi 2006: 308).

Bringing the words of the Quran that bids people to knowledge of one another together with the concept of knowledge in other Islamic texts may work towards supporting and crystallizing multiculturalism within a tripartite of other, self, and God. This tripartite of knowledge may be employed as one very helpful component of an Islamic definition of multiculturalism in a world that is made by God to be of "different nations".

Sex can be one good practice that brings people together, but now that we know that Asmahan only desires and does not love Simon, we cannot build on this affair as a useful model for multiculturalism. Nor can we build on Mustapha's cross-sexual encounters as good and constructive models for cross-cultural encounters. It is important to note that Asmahan does not end up loving any of the men she consorts with, neither Simon, nor Ricardo (Yahya), nor Jawad. Nonetheless, Asmahan's story with Simon is strikingly significant as a statement of love and love-making in times of war. At one point, time stops for Asmahan as she nails her view to a mosaic that encapsulates her fears and expectations. The mosaic depicts "[a] naked woman opening out a towel while a hawk, as big as her, is snatching the towel away in its beak" (Al-Sheikh 1996: 25). The scene portrayed in this mosaic rings a bell with Asmahan, who desires freedom from the shackles of society and culture that try to impose the Islamic veil on her. The hawk that snatches the towel, thus rendering the lady naked, may be appreciated in the form of a psychological displacement in the sense that Asmahan desires to be rescued from this 'veil imposition' by any saving power that shows up in the sky and perches down upon her. Marrying a Christian may have traversed her mind as one alternative. So, Asmahan may be attracted to Christians because they give her a substitutive satisfaction in her unveiled freedom. Nevertheless, this does not mean that multiculturalism precludes cultural uniqueness and prohibits the observation of certain rites and rituals that mark the uniqueness and exclusiveness of this culture. Through Asmahan's example, we are able to read the idea that had Lebanon been now as multicultural as it was before the war, Asmahan would not have become a victim of the Iranian cultural invasion against which she instinctively responds by becoming involved in instinctual acts (sex) with Christians as desperate statements in support of multiculturalism. A certain Shia cleric, Sheikh Nizar, says to Asmahan's mother: "God willing, Asmahan with her beautiful hair will return to the faith" (Al-Sheikh 1996: 22). Return to the faith? Asmahan the Muslim ought to return to the faith (Islam), just like any other infidel (*kafir*).

Islamic multiculturalism 185

In *SMN*, multiculturalism is also suggested as one good solution to the problems of contending cultures and cleaving creeds. At the end of the novel, the narrator goes naked into the Nile in an attempt to ritually cleanse himself from the presence of the dead Mustapha in his life. He experiences renewal and rebirth as he swims to the North (as a gesture of his openness to a peaceful experience of multiculturalism). He refuses to surrender to the "destructive forces pulling [him] downwards" (Saleh 2008: 132). Swimming to the North is a movement that holds multicultural dimensions. Swimming downwards, on the other hand, is sinking in mono-culturalism, fanaticism, and spiritual death. The narrator swims towards the North – the enemy – that Mustapha has made loveless love to. Remarkably, both the narrator and Asmahan decide to stay in their respective homelands. Their presence in the homeland is a statement that the experience of multiculturalism should be done 'here' in the East and South as it is (or as it may be) done in the West and North. Asmahan's and the narrator's decision to stick to the motherland is firm and final. They refuse to escape to lands of the western matrix of multiculturalism in a symbolic attempt to construct of themselves and of their experiences good and enduring elements for a burgeoning multiculturalism in non-western parts of the world. Asmahan and the narrator help propound the model of love-living as a more durable and a less dangerous solution to a conflict-riddled world than the model of love-making.

Multiculturalism is not a western-made (imperialistic or globalizing) innovation that is imposed on Muslims; it is part of what Islam is about. However, multiculturalism should not be understood as multi-sexualism. The two novels warn us against this misunderstanding. Living love ought not to be conflated with making love. For the experience of multiculturalism to be successful in any nation or denomination, it may be inclusive, non-exclusively, of cross-sexual encounters. Erotica may be one easy trajectory (real or imagined) to move towards the different other. The two novels I discussed reveal the need for Arabs and Muslims to embrace a multicultural world where Muslims are free enough to live love out of love, not to make love out of despair, revenge, and self-hatred. We may understand the reasons that may have lead to erotica as a para-multicultural practice, but we cannot always justify it. The two novels do not give direct or clear solutions to this problem. Awareness of the fact that cross-sexual encounters are part of the problem may be taken as a suggested solution (which may also be only partial).

Readers of these two novels may come to the conclusion that the MENA region ought to preserve the spirit and the practice of multiculturalism without having to consider itself anathema to Islam. Coexistence of Muslims with non-Muslims is not a western-made *kufr* of multiculturalism. The experience of multiculturalism in the MENA region, governed primarily by Islam, is both unique and universal. It is unique in the sense that it involves cross-cultural and intra-cultural encounters. It is also universal because, by dint of its link to the dogma and praxis of Islam, it is open to universalism.

186 George Sadaka

The novel plays a pivotal role in helping us study the history and the progress of culture and humanity. Edward Said argues that postcolonial novels are "grand narratives of emancipation and enlightenment" which "mobilized people in the colonial world to rise up and throw off imperial subjection" (Said 1993: xiii). In a rapidly growing postcolonial world, looking back at the colonial past, which involved a series of struggles and emancipations against "imperial subjection", may never be an obsolete strategy or methodology. On the contrary, anti-colonial emancipation may remain all the way relevant and alive because it encapsulates encounters with oppositional forces, which may be read as a symbiosis of the synchronic and the symbolic.

Bibliography

Accad, E. (2002) 'Beirut, the City That Moves Me', *World Literature Today* 76: 85–89.

Al-Munjid Dictionary (1956), Beirut: Catholic Printing Press.

Al-Sheikh, H. (1996) *Beirut Blues*, New York: Anchor Books.

Aschroft, B., Griffiths, G., and Tiffin, H. (1989) *The Empire Writes Back: Theory and Practice in Postcolonial Literatures*, London: Routledge.

Damrosch, D. and Pike, D. (2009) *The Longman Anthology of World Literature*, New York: Pearson.

El-Saadawi, N. (1980) *The Hidden Face of Eve*, London and New York: Zed Books.

Freud, S. (2010) *Civilization and Its Discontents*, New York: Norton.

Geesey, P. (1997) 'Cultural Hybridity and Contamination in Tayib Salih's Season of Migration to the North', *Research in African Literature* 28: 128–180.

Ibn Arabi, M. (2006) *Al-Futuhat Al-Makkiya, V 2*, Beirut: Dar Al-Kutub Al-Ilmiya.

Ibn Kathir. (1984) *The Interpretation of the Great Quran*, Beirut: Dar Ihya' Al-Turath Al Arabi.

Innes, L. (2006) 'Cosmopolitan Readers and Postcolonial Identities', in C. Joseph and J. Wilson (eds.) *Global Fissures: Postcolonial Fusions*, Amsterdam and New York: Rodopi, 178.

Jameson, F. (1986) 'Third-World Literature in the Era of Multinational Capitalism', *Social Text* 15: 65–88.

Joseph, C. and Wilson, J. (2006) *Global Fissures: Postcolonial Fusions*, Amsterdam and New York: Rodopi.

Makdidi, S. (1992) 'The Empire Renarrated: "Season of Migration to the North" and the Reinvention of the Present', *Critical Inquiry* 18: 804–820.

Mernissi, F. (1993) *The Veil and the Male Elite: A Feminist Interpretation of Women's Rights in Islam*, New York: Basic Books.

Nasr, A. (1980) 'Popular Islam in Al-Tayyib Salih', *Journal of Arabic Literature* 11: 88–104.

Said, E. (1993) *Culture and Imperialism*, New York: Vintage Books.

Saleh, T. (2008) *Season of Migration to the North*, Oxford, UK: Heinemann.

Section 4

Multiculturalism, African and African heritage

11 Toward an African recognition theory of civil rights

Christopher Allsobrook

Introduction

Studies of relations between the state and society in Africa have tended to follow a conflict between liberal systems, stressing a regime based on rights, and Africanist systems, which insist on making the old communities the centre of African politics and on defending local culture (Bidaguren and Estrella 2002). Jokin Bidaguren and Daniel Estrella argue that the solution to this impasse between Eurocentrics and Africanists must be "a synthesis which can transcend both sides" (2002: 114). While Washington consensus structural adjustment policies of the 1990s made investment conditional upon "good governance", they focused mostly on strengthening the judicial system to guarantee the stability of economic transactions and to improve states' administrative capacity. This helped to safeguard investments and markets in developing nations, but, the authors argue, "problems of active participation, remoteness and mistrust of the judicial system on the part of ordinary people and the lack of any adaptation of Western legal traditions to a multicultural reality are left as marginal issues on the agenda of reform" (2002: 115).

Patrick Heller (2009) likewise claims South Africa has fared well at consolidating democratic institutions but not at "democratic deepening", which he describes as "an increased capacity of subordinate groups to have an effective role in shaping public policy" (2009: 124). South Africa has yet to close the gap between formal legal rights and the capability of citizens to practice those rights meaningfully in the civil and political arena. At present, "pervasive inequalities distort the associational playing field", leaving a wide range of political exclusions (2009: 126). Basic institutions and procedures of electoral democracy and principles and institutions for the rule of law are firmly entrenched, but "effective democracy" remains highly constricted, leaving little room for the effective exercise of civil rights (2009: 130–131). The primary beneficiaries of transformation have been a new black bourgeoisie, occupying positions within state bureaucracies and/or "translating political connections with the ANC into rent-seeking alliances with white capital" (2009: 143). Heller argues democratic and national consolidation came at the expense of effective citizenship in South Africa (2009: 144).

190   *Christopher Allsobrook*

A common symptom of the problem of the gap between formal and effective citizenship, in South Africa and elsewhere in Africa, is that most citizens have limited access to formal justice. State law is not predominant in marginalised and outlying areas, where the "colonial, bureaucratic, incomprehensible, procedurally expensive and complicated" judicial system is poorly integrated with indigenous and traditional forms of popular justice, which enjoy greater social legitimacy (Bidaguren and Estrella 2002: 118). The legal system works alongside a parallel system of "decentralised despotism" (Mamdani 1996 in Bidaguren and Estrella 2002: 118). Traditional and vigilante courts are participative and accessible to poor, marginalised citizens but often go too far in punishments. Moreover, leaders abuse privileges with poor controls for their personal benefit. Practices cannot be allowed which call into question the very legitimacy of the state, but we should at least draw on customs which may "enrich a reformed democratic legal system, by ensuring participation, and by redefining values and principles from an intercultural perspective which takes the values and concepts of African cultures into account" (2002: 132). With appropriate reform and effective implementation, indigenous and popular courts can complement the rule of law, to serve intermediate and outlying rings of civil society and "to try new ways of organising judicial power involving the collective commitment of citizenry to respond to cultural diversity" (2002: 131). A multicultural approach must be incorporated into the concepts of political and civil liberties, to introduce reform that integrates civil and customary law, to secure equal civil rights for all citizens.

If traditional African cultural values, concepts and practices are to be better integrated in a multicultural democratic institutional framework of social rights, what can and cannot be included? Contentious traditions of patriarchy may warrant reform, just as certain Western norms may be modified for the sake of custom. African ethics of *Ubuntu* is often said to remedy weaknesses with Western political and legal norms, to better facilitate restorative (as opposed to retributive) justice, for instance, or consensual, deliberative democracy, as opposed to majoritarian, procedural democracy. The idea that one exists because of others within one's community highlights the relational character of social existence that ties an individual to a web of communal relationships and mutual obligations. Ken Kamoche (2011: 2) warns such communal thinking, including promotion of nepotism, ethnicity and tribal chauvinism, may have troublesome consequences for multicultural, democratic politics in Africa (2011: 3). He suggests further research should consider how the facilitative dimension of African ethics can be reconciled with its tendency to perpetuate ethnic rivalries (2011: 4). Geraldine Fraser-Moloketi, by contrast, claims the African philosophy of *Ubuntu* can help us to refocus African society on its inherently communal values (2007: 247). She argues *Ubuntu* must be the essence of any value system underpinning the struggle in Africa against corruption, which she blames on "values of rampant free-market capitalism under globalisation,

African recognition theory of civil rights   191

which emphasises individual wealth acquisition". Corruption, she claims, belongs not to *Ubuntu* but to Western individualism. "Our people no longer see themselves as an integral part of their communities", with the attendant responsibilities this entails (2007: 248). She claims the "market fundamentalism of contemporary global capitalism and its astonishing effect have created conditions in which corruption flourishes . . . with self-interest taking precedence over the common good" (2007: 247).

Corruption, along with problems of traditional gender inequality, is a key field of contestation in relations between rights and custom in Africa. This typically concerns the partial and exclusionary allocation of public resources, where state officials fail to honour their duty to promote universal public welfare on the basis of the equal rights of all citizens. Former general secretary of the Congress of South African Trade Unions, Zwelinzima Vavi, claims, "South African democracy is under threat from a gang of 'tenderpreneurs' who seek to build instant wealth using the power they have and the control they hold over the state", referring to officials who enrich themselves with state contracts (Okeowo 2015). Is patronage compatible with equal civil rights? Where do rights belong in African custom? Democratic socio-economic and political development is held back by unresolved tensions between customs and civil rights. It is crucial to examine the historical and normative basis of such opposition to determine what sorts of problems arise in coordinating these competing systems, of rights and custom, to promote genuine multicultural integration in South Africa.

In the following chapter I argue that disagreement regarding the relative standing of rights and custom in African societies is unlikely ever to be resolved if the normative status of rights is grounded in and conceived in terms of some particular speculative ontology of personhood. However, if rights are grounded in recognition, and in point of fact, human rights are so grounded, they may be said to follow from customary social practices. On this conceptual framework, rights and custom are not predicated from the outset in opposition and, so – considering the relative standing of rights and custom in contemporary Africa – opposed African and Western conceptions of personhood need neither thwart nor mystify their comparative analysis and desirable reconciliation.

The first section questions the status of equal rights of citizenship in African society. It is typically thought that inconsistencies between African communal norms and Western conceptions of individual rights frustrate public welfare and good governance in Africa. African ethicists typically try to dissolve the contradiction between rights and custom by showing how African communal conceptions of universal human personhood promote rights, following some attribute, such as dignity, which belongs to all. I go on toward the end of this first section to show that opposition between individual rights and communal customs has little to do with conceptions of personhood in Africa. Rather, opposition between right and custom follows an internal division in most African states, between formal systems to secure

192 Christopher Allsobrook

juridical rights and informal customary practices, neither of which remain independent of Western influence.

Section two considers how opposition between formal rights and informal patronage subverts social justice in postcolonial African states such as South Africa. In section three, I raise the problem of how, despite recognition of customary law in the South African constitution after apartheid, the bill of rights trumps customary practices in court. In the final section I outline an African recognition theory of rights which, I argue, makes better sense of the historical origins of African conceptions of social rights and of international human rights law, which is grounded in convention. Moreover, it puts to one side differences between African and Western conceptions of personhood, which complicate a problem that is complex enough, to examine unresolved inconsistencies between two systems of justice in African societies – civic and customary – neither of which remain uncompromised by colonial manipulation and both of which tend to undermine one another while their reconciliation remains undecided.

African normative theory and practice of equal rights

The following section examines a range of normative positions in African ethics on the duty of the state and of state officials to respect equal rights of public provision for all citizens. I later consider some of the historical circumstances behind the problems I outline in this normative debate. But I begin right off here with a fairly typical "Western" view, that a weak distinction in African communal culture between partial, personal obligations and impartial, public obligations undermines public welfare: Theron (2013) draws attention to the fact that 89.6% of sub-Saharan countries scored below 50 on the 2012 *Transparency International* Corruption Perception Index, indicating vulnerability to corruption. Theron aims to show how "certain traits in sub-Saharan African culture" – including communalism, gift-giving and shame – "might sanction corruption" (2013: 1). To this end she offers two key explanations. First, most African states follow a neo-patrimonial system where there is no clear separation between officials' private interests and public responsibilities. It is culturally acceptable, for instance, to receive gifts and payments for public services (2013: 2). Second, African governments are characterised by extensive patron-client networks. Patronage is used to maintain political power. State resources "nourish" personal social networks. Leaders are under great pressure to gain access to resources in order to redistribute them to subordinates, so as to stay in power (2013: 2).

Citing Kipton Jensen and Joseph Gaie (2010), Petria Theron claims "the communal notion of the self is considered by many as the cardinal point of the African worldview", adding Joseph Nyasani's claim (2013) that "sociality is one of the distinctive characteristics of African philosophy" (Theron 2013: 4). Theron agrees with Sekou Toure and Leopold Senghor that African

African recognition theory of civil rights 193

societies are "community societies" where the individual is less important than the group and solidarity in the group is more important than the needs of the individual (2013: 4). She also agrees with Kobus Van der Walt (2003) that communalism can make African societies prone to corruption, since, firstly, its social moral code, which requires people to render services and counter-services, weakens the distinction between public and private funds, and, secondly, it puts people under enormous financial pressure to family and friends. Clientelism plays a vital role in the lives of political leaders, who need to extract and redistribute state resources to their political clientele and who need to demonstrate conspicuous prosperity to attract honour. Gift-giving – a way to build personal relationships and to express gratitude – also fosters corruption (Theron 2013: 5). Finally, Theron claims, African "shame culture" fosters corruption, since offenders feel no offence has taken place unless it is discovered and leads to rejection from the group: "truth is less important than good relationships" and whistle-blowers are smeared for harming the honour of the thief (2013: 5). In African ethics, whether an act is right or wrong depends on the rules of the community, claims Theron. "An act is wrong if it is committed against the *group*". As long as corruption benefits the group, it is tolerated. And, in any case, it is rare to find a single system of rules in Africa, where official rules often differ from the "real" ones based on traditions (2013: 6).

Directly opposed to Theron's Western perspective on the shortfalls of African communal ethics for impartiality in the state, Mokoko Sebola complains that government functions are defined within frameworks that are benched against international standards of scientific rationality. He argues that the cause of escalating unethical conduct in public service lies in the imposition, upon the native cultural ethos, of ethical frameworks based on rationalist-individualist doctrines of Western Enlightenment (2014: 295). Western political systems and business practices cause major problems in developing countries, since such morality is not compatible with local norms. Sebola is not specific about how Western ethical standards are incompatible with African cultural values, but he anyway argues that local cultural norms cannot be analysed rationally or scientifically (2014: 296–297). In Africa, he claims, "culture and historical circumstances help us to interpret ethics" and "culture is dynamic and historically relative" (2014: 297). But in South Africa, "our legislative frameworks on ethics and accountability are influenced by international laws, regulations and principles . . . within rational modern conceptions that do not fit well in the African context" (2014: 298). While Theron thinks African ethics is an obstacle to good governance, Sebola thinks Western ethics is the problem. However, the authors agree, fundamental inconsistencies between the two frustrate public welfare.

Kwame Gyekye claims a certain type of corresponding social structure or arrangement tends to evolve on the basis of public conceptions of personhood (2010a: 101). For Gyekye, the rights of individuals, their duties to others and their sense of common good all follow from ontological assumptions of personhood in African ethics. Kwasi Wiredu, likewise, argues on this basis that traditional African society is moderately communitarian, implying strong family bonds and a broad scope of obligations and reciprocities, but, he notes, "to adjust the interests of the individual to those of the community is not to subordinate one to the other" (2008: 334). He admits, nonetheless, that African kinship relationships, distorted by colonists, override national allegiances. As such, mechanisms transcending traditional kinship affiliations are needed in Africa, especially in urban areas (2008: 334). Gyekye agrees with Leopold Senghor, Jomo Kenyatta and Ifeanyi Menkiti that African society puts more emphasis on the group than on individuals, on solidarity than on individual needs and on the communion of persons than on autonomy. But African leaders, he claims, have been mistaken in thinking African communitarianism would easily fit modern socialism, agreeing with Wiredu that African communitarianism does not invariably conceive of the person as *wholly* socially constituted (2010a: 101).

Gyekye argues against Menkiti's view that the ontological primacy of the community and the communal world take precedence over the reality of individual life histories in African political thinking, such that personal identity is defined on the basis of communal achievements and responsibilities alone (2010a: 102). Such a "radical, excessive and unrestricted" view, he argues, is "unsupportable", since it fails to allow sufficient room for the exercise of individual rights (2010a: 103). Personhood may reach its full realisation in community, but it is not reducible to community: "the subject of what is acquired cannot be defined by what he acquires" (2010a: 106). One's morals are not implanted or conferred by the community but depend on one's sense of responsibility and on what one has been able to achieve (2010a: 8). Personhood is only partly defined by membership in a community (2010a: 109). Gyekye and Wiredu agree that African ethics promotes a conception of human dignity that underwrites personal rights and outstrips communal values. Dignity and self-determining autonomy – two inalienable attributes of persons capable of evaluation and choice – allow for the free exercise of individual rights, which, in turn, enhances the cultural development and success of the community (2010a: 110–111).

Thaddeus Metz (2012) agrees with both Gyekye and Wiredu that interest in the common good and in provision for universal public welfare does not result in the subversion of individual rights. Metz notes that African ethical thought is typically focused on utility, dignity, community and vitality. Gyekye, he claims, sees utility or the common good as a foundational or "master" value, such that the common good is identical with social harmony and with the well-being of all individuals in society (Metz 2012: 62). Metz agrees with Gyekye that the communal good includes each and every individual – it does not imply well-being that would sacrifice the interests of an individual for the benefit of a particular group or for the greater good. He also insists, with Wiredu, on human dignity in personhood which

African recognition theory of civil rights   195

underwrites equal basic rights and duties to refrain from coercive interference with others. But, unlike them he sees friendliness as the "master value" underwriting all this (2012: 63). Whether the primary concern of African ethics is to maximise welfare or to uphold friendliness, these accounts all entail public policy positions that do not infringe on the rights of individuals but nevertheless uphold social rights and duties to others in one's community. Metz, for instance, claims his account promotes a consensus-seeking democracy that protects substantial civil liberties and distributes opportunities and wealth according to a market, after distributing funds via taxation as necessary to meet public needs (2012: 64). His ethic of friendliness supports a wide range of civil rights, including freedom from torture, trafficking, rape and genocide, since these "are well understood to be unfriendly"; sowing division and treating others as separate and inferior (2012: 75).

Metz argues that African community-based ethics best justify a consensus-based democracy which gives each person an equal vote. What confers our dignity is our capability to exhibit identity and solidarity with others. So, he concludes, "an egalitarian-unanimity rights-oriented model of democracy follows fairly easily" (2012: 72). Consensus-seeking democracy is different from a typically Western majoritarian model in that each citizen has an equal right of representation with respect to every decision, that is, the right not to be utterly marginalised when major laws or policies are formulated or adopted. "If we are *equally* special by virtue of having the requisite capacity to share a way of life", Metz adds, "this means according people the equal ability to influence collective decision-making, which, in turn, means having an equal vote" (2012). African ethics supports re-distributive capitalism due to its communal content and deontological form, promoting public policies such as progressive taxation to prevent large inequalities, which undermine solidarity and identity (2012: 79). Jason Van Niekerk (2011: 62) clarifies the relationship between *Simunye* and *Ubuntu* in African ethics as such: *Ubuntu* (a normative ethical system promoting *harmony*) is irreducible to *Simunye* (a claim of metaphysical oneness and *solidarity* with one's community). The latter is a necessary, but insufficient, component of *Ubuntu*, which runs alongside an equal duty to be *responsive* to others.

Gyekye, Wiredu, Metz and Van Niekerk agree that individual rights are compatible with African ethics. Metz argues further that the basic obligation of *Ubuntu*, to live communally with all other persons, forbids corruption. Although *Ubuntu* forbids *impartialism*, which insists, for instance, that those working for a liberated state, such as South Africa, should act only for the sake of the public as a whole (Metz 2009: 349), *Ubuntu* also forbids *strong partialism*, which would permit state officials to favour members of their families or political parties (2010: 336). This is because strong partialism involves unfriendly behaviour toward excluded strangers, fostering substantial discord and exploiting others as if they exist merely to serve a purpose (2009: 346). "A procurement official who awards a contract to a member of his family or political party fails to secure the kind of state

196 *Christopher Allsobrook*

required by an ethic of harmony", writes Metz (2009: 345). On the other hand, *Ubuntu* does promote "moderate partialism", holding that – although government officials should distribute resources so as to benefit the public as a whole – in certain cases, where individuals have made great sacrifices for it or have been seriously wronged by it, some may be favoured over others (2009: 343). For instance, preference in tie-breaking job applications or state contracts should be given to those disadvantaged by apartheid, since a person's duty to be friendly implies mending discordant relationships. Veterans of the struggle against apartheid may also be given such preference since it is unfriendly to fail to show gratitude to those who have risked their life for their country (2009: 349).

Historically speaking, it is problematic to assume Africans all share one typical and unique set of ethical intuitions. This overlooks, for instance, the deeply ambivalent character of the "bifurcated state" in Africa, where two inconsistent, parallel political systems, historically distorted by colonial and imperial ambitions, tend to operate alongside one another so as to generate systemic instability (1996: 16–18). Mamdani emphasises the case that the colonial state was a "double-sided affair": while its one side governed *citizens* "bounded by the rule of law and an associated regime of rights", its other side, which ruled *subjects*, involved "a regime of extra-economic coercion and administratively driven justice" (1996: 19). Colonialists and missionaries tended, through indirect rule, to "capture" indigenous practices and concepts and reorient them to suit administration of the local population. Moreover, although a basic cause of persistent underdevelopment in Africa stems from the weak institutional structure of the state inherited from colonial times, Ola Olsson's survey of postcolonial states finds "a general positive relationship between the duration of colonial rule and current democracy . . . driven by the experience of former British colonies . . . colonized after 1850 during a more liberal era" (2009: 535). He demonstrates that the timing and duration of colonial activities proved significant determining factors for later economic performance. Later direct rule, more so than indirect rule, proved relatively beneficial for subsequent development (2009: 535).

British policy promoted property rights, free trade and capitalism, which proved more fruitful for democratic ideas later on (Olsson 2009: 539). While weak democratic institutions and civil rights are often associated with the imposition of Western values and norms in Africa, Matthew Lange (2004) shows that direct forms of colonialism ensured better state capacity and equality before the law. Indirect rule, which relied on indigenous customs, institutions and authorities, tended to prove worse later on for institutional development in general. This is because in directly ruled colonies the state centralised control of territory, while colonial settlers and administrators helped to construct institutions that secured political stability and the rule of law, to protect property, to improve bureaucratic effectiveness and to control for corruption. Indirect rule left behind a fragmented state unable

African recognition theory of civil rights 197

to regulate local power-holders (2004: 905–906). Direct rule established administrations grounded in formal rules as opposed to individual decisions and centralised legal-administrative structures with a formal chain of command linking officials to the state. These were positions which could not be owned but were based on criteria of merit, and they provided a sole source of income and a career offering advancement for the civil servants who occupied them. Civil society was regulated by rules and enforced by a large police force and court system grounded in European law. Indirect rule, by contrast, created two separate and incompatible sets of rules, one dominated by a tiny colonial administration, concentrated in the capital, and the other by patrimonial chiefs (2004: 907). Chiefs were given substantial institutional powers at the local level, with control of communal lands and the police and with "customary law" typically manipulated for the benefit of the coloniser and chief, whose unchecked power, backed up by a foreign army, fostered rent-seeking behaviour (2004: 908). Such "dispersed domination" hindered effective state governance, creating extremely powerful intermediaries "who limit state infrastructural power and ability to provide basic public goods" and "weaken regulation of social relations through law, governance and broad-based development" (2004: 917).

What is crucial to understand here is that "the day-to-day violence of the colonial system was embedded in customary Native Authorities in the local state", not in civil power at the centre, although it was indeed backed up by central civil, and ultimately, imperial military, power. Colonial despotism was decentralised to the legislative, judicial, executive and administrative head of local government, the chief, "whose authority lay behind the regime of extra-economic coercion" (Mamdani 1996: 23). Trusteeship or Indirect Rule was intended "to be no more than a deference to local tradition and custom" (1996: 24). Yorubu customary social thought, for instance, stipulates the norms, values and expectations expected within relationships where patrons exchange goods for the loyalty of less privileged clients (Omobowale 2008: 203). But, as Ayokunle Omobowale argues, "by gaining control of the socio-political system and reducing indigenous languages to writing, [colonialists] were able to redefine what was acceptable socially through the imposition of European philosophies (i.e. social thought) and cultures using the languages of the colonised people" (2008: 206). Official, formalised African customs, laws and leaders thus share with the West deep imperialist culpability.

Traditionally, patronage relations with respected elders, who justify decisions with reference to traditional proverbs, are often the basis of social order in African communal cultures, but elders are also expected to engage in reciprocal respect and to provide support if they are to avoid losing followers (2008: 216–218). Such reciprocity was undermined by colonialism and capitalism. Achievement became highly personalised; local customs were adapted to secure the extraction of resources and to sustain vast exclusionary neo-patrimonial networks that continue to undermine public

198 *Christopher Allsobrook*

well-being (2008: 219). Shmuel Eisenstadt first employed the term neo-patrimonialism to distinguish – from traditional forms of social capital and political cohesion – the hybrid form now regarded as a fundamental threat to African political development. Neo-patrimonial regimes, Le Vine argues (1980: 666), tend to be personalist, but they also rely on practices derived from tradition. The modern neo-patrimonial bureaucratic African state mixes up traditional legitimacy and patrimonial rule with modern administrative governance (1980: 670). Neo-patrimonialism does not depend like traditional patrimonialism on charismatic domination, but it also does not restrict advancement in the ranks to criteria of experience, training or efficiency, like most modern legal-rational bureaucracies. With neo-patrimonialism both elements coexist, uncertainly, alongside one another (Erdmann and Engel 2007: 98).

Gero Erdmann and Ulf Engel stress the point that the bureaucratic element in Africa "is more than a legal-rational façade" – not all political and administrative decisions are made according to informal rules determined by partial interests (2007: 104). Administration is usually fixed by procedures that follow the formal course of a legal rationality even as many of these are accorded to private discretion (2007: 104). Formal public rule structures and informal private and political interests are not isolated from one another: "people, hypothetically, have a degree of choice as to which logic to employ" (2007: 105). "There are many circumstances where the interests of the politically or economically strong are better supported by the official legal-rational rules than by informal political relations" (2007: 108). But we do not see here a state of harmonious multicultural reconciliation. The exercise of power in such regimes is often erratic and unpredictable, unlike the calculable power of traditional or universal rules (2007: 114). As such, insecurity about the role of the state and public officials leads actors to try to overcome their insecurity at both levels, reproducing the system such that state institutions fail to accomplish the universalistic purpose of public welfare (2007: 105).

Reconciling African customs and multicultural rights

The previous section discussed various attempts to underwrite rights in African ethics according to some conception of personhood. I argued that African ethicists typically try to reconcile rights and customs by showing how African communal conceptions of personhood promote rights, due to some special characteristic belonging to all of humanity. I then argued that opposition between individual rights and communal customs has little to do with ontology of personhood and more to do with an historical divide between two inconsistent systems in African states, neither of which remains independent of Western influence, that is, between formal civil institutions, meant to secure equal rights for all citizens, and informal customary practices, sanctioned by traditional authorities. In the following

African recognition theory of civil rights 199

section I consider how this tension between rights and customs tends to play out in practice.

John Yoder puts it plainly that the failure of democratic pluralism in the Congo and other neighbouring states is due to African political culture (1998: 484). He argues that a stable democracy requires mass habituation to democratic values and orientations over time, including an inclination to play by the rules, to support the community as a whole, to respect individual rights and to engage in moderate compromise. Adherence to civic values at the elite and popular level is what sustains democracy and what prevents establishment of patrimonial, authoritarian or statist regimes that abuse state power (1998: 488). Yoder warns that traditional African thought is more compatible with a corporatist or bureaucratic-authoritarian political system than democracy, but, then again, it is "not anti-democratic" either, containing expectations to demand responsive government, which responds to the views of the people and to support tolerance, accountability, stability and flexibility (1998: 506). Yoder claims the weight of traditional opinion, in Kanyok thought, for example, favours a powerful chief who makes decisions which are unconstrained by direct checks on power, but his administration is also expected to be generous and to provide economic rewards (1998: 504).

Especially where local state structures are weak, social demands of collectivism in African ethics may in fact predispose officials to engage in corruption. General failure by the state to deliver basic services can lead the public to see representatives as special interest providers rather than representatives of contending views on public policy, such that they begin to put pressure on councillors to lobby the state for resources (Bukuluki 2013: 34). Public provision thereby becomes subject to rent-seeking by the individuals who represent different ethnic groups, which further perpetuates ethnic divisions (Kimenye 2003: 3). Ethnic groups maximise members' welfare at the expense of others to gain advantage in influencing policy (2003: 8). In surveys of ethnic identity across Africa, policies of national democratic solidarity are of lowest salience before elections. People are most mindful of their ethnic identities at this time, since it is when those who control allocation of resources are chosen (Eifert et al. 2010: 31). Institutions of governance are, however, weakened by heightened ethnic identification, since it increases transaction costs in provision of public goods at the national level (Kimenye 2003: 4). Furthermore, in many diffuse African countries, the state, by contrast with one's community, is seen as an abstract entity, such that "when you steal from governments you are stealing from nobody". So, as a senior lecturer in Theology at Kampala responded, "Government is impersonal, you cannot identify with it . . . it is absent. If you steal from something abstract you are not touched or cannot be felt. . . . Community sanctions . . . do not know how to react" (Bukuluki 2013: 33). Competition to control state resources heightens cultural identity and ethnic identification among sub-Saharan Africa's 2000 ethnicities, which, in turn, generates chronic underdevelopment (Kimenye 2003: 26). There is thus an urgent need to find ways to shift politics away from ethnic cultural identities and the division of state resources toward policy issues of social justice and governance (Szeftel 2000: 427).

Does a poor fit between Western civil liberties and indigenous communal values and practices hold back effective citizenship and democratic deepening in South Africa? Where do the problems arise in this regard? In many African countries, arguments based on resistance to Westernisation and the need to protect cultural values are raised in opposition to universal rights. Women's rights, in particular women's claim to equality, are one of the key areas of disagreement (Grant 2006: 2). In constitutional negotiations, lobbying by traditional leaders to exclude culture from the reach of the Bill of Rights in constitutional negotiations was motivated in part by suspicion of imposed Western values "swamping" customary law and tradition with "individualistic influences". Traditional leaders attempted to exempt customary law and traditional practices from the requirements of the right to equality in Section 9 of the Constitution (2006: 8). However, in light of the overriding importance of equality in the Constitution, commentators have concluded in the inevitable clash between culture and equality, equality must necessarily take priority (2006: 9).

South Africa's 1996 Constitution enshrines a range of internationally recognised human rights in its Bill of Rights, which is described as the "cornerstone" of our democracy (Grant 2006: 3). Cultural rights are also protected in the South African Constitution. While explicitly describing South Africa as a sovereign democratic state with one common citizenship, the Constitution also recognises and protects the multicultural and linguistic diversity represented within that commonality (2006: 6). Sections 30, 31 and 185 provide for the protection of culture. Separate provision is made for the application of customary law in section 211(3), which states, "The courts must apply customary law when that law is applicable, subject to the Constitution and any legislation that specifically deals with customary law" (2006: 6). The right to culture is limited in Section 30 by a proviso, which states, "No one exercising these rights may do so in a manner inconsistent with any provision of the Bill of Rights" (in Grant 2006: 7). Section 211 requires customary law to be consistent with the Constitution, and Section 39 obliges the courts to promote the "spirit, purpose and objects of the Bills of Rights" in interpreting and developing common and customary law (in Grant 2006: 7).

Thus far, the strategy adopted by the Constitutional Court has been to interpose common law in those areas of customary law found incompatible with the Constitution. While practically beneficial, however, the historical significance of Roman-Dutch common law trumping African customary law in this way is "deeply troubling" (Grant 2006: 18). A better solution would be to develop customary law to ensure compatibility with the Constitution, maintaining both customary and common law on the basis of legal dualism, subject to the Bill of Rights. But a major problem here is that the official version of customary law is "frozen in time and skewed by gender" (2006: 19). Thus, the starting point for development of customary law must be *living* customary law rather than *official* customary law, since the former is relatively less compromised by the past. Moreover, the validity of customary law is not dependent on formal written sources, but it is proved on the basis of evidence of its current social practice, making codification problematic, especially if homogenous formal rules often do not apply across different communities that value particular practices (2006: 19).

Although South Africa has established a formal democracy, with full legal and political rights for all citizens, high inequality prevents the effective practice of citizenship in the public sphere and in local decision-making. Formal constitutional democracy has not given citizens the capacity to shape public policy. Rather, many of the most vulnerable citizens are dependent on networks of patronage for the delivery of public services, with the public domain characterised by lobbying by powerful interests and daily inchoate street-level "popcorn" protests calling for local service delivery. In some ways effective democracy has diminished since the new Constitution came into place in 1996, since the government, which considers itself the true voice of the majority, as Herman Wasserman and Anthea Garman put it, "narrowed the identity of the citizen, from the Constitution's rights-bearing, issue-expressing person to an essentialised African identity as the hallmark of the authentic citizen" (2012: 393). Equivalence of race with loyalty is increasingly typical of public discussions. Citizenship is expressed in essentialist terms which question the right of the white elite to criticise the government (2012: 394).

Ubuntu is based on village values and family norms that define reciprocal communal exchanges in a traditional setting. This includes compassion for others, consensus-seeking and cooperation, as we have heard. The moderate communitarians we have discussed are at pains to emphasise that African ethics values universal human dignity, welfare or responsiveness to others, which underwrites some conception of basic individual rights. Xenophobic attacks on foreigner Africans in South Africa in 2008 and again in 2015 were rightly condemned as being contrary to the spirit of *Ubuntu*. Yet, with the notion of *Ubuntu*, the local elite also "systematizes and articulates a set of values and practices that at the grass roots level are largely intuitive and unsystematic" (McAlister 2009: 7). Instead of developing democratic institutions that can help to ensure social justice for all citizens, post-apartheid South Africa has seen a resurgence of cultural nationalism presenting itself in the form of *Ubuntu*, in an obsession with moralising, exclusionary and anti-democratic nation-building (Marx 2010: 51). Alongside *Ubuntu*'s "Christianised" compassionate solidarity, Christof Marx warns of a nationalist ideology of compulsory conformity and ostracism (2010: 52). "African communalism" emerges as a formula that excludes and includes, interpreting all deficits in the present order in one-dimensional terms of "Western individualism", to suppress dissidence and to ensure conformity (2010: 53).

202 Christopher Allsobrook

The real meaning of such collective identity is pitched against those who are different (Marx 2010: 59). Authoritarian emphasis on unity, integration and harmony at the same time presents the "West" in ahistorical, culturally essentialist and dichotomous terms against the communal interactions of quintessential African village life. Such simplistic conceptions are dangerous. Marx remarks with irony that the same sense of traditionalism which comes to the fore in the nationalist ideology of *Ubuntu* was also consecrated by the apartheid government. This reveals continuity with, and adoption of, the ideology of the former apartheid state by its adversaries, reviving structures of domination controlled by traditional authorities who profited by colluding with white supremacists (2010: 62). Voices of the past echo in the present. The Afrikaner nationalist Nico Diederichs claimed in the 1930s, "The individual or single human being as such is an abstraction that does not exist in reality. Outside of the community and the communication with other human beings the human being is not really human" (in Marx 2010: 56). When each person can find fulfilment only within the nation, every form of individualism can be rejected as alien, outside and hostile to the community.

Constitutionalism in Africa depends on consultation with traditional culture and customary precedents to draw out suitable institutional structures. Constitutionalism must reflect the customary norms and practices of African societies, drawing on compatible elements of different cultural practices in an ongoing process of incremental reform (Hessebon 2013: 35). In this there are no reliable criteria for African authenticity. Ancient African thought has been essentialised and perverted by imperialists and nationalist elites. Local level democracy should draw on deliberative and consensus-seeking aspects of traditional African values and customs. If the state neglects effective oversight, conditions of decentralised despotism will continue to thrive (Koelble 2005: 30).

An African recognition theory of social rights

The chapter has so far argued for an improved synthesis of systems of civil rights and traditional customs that presently interact inconsistently in the typically bifurcated postcolonial African state. Civil rights should not automatically trump customary practices as they currently do in South African constitutional practice, nor should they be subverted at the discretion of decentralised despots as they are in unofficial practice. Effective citizenship and democratic deepening depend on acknowledgment of how African customary practices of communal reciprocity are tied up in coercive and undemocratic networks of neo-patrimonial patronage and clientelism. Consensus-seeking aspects of African communitarian political philosophy should be promoted, but customary communal obligations can undermine equal rights and equitable distribution of public resources. Acknowledging such dangers, moderate communitarians emphasise the space in African

African recognition theory of civil rights   203

communal identity for rights grounded in dignity, collective well-being or the mutual identity and solidarity of friendly relations with others. Sebola overstates the incompatibility of Western rationally institutionalised ethical demands with intuitive African customary practices, but it is worth considering that conflict between African customs and civil rights often stems from essentialised conceptions of cultural identity or rights. African customary norms have been decontested and reified, shorn of reciprocal obligations, for the ideological convenience of imperialists and nationalists, supported by decentralised despots.

Tension between rights and customs in Africa is commonly conceived of as if an institutional framework of liberal individualism was simply imposed on an ill-fitting indigenous communitarian ontology of personhood. This is not inaccurate as much as it is misleading. Problematic as it is, the imposition of an institutional framework supporting constitutional civil liberties has generally been well received and relatively successful, certainly in South Africa, as argued earlier. Moreover, colonies ruled directly, for an extended duration, by a Western liberal institutional framework have generally proved better equipped to secure democratic development after independence than those governed by indirect rule, which manipulated and recoded customary leadership, resulting in patterns of neo-patrimonialism, ethnic rivalry and chronic corruption that undermine equal rights of citizenship. Essentialised cultural identities are perpetuated where conflict between rights and customs is framed in terms of contestation between African communal culture and external Western liberties. Just like Afrikaner nationalists before them, African nationalist elites manipulate such an essentialised cultural identity to promote narrow, conformist and exclusionary ideology.

I would suggest that these problems regarding rights and customs in African political philosophy may be better understood, not as a conflict between Western individualism and African communal identity, but, rather, in terms of an internal tension within African political philosophy between an essentialist conception of the status of customary rights and a recognition theory, which I advance. In doing so, I agree with David Boucher that theories which ground the origin and acquisition of moral rights in an ontology of the person are a "convenient fiction". Customary international law and the "rights recognition thesis" offer more adequate accounts of what it means to have universal rights and obligations and articulations of the obligations of states to hold these to account (Boucher 2011: 752). Recognition theory arises in the context of customary international law. Since there is no sovereign at the international level to enforce a universal constitution, establishing which rules are genuinely universally binding is a discursive activity underpinned by customary rules of interpretation and evidentially based on the practices of states, precedent and the opinions of learned jurisprudents (2011: 753).

The rights recognition thesis helps us make sense of customary international law in two ways. First, recognition of customary practices creates

204   *Christopher Allsobrook*

rights. Second, customary recognition is a way of acknowledging and knowing those rights, in the sense of formal interpretation (2011: 754). On TH Green's British Idealist formulation, recognition theory deems rights to be those powers possessed by an individual that others recognise as necessary for the achievement of a shared good (2011: 756). Rights are defined not by principles of natural law, nor by attributes of personhood, but by their customary recognition in moral communities both below and beyond the level of the state. Rights are said to be "immanent in social practices" in that their formal recognition may come long after they are established. They are established by demonstrating customary observance, whose continued use endows them with obligatory power evidenced by enduring public recognition and participation. Rights are also acknowledged and recognised as fundamental to the social, moral and political fabric of a society in the form of customary if not fully articulated rules (2011: 760–761).

Although much has been made of Gyekye's moderate communitarian account of personhood over the past twenty years in African philosophy, as Metz rightly acknowledges (2012: 61), I would argue that more attention should be paid to an alternative account of good governance in Akan political thinking, which he presents elsewhere (2010b). Gyekye insists that any attempt to reconcile traditional custom with democratic rights in Africa depends on inquiry into the status, nature of authority, roles and power relationships holding between the people and the chief, where chieftaincy has long been the outstanding feature of the political landscape. The way Gyekye describes such practices, at least in principle, supports a recognition theory of rights, which would avoid problems of cultural essentialism associated with framing this tension in terms of a contrast between African communal personhood and Western individualism. In his account Gyekye stresses the point that the hereditary position of the Akan village chief was traditionally elected from the royal lineage in consultation with members of the lineage and only chosen if he was deemed acceptable by councillors and the body of citizens. Limits of monarchical power were clearly set by custom and by the concurrence of councillors, who would listen to arguments in the public village where anyone was free to express dissent until consensus was achieved through the reconciliation of opposed views (2010b: 242–244). The chief was enjoined not to be dogmatic but to be tolerant of the views of others, by a set of injunctions publically recited before him and acknowledged by him. He was bound not to deliberate or enact policy but, rather, to authorise and to represent a position of public consensus (2010b: 245).

In Gyekye's account, chiefs are constrained by custom and the consensus of councillors representing the body of citizens. The role of chief is not to stipulate, define or impose his views or his rules but, rather, to secure and enforce the customary practices of the community the executive represents. Norms of governance and rights of citizenship, on this account, are not derived from any necessary or essential properties, natural or otherwise, belonging to human personhood or community, such as dignity or a duty to collective well-being or friendliness. Rather, social rights and customary norms of governance are just those practices which the community recognises and the chief represents. Much antipathy shared by Africanists toward a liberal Western institutional framework of rights owes to associations with abstract, reified principles that are poorly integrated with practical living. Likewise, problems of neo-patrimonialism and corruption associated with communal African customs belong to essentialist conceptions consolidated by imperialists and nationalist elites. Recognition theory accommodates the common practice, at least in South Africa, of distinguishing "official" from "living" customary law, and it works against the reified terms coded into the body of complicit norms that prove convenient for colonialism, apartheid and nationalist despotism. A recognition theory of rights best accounts for "cultural relativist" intuitions shared by sub-Saharan African people regarding the status of social rights, and it avoids exclusive, essentialist ethnic identity. In actual practice it underwrites all human rights as codified in international customary law.

There is evidence to suggest, at least in Gyekye's description of good governance in Akan society, that there is scope in African political thinking for a recognition theory of rights. Not only are rights recognised in traditional Akan social practices without recourse to Western discourse, but the status of these rights may be seen to derive from the fact that they are recognised – i.e., their legitimacy stems from the fact that they are embedded in widely acknowledged customary practices and enforced by a leader whose duty is to enforce this order, not to impose arbitrary orders. Although Gyekye argues that rights are grounded in personhood, his accounts of Akan political thinking show that a recognition theory of rights may have some purchase in this society. It is possible both views may be found in Africa – that rights derive intrinsically from certain basic attributes of human personhood or that rights derive from recognised customs. On certain matters, Westerners have such different customs that the set of rights recognised in their part of the world is not quite the same as the set of rights Africans typically recognise. But, on fundamental human rights, all customs coincide, as we see in their near universal recognition. This coincidence is not necessary but fortunate; it belongs not to traits of personhood but to likely and actual consensus.

If rights are thought to belong to personhood, a tension is typically presumed to follow between Western individualist ontologies of personhood, grounding individual rights, and African communal ontologies of personhood, which uphold customary practices. This way of thinking frustrates reconciliation of rights and custom, citizenship and subjecthood, in the postcolonial bifurcated state. Communalist and communitarian Western political thinking fits uneasily into this polarising narrative, the distorted colonial history of African customs is under-scrutinised by it and individualistic attributes of African political thinking become difficult to integrate with the core solidarity at stake in moderate Afro-communitarian political theory. Tensions between individualism and communalism anyway persist in political thinking across most cultures. It is unhelpful to project this neat distinction

206 _Christopher Allsobrook_

onto an historical bifurcation facing postcolonial states, between citizens' rights and subjects' customs, neither of which are either authentically Western or African and neither of which belong intrinsically to individualist or communalist social ontologies. Recognition theory, by contrast, can claim some African heritage with respect to the status of rights in traditional African communities, and its framework accounts for relations of power in a way that helps to better articulate the Africanist critique of hegemonic Western principles of right, which seems typically to motivate African political theorists to draw distinctions between different ontologies of personhood.

Conclusion

Although I have not provided a detailed account of a particular African recognition theory of rights, I have argued that such a theory may and should be elicited from Gyekye's accounts of traditional Akan political thinking. Moreover, I have argued that a recognition theory of rights is better able (than one underwritten by an essentialist ontology of personhood) to account for and to reconcile divisions between citizenship and subjecthood whose persistence perpetuates underdevelopment in the typically bifurcated postcolonial African state. Prescribed constitutional rights, I have argued, should not automatically trump inherited customary practices, wherever the latter prove inconsistent with the former. Customary authority and customary law have been poorly integrated with democratic authority and civil rights. The two systems, operating alongside one another, are not reconciled in practice. Thus they undermine each other's legitimacy, breeding insecurity, institutional weakness, weak accountability and opportunities for abuse. I have argued that an essentialist conception of _Ubuntu_, belonging to a unified conception of African personhood, set in contradistinction to Western personhood, tends to perpetuate apartheid nationalist thinking. Ethnic identification in African politics distracts attention from the details of candidates' public policy platforms and typically increases transaction costs in provision of public goods at the national level.

Essentialist distinctions between African and Western personhood, conceived independently of their politically contested historical conditions, are not helpfully projected by applied ethicists onto the bifurcated postcolonial state to explain conflict between individual rights and communal customs. Recognition theory avoids such reified ethnic stereotyping to help reconcile and adapt to living customary practices as they evolve through changing historical conditions over time. Unlike static ontologies of personhood, recognition theory is open to ongoing reform of regulations, in accordance with operative customary practices. By explicitly acknowledging and putting into question the historically contested status of political identities, a recognition theory of rights avoids the narrow conformism of essentialist ethnic African identities that have historically played into the hands of imperialists and nationalist elites. The explicitly contingent normative foundations of

African recognition theory of civil rights 207

recognition theory better express the critique of Western conceptual hegemony that motivates distinctions in African political philosophy between African and Western personhood. Finally, unlike any theory of rights underwritten by one particular set of attributes of personhood that African political thinking may be said to uphold, a recognition theory of rights aims to integrate compatible elements of various cultural practices in an incremental process of avowedly multicultural reform.

Bibliography

Bidaguren, J. and Estrella, D. (2002) 'Governability and Forms of Popular Justice in the New South Africa and Mozambique', *Journal of Legal Pluralism and Unofficial Law* 34(47): 113–135.

Boucher, D. (2011) 'The Recognition Theory of Rights, Customary International Law and Human Rights', *Political Studies* 59: 753–771.

Bukuluki, O. (2013) ' "When I Steal, It Is for the Benefit of Me and You": Is Collectivism Engendering Corruption in Uganda?' *International Letters of Social and Humanistic Sciences* 5: 27–44.

Eifert, B., Miguel, E. and Posner, D. (2010) 'Political Competition and Ethnic Identification in Africa', *American Journal of Political Science* 54(2): 494–510.

Erdmann, G. and Engel, U. (2007) 'Neopatrimonialism Reconsidered: Critical Review and Elaboration of an Elusive Concept', *Commonwealth and Comparative Politics* 45(1): 95–119.

Fraser-Moloketi, G. (2007) 'Toward a Common Understanding of Corruption in Africa', *African Renaissance Studies* 2(2): 239–249.

Grant, E. (2006) 'Human Rights, Cultural Diversity and Customary Law in South Africa', *Journal of African Law* 50(1): 2–23.

Gyekye, K. (2010a) 'Person and Community in Akan Thought', in K. Gyeye and K. Wiredu (eds.) *Person and Community. Ghanaian Philosophical Studies, I*, Washington, DC: Council for Research and Values.

Gyekye, K. (2010b) 'Traditional Political Ideas: Their Relevance to Contemporary Africa', in K. Gyekye and K. Wiredu (eds.) *Person and Community. Ghanaian Philosophical Studies, I*, Washington, DC: Council for Research and Values.

Heller, P. (2009) 'Democratic Deepening in India and South Africa', *Journal of Asian and African Studies* 44(1): 123–149.

Hessebon, G. T. (2013) 'Come Major Themes in the Study of Constitutionalism and Democracy in Africa', *Vienna Journal on International Constitutional Law* 28(1): 28–48.

Jensen, K. and Gaie, J.B.R. (2010) 'African Communalism and Public Health Policies: The Relevance of Indigenous Concepts of Personal Identity to HIV/AIDS Policies in Botswana', *African Journal of AIDS Research* 9(3): 297–305.

Kamoche, K. (2011) 'Contemporary Development in the Management of Human Resources in Africa', *Journal of World Business* 46: 1–4.

Kimenye, M. S. (2003) 'Ethnicity, Governance and the Provision of Public Goods', *University of Connecticut Economics Working Papers* 49: 1–41.

Koelble, T. (2005) 'Democracy, Traditional Leadership and the International Economy in South Africa', *South African Centre for Social Science Research Working Paper* 114: 1–42.

Lange, M. (2004) 'British Colonial Legacies and Political Development', *World Development* 32(6): 905–922.

Le Vine, V. T. (1980) 'African Patrimonial Regimes in Comparative Perspective', *The Journal of Modern African Studies* 18(4): 657–673.

Mamdani, M. (1996) *Citizen and Subject: Contemporary Africa and the Legacy of Late Colonialism*, Princeton, NJ: Princeton University Press.

Marx, C. (2010) 'Ubu and Ubuntu: On the Dialectics of Apartheid and Nation-Building', *Politikon: SA Journal of Political Studies* 29(1): 49–64.

McAlister, P. (2009) 'Ubuntu – Beyond Belief in Southern Africa', *Sites: New Series* 6(1): 1–10.

Metz, T. (2009) 'African Moral Theory and Public Governance: Nepotism, Preferential Hiring and Other Partiality', in M. F. Murove (ed.) *African Ethics: An Anthology for Comparative and Applied Ethics*, KwaZulu-Natal: UKZN Press.

Metz, T. (2012) 'Developing African Political Philosophy: Moral-Theoretic Strategies', *Philosophia Africana* 14(1): 61–83.

Nyasani, J. M. (2013) 'The Ontological Significance of "I" and "We" in African Philosophy', *Foundation for Intercultural Philosophy and Art*. [Online] Available at http://www.galerie-inter.de/kimmerle/frameText8.htm (Accessed: May 1, 2016).

Okeowo, A. (2015) Can Thuli Madonsela Save South Africa From Itself? *The New York Times* [Online] 21 June 2015. Available at http://www.nytimes.com/2015/06/21/magazine/can-thulisile-madonsela-save-south-africa-from-itself.html (Accessed 2 August 2015).

Olsson, O. (2009) 'On the Democratic Legacy of Colonialism', *Journal of Comparative Economics* 37: 534–551.

Omobowale, A. O. (2008) 'Clientelism and Social Structure: An Analysis of Patronage in Yoruba Social Thought', *Africa Spectrum* 43(2): 203–224.

Sebola, M. P. (2014) 'Ethics in the Public Service: A Paradox of Culture, Politics and Ethics in the World of Work', *Journal of Social Science* 40(3): 295–304.

Szeftel, M. (2000) 'Clientelism, Corruption and Catastrophe', *Review of African Political Economy* 27(85): 427–441.

Theron, P. M. (2013) 'Corruption in Sub-Saharan Africa: A Practical-Theological Response', *In die Skriflig/In Luce Verbi* 47(1) Art: 676, 8 pages.

Van der Walt, B. J. (2003) *Understanding and Rebuilding Africa: From Desperation Today to Expectation for Tomorrow*. Potchefstroom: Institute for Contemporary Christianity in Africa.

Van Niekerk, J. (2011) 'On the Tension between *Simunye* and *Ubuntu*', in G. Walmsley (ed.) *African Philosophy and the Future of Africa*, Washington, DC: Council for Research and Values.

Wassermann, H. and Garman, A. (2012) 'Being South African and Belonging: The Status and Practice of Mediated Citizenship in a New Democracy', *Social Dynamics: A Journal of African Studies* 40(2): 392–407.

Wiredu, K. (2008) 'Social Philosophy in Post-Colonial Africa: Some Preliminaries Concerning Communalism and Communitarianism', *South African Journal of Philosophy* 27(4): 332–339.

Yoder, J. (1998) 'Good Government and Traditional African Political Philosophy: The Example of the Kanyok of the Congo', *The Journal of Modern African Studies* 36(3): 483–507.

12 The Pan-African philosophy and movement

Social and educational praxis of multiculturalism

Kersuze Simeon-Jones

We love humanity. We are working for the peace of the world, which we believe can only come about when all races are given their due.[1]

Thus, this historic struggle for Black Studies was in fact a struggle for multicultural education as opposed to a Eurocentric one.[2]

The Pan-African philosophy and movement grew out of the necessary response to re-establish individuals and communities of African ancestry within their social and cultural traditions, as well as their political and economic rights. Through national and international organizations, as well as through various publications, Pan-Africanists advocated for a respectable and equitable re-integration into a shared world community – after the effects of the Slave Trade, the slavery system in the New World, global disenfranchisement, colonialism and neo-colonialism. From its *de facto* modern existence in the 1700s – and the influences that date back to the experiences of the Middle Passage – to its formal inception in the early 1900s, Pan-Africanism has been inherently multicultural in its philosophy and practice. From the outset, the present chapter will distinctively examine the Pan-African philosophy of the 1700s in relation to the ensuing movement of the 1900s. Moreover, it will offer a comprehensive analysis of the two intrinsic dimensions of multiculturalism within the Pan-African movement: 1) its intra-racial and transnational scopes; 2) its humanist/multiracial and international components. On the one level, Pan-Africanism's fundamentally diasporic characteristic, which encompasses numerous African ethnicities, languages, religions and cultures within the African continent and among those of African descent throughout the world, fostered invaluable exchanges. On the other level, Pan-Africanists' forthright and resolve conversation with the global world opened a space – very early on in modern human history – for a multicultural approach to the world, in terms of addressing social and economic ills, as well as promoting humane participation and varying contributions to society. Thus, Pan-Africanism introduced the concept of multiculturalism *avant la lettre*. Moreover, the Pan-African Movement, and the movements it influenced transnationally,

210 Kersuze Simeon-Jones

went beyond the articulation of a multicultural philosophy and framed the blueprint of a multicultural social program that is embedded in education.[3] Pan-Africanism's multi-national/multi-dimensional program set forth the urgent re-evaluation of educational, intellectual, social and political praxis within the global world.

The term "multiculturalism" and its advocacy gained momentum in the Western world throughout the second half of the 1900s, due to the increasing number of multi-ethnic and multi-racial societies. Multiculturalism became particularly significant in the United States following the Long Civil Rights and the Civil Rights Movements for African descendants in the United States and the growing number of citizens with origins from Asia, Africa, the Caribbean and South America.[4] To address the foundational contribution of African descendants to the creation and prosperity of the United States, while relegated to an unmitigated destitute disposition, proponents of Pan-Africanism – and other movements such as the New Negro Movement, the Civil Rights Movement and the Black Power Movement in the U.S. context[5] – called for their appropriate education (Woodson 2005: 83). The appropriate education that Pan-African proponents advocated in the United States, Africa, the Caribbean and Europe was based on multiculturalism; that is, the valorization and teaching of African history, along with European history and the histories of other regions. In his *Introduction to Black Studies*, first published in 1982, Maulana Karenga situates the emergence of multiculturalism in the United States to highlight the following:

> The struggle for a multicultural education begins in full form in the 60's with the Black Student Movement demanding the end to the exclusive white studies instruction . . . the Black students' struggle for Black Studies and the end to the Eurocentric curriculum was joined and aided by Third World groups who formed with Blacks the Third World Liberation Front. Thus, this historic struggle for Black Studies was in fact a struggle for multicultural education as opposed to a Eurocentric one. . . . Therefore, other ethnic studies, i.e., Native American, Latino and Asian Studies, and women's studies built on this tradition and joined in demanding an education of quality and relevance. It is at this point that quality education unavoidably requires a multicultural content.
>
> (Karenga 1993: 44)

Within the framework of political and social rights, Pan-Africanism's most salient prescription to the plight of African descendants and, by extension, the practice of true multiculturalism within society, lies in the group's advocacy for, and relentless effort towards the implementation of *proper* or *appropriate* education. Education became the key factor for the Pan-African program as early as the mid-1800s, with the work of Edward Wilmot Blyden (Caribbean born) in Liberia. Proponents of the Pan-African movement – and other sociopolitical movements of the Black world – understood that without

The Pan-African philosophy and movement 211

the proper education of African descendants and the proper education of other groups in African history and Afro-Diasporic histories, the identity of Africa's descendants will continue to carry the imposed stigma that was constructed for the justification of the Transatlantic Slave Trade, slavery and lasting multifaceted exploitation. Africa's descendants will continue to lack an autonomous or influential voice in the political processes of their respective nations and the global world. Without a prominent political voice it will be quasi-impossible – or simply impossible – for the majority of Africa's descendants to climb out of the economic pit within which they found themselves since the dehumanizing system of the Slave Trade to the current days. It is an established fact that the political and economic structures of modern society – in relation to the confining destitution of Africa's descendants – have been established since the fifteenth century. Consequently, as early as the 1800s Pan-Africanists understood that *without* the re-education of the world, without a political voice that is able to effect change, the political and economic structures will remain the same. It follows that without such fundamental transformation, multiculturalism in general, and intellectual and political multiculturalism, more specifically, will remain an ambiguous term and an unfulfilled agenda. Within the context of the United States, Malcolm X astutely posited the following in 1965, in order to unveil the education problem that thwarts communities. His statement holds true on a global level. In fact, one could substitute "the global population" for "the entire American population" while reading his analysis at length. He explained:

> If the entire American population were properly educated – by properly educated, I mean given a true picture of the history and contributions of the black man – I think many whites would be less racist in their feelings. They would have more respect for the black man as a human being. Knowing what the black man's contributions to science and civilization have been in the past, the white man's feelings of superiority would be at least partially negated. Also, the feeling of inferiority that the black man has would be replaced by a balanced knowledge of himself. He'd feel more like a human being. He'd function more like a human being, in a society of human beings. So it takes education to eliminate it.
>
> (Malcolm X 1993: 196)

Grounded in the principle and advocacy of proper education, this chapter will, thus, underscore the extent to which the praxis of multiculturalism has been central not only to the Pan-African movement, but also intrinsic to the movements it influenced diasporically – such as the New Negro Renaissance, the Indigénisme, Garveyism, Négritude, the Afro Criollo Movement, the Civil Rights Movement and the Black Power Movement. Examining Pan-Africanism's fundamental philosophy, the chapter will pay particular attention to the current aims of multiculturalism, which include: 1) recognition and preservation of different histories and cultures; 2) an education approach that takes into

212 *Kersuze Simeon-Jones*

account the teaching of various histories and cultures within a society, for a better understanding of such society and peaceful interactions among its citizens. However, it is crucial to note that while Pan-Africanism and the various sociopolitical movements of the Black Diaspora put forth persistent efforts in revealing and exposing indispensable solutions to the plight of African descendants, the ethical and social problems of an incomprehensive education in history – for all, and African descendants in particular – remain in the twenty-first century. The global application of the Pan-Africanist education program, from grade schools to the universities, would lead to viable social transformations embedded in true multiculturalism.

Pan-Africanism and the African Diaspora

As examined in *Literary and Sociopolitical Writings of the Black Diaspora*, it is a difficult – if not impossible – task to formulate an exact definition of Pan-Africanism, as it "cannot be indisputably periodized, nor can it be a definitive concept" (Esedebe 1982: 3). Nonetheless, examining the different facets of Pan-Africanism, from its practices in the 1700s to the nominal movement, a number of confluent definitions were expounded throughout the twentieth century. Amongst which, the respective definitions of Chief Anthony Enahoro, W. E. B. Du Bois, P. Olisanwuche Esedebe and Alioune Diop require some attention. Anthony Enahoro defines Pan-Africanism as a continental affair, where "the economic, social and cultural development of the continent, the avoidance of conflict among African states, the promotion of African unity and influence in world affairs" is paramount. From W. E. B Du Bois's perspective, Pan-Africanism is "an intellectual understanding and co-operation among all groups of African descent in order to bring about the industrial and spiritual emancipation of the Negro people". P. Olisanwuche Esedebe concludes that "with some simplification we can say that Pan-Africanism is a political and cultural phenomenon which regards Africa, Africans and African descendants abroad as a unit. It seeks to regenerate and unify Africa and promote a feeling of oneness among the people of the African world". Furthermore, Esedebe underlines that Pan-Africanism teaches pride in African values. Thus, "any adequate definition of the phenomenon must include the political and cultural aspects". Lastly, Alioune Diop views Pan-Africanism as "more or less synonymous with the concept of 'African Personality' or 'Négritude'" (Esedebe 1982: 3).

It is imperative to underline that the group consciousness of the African condition started to form during the Middle Passage, in the belly of the slave ship, where the multi-ethnic African concepts of life were altered and a new reality was conceived. In the documentary entitled *The Middle Passage*, the narrator – the spiritual voice of an ancestor – reminds the audience:

> We were from every corner of the continent. We were Igbos . . . Fantis, Ashantis . . . Yorubas, and Wolofs from Senegambia . . . we were

The Pan-African philosophy and movement 213

Mandigas, Bambaras. . . .We were all foreigners to each other, but it wouldn't be long before we became one people. And, in that unity we shared not only our languages and our customs, or even common gods, but rather a question that goes forever unanswered.

(Chamoiseau, Deslauriers, et al. 2003: 1)

That question – for the enslaved and their progeny – is how the Africans will be able to change the condition within which they found themselves. To what extent will rebirth/regeneration or transformation be possible and successful? While the enslaved Africans came from diverse family and community structures, different regional cultures, as well as a myriad of agricultural skills, languages, religions and concepts of life and society, the new African condition became that of a common suffering: dehumanizing physical distress and chronic psychological affliction. Equally significant is the *awareness* that their general African origin became indissolubly linked to their common condition; as such, their liberation would necessitate a group or groups of concerted response. As connections began to form on the ship, as alliances and kinships crystalized in the new world, Pan-Africanism emerged as both a mindset and a way of life that united for the attainment of liberation and social transformation. Their Pan-Africanism was rooted in the need for unity while recognizing the multifarious diversity among the unified group. If Pan-Africanism, in its multi-dimensional definitions, is a "co-operation among *all groups* of African descent in order to bring about the industrial and spiritual emancipation of the Negro people" (emphasis added), the slave rebellions and revolutions throughout the plantations of the Americas marked the actualization of a Pan-Africanist ideology that pre-ceded the eventual movement. To eradicate common suffering, the group's ideology and common goal *became* liberty from the yoke and drudgery of slavery. The elemental aim was: 1) basic human freedom and natural rights – that is, spiritual, psychological and physical freedom – followed by 2) political and civil organizations as Africans and their descendants began to organize into communities and nations.

The New World's most notable African leader of the nineteenth century – Toussaint Louverture – succeeded in assembling Africans under the umbrella of revolution. Approximately a century before the leadership of Louverture, the marooned Makandal conceived a plan where Blacks would unite to gain control over the colony and end slavery. The Makandal rebellion fell short of its intentions. Makandal was betrayed, captured and burned alive; however, the spirit of liberty lived on. In 1791 Boukman organized thou-sands of Africans and their descendants for the rebellion that introduced the beginning of a new era; it marked the end of slavery in Saint-Domingue and, subsequently, the Black world. The enslaved and marooned Africans organized under the umbrella of a general religion, blending various tenets of African religions and philosophies into *a* religious philosophy of libera-tion. After solemn chants during their ceremony of August 1791 – which preceded the revolt – Boukman and his followers asserted the following among themselves: "The god who created the sun which gives us light, who rouses the waves and rules the storm, though hidden in the clouds, he watches us. . . . Our god who is good to us orders us to revenge our wrongs. He will direct our arms and aid us. Throw away the *symbol* of the god of the whites who has so often caused us to weep, and listen to the voice of liberty, which speaks in the hearts of us all" (James 1989: 87). The *symbol* of "god" and religion they were given at enslavement was a "god" who sanctions abject African subjugation and dehumanization. To supplant the symbol as well as the destructive reality such a symbol assured, it was imperative that the multi-ethnic Africans assembled under a shared belief, under common symbols and religious principles. The symbol of enslavement was replaced by the symbol of liberty and all that came with it.

The momentum of the Garvey movement in the 1920s represents the zenith of Pan-African thoughts and actions, before the independence of many African nations in the 1960s. From its inception (in the 1910s) to the 1930s, Garveyism was unique on three levels. These were the call for: 1) the psychological renaissance of people of African descent throughout the globe, 2) their political and economic freedom and 3) the movement's global and diasporic dimension – a dimension Garvey's predecessors could not encompass; a dimension that remains incomparable to other historic movements, well into the twenty-first century.[6] In 1940 W. E. B. Du Bois wrote: "Garvey proved not only an astonishing popular leader, but a master of propaganda. Within a few years, news of his movement, of his promises and plans, reached Europe and Asia, and penetrated every corner of Africa. . . . My first effort was to explain away the Garvey movement and ignore it; but it was a mass movement that could not be ignored" (Du Bois 1975: 277–278). In the late 1800s Edward Wilmot Blyden (1832 to 1912) espoused "Africa for the Africans" – including African descendants – also as a response to debilitating racism he observed in the Caribbean and experienced in the United States. He worked to dismantle religious and ethnic factions in Africa in order to unify for progress; for intra-racial and ethnic prejudice – in Africa and abroad – national conflicts and wars only contribute to the regression of the race's agenda. Moreover, inter-racial and ethnic disenfranchisement and aggression, engendered from prejudice, hinder the potential for global productivity and security. Blyden's Pan-African program, similar to his ideological successors, connected the prosperity of the land and its people to their pertinent education. "If in the future Africans are to control their own land, achieve social and political success, and be regarded as full citizens, their children must first receive a relevant education. . . . Blyden associated the political impotence to the dispersion of blacks throughout the world and to a politically disunited Africa" (Simeon-Jones 2010: 53). Although Blyden's writings and the work he undertook in Liberia remain invaluable to the formation of the Pan-African movement and beyond, they did not reach the masses of African descendants on a global scale comparable to Garveyism.

The Pan-African philosophy and movement   215

In the first half of the 1900s, after his travels throughout the Caribbean, South America and the United States, Marcus Garvey came to re-launch Blyden's idea of a necessary repatriation to Africa. The decision to build a nation in Africa, as he viewed it, was forced upon them, given the reality of the era. He reasoned that "the Universal Negro Improvement Association is not seeking to disrupt any organized system of government". Instead, "the Association is determined to bring Negroes together for the building of a nation of their own. And why? Because we have been forced to it. We have been forced to it throughout the world; not only in America, not only in Europe, not only in the British Empire, but wheresoever the black man happens to find himself, he has been forced to do for himself" (Garvey 1986: 96). Aside from a Back-to-Africa effort that was never realized, Garvey's commitment to ideologically rally African descendants was grounded in a complex program of psychological, economic and political renaissance. From his own experiences – lived through the international sojourns – and the examination of the African condition globally, Garvey drafted the *Declaration of Rights of the Negro Peoples of the World*. The *Declaration* assessed the contemporaneous state of African descendants and proposed the necessary modifications that must take place for a prosperous, dignified and fulfilled future. The document was judiciously drafted: "in order to encourage our race all over the world and stimulate it to a higher and grander destiny, we demand and insist on the following Declaration of Rights" (Garvey 1986: 136). Garvey's first emphasis, before the enumeration of the demands, is one of origin and connection:

> Be it known to all men that whereas, all men are created equal and entitled to the rights of life, liberty and the pursuit of happiness, and because of this we, the duly elected representatives of the Negro peoples of the world, invoking the aid of the just and Almighty God do declare all men women and children of our blood throughout the world free citizens, and do claim them as free citizens of Africa, the Motherland of all Negroes.
>
> (Garvey 1986: 137)

If Garvey's Pan-African philosophy was overall global – in spite of its unrealized territory intention – the second half of the 1900s witnessed a continental Pan-African agenda, which facilitated the political independence of many African nations throughout the late 1950s into the 60s. The official Pan-African Congresses, from the first in 1900 to the last in 1945, advocated political and economic freedom as well as social and cultural valorization for Africans and African descendants. From its multi-dimensional analysis, the Pan-African congresses requested substantive change in the matters of land ownership, capital, labor regulations and proper education in Africa, as well as for African descendants born and/or living in the Western Hemisphere. Among the demands that continue to be of

216 *Kersuze Simeon-Jones*

pertinence to Africa's economic and political state in the twenty-first century, one would note:

a   *The Land.* The land and its natural resources shall be held in trust for the natives and at all times they shall have effective ownership of as much land as they can profitably develop.

b   *Capital.* The investment of capital and granting of concessions shall be so regulated as to prevent the exploitation of the natives and the exhaustion of the natural wealth of the country. Concessions shall always be limited in time and subject to state control. The growing social needs of the natives must be regarded and the profits taxed for social and material benefit of the natives (Padmore 1956: 118–130).

As African leaders began to rally for independence, the Pan-African Congress of 1945 underlined the following:

a   Since the advent of the British, French, Belgian, and other European nations in West Africa, there has been regression instead of progress as a result of systemic exploitation by these alien imperialist powers. The claims of "partnership", "trusteeship", "guardianship", and the "mandate system" do not serve the political wishes of the people of West Africa.

b   That the artificial divisions and territorial boundaries created by the imperialist powers are deliberate steps to obstruct the political unity of the West African people (Padmore 1956: 152–170).

In 1949 Nkrumah formulated the program of the Convention People's Party (C. P. P.). One of the objectives of the C. P. P., in addition to its national preoccupations, was "to assist and facilitate in any way possible the realization of a united and self-governing West Africa" (Nkrumah 1976: 101). In establishing a united West Africa, the role of language within the general education program was a key element. In addition to the diverse ethnicities and nations in Africa, the variety of languages among them remains one of the important components of multiculturalism.

In *Decolonising the Mind: The Politics of Language in African Literature*, Ngũgĩ wa Thiong'o theorizes on the influential use of language. He explains:

> The choice of language and the use to which language is put is central to a people's definition of themselves in relation to their natural and social environment, indeed in relation to the entire universe. Hence language has always been at the heart of two contending social forces in the African of the twentieth century.
>
> (Thiong'o 1986: 4)

Within a world that is increasingly multicultural, multi-racial and multi-ethnic, decolonizing the African mind is primordial for effective participation

The Pan-African philosophy and movement 217

in global affairs. One of the mediums through which the African can experience the benefits of multiculturalism is through the incorporation of its languages – particularly in national affairs – and the respect of its cultural traditions in Africa and abroad. In 1951 the Bureau of Ghana Languages was established. Initially the bureau focused solely on Ghanaian languages and cultures. To move towards a Pan-African and multicultural practice, in 1961 the Ghana Institute of Languages was created. It included numerous national African languages, as well as the teaching of Western languages such as English, French, Spanish and Portuguese. In founding the institute of languages, Kwame Nkrumah envisioned that it "would educate individuals who would eventually make possible and facilitate communications among black nations, particularly in Africa. In other words, the dissemination of Pan-Africanist philosophy and movement was the principle objective for the founding of the Ghana Institute of Languages" (Simeon-Jones 2010: 182).

It is worth noting that beyond the agenda for cooperation among African states in Africa (Pan-Africanism as a continental affair), throughout the 1920s and 60s Pan-Africanism consistently reiterated its global, multi-lingual and multi-national program. Notably, it called for relevant education and requested fulfilled citizenships – for Blacks in Africa and throughout the world – based on true liberty and respect, not the simple nominal freedom or empty de jure citizenships. With similar international and global vision, the U. N. I. A. (Universal Negro Improvement Association) disseminated the *Negro World* in English, French and Spanish, throughout Africa, North America and South America. The N. A. A. C. P.'s (National Association for the Advancement of Colored People) *Crisis* published works from various regions of the Diaspora. In 1926, Du Bois published an article on the importance of foreign languages for Blacks.

> He posited that foreign languages should be considered as an essential subject in education, particularly for blacks, because it is a vital tool of communication and a sociocultural bridge. He viewed foreign languages as an agent without which the Pan-African movement cannot reach its full potential. . . . Du Bois argued that the language barrier within the Diaspora adds strength to the existing territorial boundaries. The conclusion to such analysis is that without the dismantling of lingual, intellectual, and territorial barriers, unity and cooperation among black nations will remain difficult, if not impossible, to attain.
>
> (Simeon-Jones 2010: 110)

The Pan-Africanist education program for a multicultural world

The philosophy undergirding the principles the leaders of the twentieth century came to denominate Pan-Africanism *is* proper education. It is proper education for the benefit of social, political and economic advancement.

218 *Kersuze Simeon-Jones*

Rooted in a comprehensive education philosophy, Pan-Africanism sought the cooperation of Africans on the continent as well as within the global and, inescapably, multicultural world. Edward Blyden, who is recognized as one of the forefathers of an articulated Pan-African philosophy and the progenitor of the movement, arduously worked for the general religious and secular education of Blacks in African history, language and culture, as well as in European history, language and technology. During the Pan-African Congresses, the representatives emphasized the transformative impact of an appropriate education tailored from Africa's general history and its national histories, as well as the histories and cultures of African descendants abroad. The Congresses also placed consistent attention on the role of Africans in their own affairs and their freedom of religion. Ultimately, in their extensive and inclusive requests, the representatives of the Second Pan-African Congress – 28 to 29 August 1921 – called for "Co-operation with the rest of the world in government, industry, and art on the basis of justice, freedom and peace" (Padmore 1956: 130–136).

In his *Declaration of Rights* Garvey underlined the eventual result the U. N. I. A. envisioned. He reminded his audience – supporters and opponents:

> The Universal Negro Improvement Association has been misrepresented by my enemies. They have tried to make it appear that we are hostile to other races. This is absolutely false. We love all humanity. We are working for the peace of the world, which we believe can only come about when all races are given their due.
>
> (Garvey 1986: 132)

At this juncture of human history it is clear that the term *humanity*, which can only be understood through multiculturalism, is "an abstraction" (as Dr. Maulana Karenga puts it), "a mere construction for the convenience of conversation *unless* it is seen in its diversity and particularity as well as its unity and universality" (Karenga 1993: 15, emphasis added). From that perspective one can affirm that Black Studies (Africana Studies or Afro-Diasporic Studies) – the offspring of Pan-Africanism and the many intellectual and political liberation movements of the nineteenth and twentieth centuries – effectuated the first step towards multiculturalism. It transcended the abstract in order to reconcile the theory and praxis of true humanism.

Building on the multi-ethnic and diasporic vision of the Pan-African movement, in 1989 Martinican writers Patrick Chamoiseau, Raphaël Confiant and Jean Bernabé published *L'Eloge de la Créolité* (*In Praise of Creoleness*) to emphasize the multicultural reality of the Caribbean and promote the Pan-Caribbean ideology through Creoleness. As Aimé Césaire – the co-founder of the Négritude Movement – underlines in reference to the Afro-Caribbean: ("s'il n'y avait pas le Nègre en premier lieu, l'Antillais [le Créole] n'existerait pas") "if the Negro did not exist in the first place, the Antillean [the Creole] could not exist" (Césaire 1994: II). In other words, the multiculturalism

The Pan-African philosophy and movement 219

of the Caribbean includes the genealogical and philosophical contributions of the African descendant, the so-called Negro. For the proponents of Négritude, "Africa was not some sort of blank page in the history of humanity", its effects were/are lasting (Césaire 2000: 91–92). Négritude, similar to Pan-Africanism, emphasized diversity within the global world. As humanist movements, their commitment was to re-establish Blacks in their humanity – after the dehumanizing effects of slavery – in order to help lead the regeneration of the race and the progress of the world. It is "an effort at reconciliation", Césaire reasoned. "The West told us that in order to be universal we had to start by denying that we were black. I, on the contrary, said to myself that the more we were black, the more universal we would be. It was a totally different approach. It was not a choice between alternatives, but an effort at reconciliation" (Césaire 1994: II). Hence, the Pan-Caribbean multiculturalist analysis of the writers of *In Praise of Creoleness* was certainly embedded within the Pan-African and Négritude movements' objective of reconciliatory diversity: racial, lingual, ethnic and national cultures. In a 1998 interview published in 2000 in *The French Review*, Patrick Chamoiseau expressed his concept of diversity in the world. He examined:

Pour préserver la diversité du monde, la diversité des cultures, des langues, des races, des conceptions du monde, pour éviter la standardisation et l'uniformisation du monde qui risque de se faire, il faut penser au fait que nous sommes *en train de construire non pas des territoires mais des lieux*, des lieux multiculturels, multilingues, multiraciaux, avec des différentes histoires qui s'entremêlent.

. . . Mais si on se projette dans cette réalité-monde, en perdant ses assises, en faisant table rase de ce qui nous représente, comme un vieux citoyen du monde désincarné en parlant de l'universel complètement inodore et incolore, à ce moment-là on se perd dans le désordre ou dans le chaos du monde.

To preserve the diversity of the world, the diversity of cultures, of languages, of races, as well as the diversity of conceptions of the world; to avoid standardization and uniformity of the world, which risk of happening, one must think of the fact that we are in the process of constructing not territories but "spaces", multicultural, multilingual, multiracial spaces, with different histories that are connected.

. . . However if one embarks in this real-world losing his/her ground or, engaging in making a tabula rasa of what represents us, similar to an old citizen of an unreal world who speaks of the inodorous and colorless, universal, at that point we would be lost in the disorder or chaos of the world.

(Simeon 2005: 151)

In his proposal to maintain and further develop a multicultural world, Chamoiseau makes the distinction between uniformity/*unicité* and unity/*unité*. As

220 *Kersuze Simeon-Jones*

he reminds us, as a manoeuvre to perpetuate uniformity and hegemony, many languages and cultures have been devalued, if not erased. In the Caribbean, he proposes the formation of psychological spaces/*lieux* instead of the perception of the Caribbean as territories whose cultures and idiosyncrasies are stifled for the practice of conformity. For, "in the transformation to unicité or standardization, territories were for the most part constituted in a monolithic manner, where History erased the histories of each region, just as the official language crushed regional languages" (Simeon 2005: 152).

It is in the acknowledgement of various histories, cultural traditions and a defined call to social transformation that such multicultural focus as Creoleness in the Caribbean and Europe, multi-racial and multi-ethnic education in the United States and multi-ethnic political collaboration in Africa *are* all connected to the Pan-African philosophy of the 1700s and the Pan-African movement of the 1900s. Hence, throughout the 1800s and the 1900s Black intellectuals writing from the Caribbean, the United States, Europe and Africa addressed the evolutionary effect of an education program grounded in cultural awareness, historical specificities and factual current circumstances. This cultural and multicultural awareness also took into consideration a program of serious intellectual education for women of African descent. In 1886 Anna Julia Cooper – writing from the United States – expounded that "the regeneration, the retraining of the race, as well as the ground work and starting point of its progress upward, must be the black woman . . . with all the wrongs and neglects of her past, with all the weakness, the debasement, the moral thralldom of her present", the Black woman is the source of nurture, education and elevation (Cooper 1988: 62). As "no people are elevated above the condition of their females; hence the condition of the mother determines the condition of the child" (Delany 1993: 38).

For the general education of African-descended Americans, Cooper further explained:

> It cannot be denied that the wisest plan of education for any people should take cognizance of past and present environment, should note the forces against which they must contend, or in unison with which they must labor in the civilization of which they form a part. It should not be ignored, further, that the colored man in America, because of his marked appearance and his unique history, will for a long time need peculiar equipment for the intense, the unrelenting struggle for survival amid which he finds himself in America today.
>
> (Cooper 1988: 250)

Pondering the state of the Black world up to the late 1800s, Edward Blyden wrote from Africa in reference to the Africans and those of African ancestry:

> It is true that culture is one, and the general effects of true culture are the same; but the native capacities of mankind differ, and their work

The Pan-African philosophy and movement 221

and destiny differ, so that the road by which one man may attain to the highest efficiency, is not that which would conduce to the success of another. The special road which has led to the success and elevation of the Anglo-Saxon is not that which would lead to the success and elevation of the Negro.

(Blyden 1967: 83)

In 1919 Jean Price-Mars wrote on the purpose of education in general, and within the context of Haiti in particular:

> Si l'éducation est une tentative de modeler l'homme selon un idéal déterminé, il me semble que tout système de pédagogie doit d'abord connaître le tempérament du peuple auquel on se propose de l'appliquer. C'est la première considération, je suis tenté d'affirmer que c'est la considération essentielle qui doit dominer une entreprise d'éducation collective.
>
> If education is an attempt to shape the human based on a well-defined ideal, it seems to me that a pedagogical system must first know the personality of the people that it proposes to educate. That is the first consideration. I am tempted to affirm that it is the essential consideration that must take precedence in a collective educational system.

(Price-Mars 2001: 68)

In *Introduction to Black Studies*, Karenga contextualizes the creation of Black studies programs and their multicultural agenda – Black Diaspora Studies, African Diaspora Studies, Africana Studies, Caribbean, African and African-American Studies, depending on the institution. These programs were born from a longstanding educational history that reached its highest point of practice in the 1960s and 70s, with the implementation of the discipline.[7] In the "Origins of the Discipline", Karenga explains:

> The discipline of Black Studies is rooted in the social visions and struggles of the 60's which aimed at Black power, liberation and higher level of human life and thus from its inception, it has had both an academic and social thrust and mission. . . . Fixing the starting point of the discipline firmly in the Sixties does not deny the pre-discipline intellectual history which laid fundamental ground for its emergence in the 60's. . . . Thus Black Studies defines itself and its mission in the historically evolved intellectual-activist tradition which extends back to the freedom-directed and life-affirming work during the Holocaust of Enslavement and extends thru other periods of crisis, challenge, struggle and achievement, culminating in the liberational projects of the 60's.

(Karenga 1993: 3)

Karenga emphasizes the role of the "pre-discipline" history as fundamental in establishing an academic field whose mission is at once intellectual and *corrective* – in terms of addressing social ills and transforming society. Indeed, it is from the multi-ethnic rebellions throughout the Middle Passage and the Slavery era that the multicultural Pan-African practice began to take shape. Such rebellions *are* the pre-movement history and, by extension, the pre-discipline history. The Pan-African philosophy continued to crystalize in the writings and deeds of intellectuals of the 1800s. By 1900 an official movement was recognized through the First Pan-African Congress in London. The Pan-African Movement, along with the New Negro Movement, Garveyism, Indigénisme and Négritude laid the foundation for the consistent advocacy of appropriate education for Blacks. If the historical circumstances of the Pan-African philosophy of the Middle Passage and the Slavery era were rooted in the physical and spiritual liberation of African descendants, the Pan-African movement of the 1900s (and the philosophy it inherited from the 1800s) had as its principles the psychological and intellectual liberation of African descendants. Such liberation can only be obtained through appropriate and multicultural education.

Conclusion

The praxis of Pan-Africanism is framed within multi-sociopolitical approaches, multi-intellectual perspectives and multicultural vistas, embedded in appropriate education. In the *Declaration of Rights of the Negro Peoples of the World*, Garvey emphasized this goal: "we demand that instructions given Negro children in schools include the subject of 'Negro History,' to their benefit" (Garvey 1986: 142). The significant attention here is on *children* (before adulthood and the University); children who may or may not attend a university in their future. Regardless of their professional choices or circumstances, these children – grown into adulthood – would be grounded in history, as well as self-knowledge and well-rounded social consciousness. Stated differently, the call for the re-valorization of the Africans' identity and that of their descendants, the call for a respected political voice and effective political participation in world affairs, the call for fair and equitable economic programs, can only be achieved through appropriate education. Ultimately, Pan-Africanism's salient educational and multicultural philosophy remains a global challenge in the twenty-first century. For, to restate Du Bois and Garvey respectively, Pan-Africanism is the "intellectual understanding and co-operation among all groups of African descent in order to bring about the industrial and spiritual emancipation of the Negro People". "We love all humanity. We are working for the peace of the world, which we believe can only come about when all races are given their due". In the final analysis, Pan-Africanism is a call for coexistence. It is a call for the *reconciliation* of foundational cultural traditions in dialogical harmony with the continuous cultural evolutions of the global world.

Notes

1 Garvey, *Philosophy and Opinions of Marcus Garvey*, Dover: The Majority Press, 1986, p. 132 of volume II.

2 Karenga, *Introduction to Black Studies*, Los Angeles: The University of Sankore Press, 1993, p. 44.

3 The successive and contemporaneous movements connected to the philosophy and the program of the Pan-African Movement, include: the New Negro Movement, the Mouvement Indigéniste, Garveyism, Négritude, and the Movimiento Negrista.

4 For some historians, the sociopolitical atmosphere and events leading to the Civil Rights Movement date from the 1930s and continued until the 1970s. Others may argue that the so-called "Long Civil Rights Movement" dates further back. It is clear, however, that in spite of a system of periodization, long continuance of communal psychological preparation and events are necessary before the crystallization of an eventual movement.

5 In his influential and multi-layered analysis, Woodson argues that the "the leading facts of the history of the world should be studied by all, but of what advantage is it to the Negro student of history to devote all of his time to courses bearing such despots as Alexander the Great, Caesar, and Napoleon, or the record of those nations whose outstanding achievement has been rapine, plunder, and murder for world power? Why not study the African background from the point of anthropology and history, and then take up sociology as it concerns the Negro peasant or proletarian. . . . Why not take up economics as reflected by the Negroes of today and work out some remedy for their lack of capital, the absence of cooperative enterprise, and the short life of their establishments".

6 In 1914 Garvey founded the Universal Negro Improvement and Conservation Association of African Communities' League. The League was later renamed the Universal Negro Improvement Association. In 1916 Garvey moved to Harlem and continued to lead the organization in the United States. The U.N.I.A. (Universal Negro Improvement Association) was incorporated in 1918.

7 In its evolution the discipline has come to include: Classical African Studies (with a focus on Africa's intellectual and political contributions to the Ancient World and the New World), Black Women's Studies, the Caribbean and Latin America and Multiculturalism (beyond North, Central and South America). The subfields or subject areas of the discipline encompass: History, Politics, Religion, Economics, Women's Studies, Creative Production, Psychology and Natural Sciences. All within the context of, and in relation to, the global world, as well as specific to the Black experience.

Bibliography

Blyden, E. W. (1967) *Christianity, Islam, and the Negro Race*, Edinburgh: Edinburgh University Press.

Césaire, A. (1994) *Aimé Césaire: A Voice for History*, San Francisco: California Newsreel.

Césaire, A. (2000) *Discourse on Colonialism*, New York: Monthly Review Press.

Chamoiseau, P. and Deslauriers G., et al. (2003) *The Middle Passage*, New York: HBO Video.

Cooper, A. J. (1988) *The Voice of Anna Julia Cooper: Including a Voice from the South, and Other Important Essays, Papers, and Letters*, C. Lemert and E. Bhan (eds.), New York: Rowman and Littlefield Publishers.

Delany, M. (1993) *The Condition, Elevation, Emigration, and Destiny of the Colored People in the United States*, Baltimore: Black Classic Press.

Du Bois, W. E. B. (1975) *Dusk of Dawn*, New York: Kraus-Thomson Organization Limited.

Esedebe, O. P. (1982) *Pan-Africanism: The Idea and Movement, 1776–1963*, Washington, DC: Howard University Press.

Garvey, M. (1986) *Philosophy and Opinions of Marcus Garvey*, Dover: First Majority Press Edition.

James, C. L. R. (1989) *The Black Jacobins*, New York: Vintage Books.

Karenga, M. (1993) *Introduction to Black Studies*, Los Angeles: The University of Sankore Press.

Malcolm, X. (1993) *Malcolm X Speak: Selected Speeches and Statements*, New York: Betty Shabazz and Pathfinder Press.

Maulana, K. (1993) *Introduction to Black Studies*, Los Angeles: The University of Sankore Press.

Nkrumah, K. (1976) *Ghana: The Autobiography of Kwame Nkrumah*, New York: International Publishers.

Padmore, G. (1956) *Pan-Africanism or Communism? The Coming Struggle for Africa*, New York: Roy Publishers.

Price-Mars, J. (2001) *La Vocation de l'élite*, Port-au-Prince: Editions de Presses Nationales d'Haïti.

Simeon, K. (2005) 'Free Poetics, Nation Language in Caribbean Literature', *Journal of Caribbean Studies* 19(3): 151–169.

Simeon-Jones, K. (2010) *Literary and Sociopolitical Writings of the Black Diaspora in the Nineteenth and Twentieth Centuries*, Lanham: Lexington Books.

Thiong'o, N. (1986) *Decolonising the Mind: The Politics of Languages in African Literature*, London: J. Currey.

Woodson, C. G. (2005) *The Mis-Education of the Negro*, Washington, DC: The ASALH Press.

Contributors

Christopher Allsobrook is the Director of the Centre for Leadership Ethics in Africa at the University of Fort Hare. His research is in Political Philosophy, Critical Theory and Intellectual History. He leads the Research Niche Area in "Democracy, Heritage and Citizenship" at Fort Hare and is an editor of *Theoria: a Journal of Social and Political Theory*. His recent work includes, "A Genealogy of South African Positivism" for the edited volume, *Intellectual Traditions in South Africa* (UKZN Press, 2014) and "Pale Skin of the Kat: James Read Junior", written with Dr. Camilla Boisen for an edited volume on *Coloured Intellectuals* (SunMedia, 2015). Dr. Allsobrook is currently working with Dr. Camilla Boisen (University of the Witwatersrand) on the history of Trusteeship in South Africa and its impact on the peace negotiations at Versailles and subsequent colonial settlement after the First World War.

Rebecca Bamford is Associate Professor of Philosophy in the Department of Philosophy and Political Science at Quinnipiac University, and is also Adjunct Professor at the University of Fort Hare. Her research is done at the interface of nineteenth-century philosophy, ethics, social and political philosophy, and the history and philosophy of science and mind. She is the editor of *Nietzsche's Free Spirit Philosophy* (2015), and has published multiple articles on Nietzsche's philosophy and on problems in contemporary bioethics.

Luís Cordeiro-Rodrigues is a postdoctoral researcher at CLEA, The University of Fort Hare. He holds an MA and a PhD in Politics and Philosophy from the University of York. He has taught politics and political theory at the University of York and has published in Portuguese and English. He has contributed papers to *Critical Studies on Terrorism, Journal of Critical Animal Studies, Theoria* and *South African Journal of Philosophy*, among other journals.

Demin Duan has an MA in Law from Peking University and a PhD in philosophy from the Katholieke Universiteit Leuven. His research focuses on the history of political thought and especially in the philosophy of

226 Contributors

Tocqueville. He has published in English, Portuguese and Chinese journals. He is currently an associate professor at the School of Government at the University of Peking.

Uri Gordon, DPhil (Oxon.) is Lecturer in Political Theory at Loughborough University and co-convenor of the Anarchist Studies Network. An Israeli-born activist and academic, he is the author of *Anarchy Alive! – Anti-authoritarian Politics from Practice to Theory* (Pluto Press, 2008) and has published contemporary anarchist perspectives on political philosophy, technological politics, radical geography, environmental history and the Israeli-Palestinian conflict. His work has been translated into thirteen languages.

Lisa Kemmerer, Professor of philosophy and religions at Montana State University Billings, is a philosopher-activist working on behalf of nonhuman animals, the environment and disempowered human beings. A graduate of Reed, Harvard and Glasgow University (Scotland), Kemmerer has written/edited nine books, including *Eating Earth: Dietary Choice and Environmental Health, Animals and World Religions, Animals and the Environment: Advocacy, Activism, and the Quest for Common Ground*, and *Sister Species: Women, Animals, and Social Justice*.

Eric Russet Kraemer, PhD Brown University, is Professor of Philosophy at the University of Wisconsin-La Crosse. He publishes in the fields of philosophy of mind, epistemology and social ethics in journals such as *Mind, Journal of Holocaust Studies* and *Metaphilosophy*.

Lin Ma received her PhD and MA from the Higher Institute of Philosophy, KU Leuven (Belgium) in 2006 and 2001 respectively. She also obtained an LLB in International Intercultural Communication and BA in English Language and Literature from Beijing University in 1993 and 1991 respectively. She is the author of *Heidegger on East-West Dialogue: Anticipating the Event* (New York/London: Routledge, 2008) and has published research papers in such journals as *Continental Philosophical Review, Journal of the British Society for Phenomenology, Philosophy East and West* and *Journal of Intercultural Communication*. She has taught both in China and in Belgium and has presented papers at academic conferences held in Norway, Austria, Germany, Denmark, the United States and Canada. Her major research field is comparative studies of Continental European philosophers (Heidegger, Levinas) and Chinese philosophy (in particular, Daoist philosophy).

Andrew Ryder is a Visiting Lecturer of Gender Studies at Central European University in Budapest, Hungary. Dr. Ryder previously taught in Pittsburgh, Pennsylvania; Abu Dis, Palestine; Atlanta, Georgia and Prague,

Czech Republic. He has published numerous articles on Continental philosophy, Marxism and literature. These essays include: "The Plurality of Jihad," "Charlie Hebdo and the Limits of Nihilism" and "Gastropolitics in the Conflict Kitchen" (in *Warscapes*), "Foucault and Althusser" (in *Foucault Studies*), "Baudelaire, Rimbaud, Toomer" (in *Callaloo*), "Derrida and the Crisis of French Zionism" (in *Jadaliyya*), "Badiou's Materialist Reinvention of the Kantian Subject" (in *Badiou Studies*), "On the Left-wing Reading of Levinas" and "Bataille against Heidegger" (in *Studies in Social and Political Thought*), "'Le plus beau récit de notre temps'" (in *Symposium*), "Revolution without Guarantees" (in *Journal of French and Francophone Philosophy*), "The Skull-Bone and the Bloody Head" (in *International Journal of Žižek Studies*), "Politics after the Death of the Father" (in *Mosaic*), "Inner Experience is Not Psychosis" (in *Parrhesia*) and "Sartre's Theater of Resistance" (in *Sartre Studies International*).

George Sadaka is a full-time Lecturer of English Literature and Cultural Studies at the Lebanese American University (Byblos Campus). He earned his PhD in English at the University of Lancaster in 2012. He has research interests in cultural and literary tropes of modern (colonial and postcolonial) English and American literatures.

Marko Simendić is a lecturer at the University of Belgrade – Faculty of Political Sciences. He obtained his PhD at the University of York (UK) and has two MA degrees – an MA in Political Philosophy (The Idea of Toleration) from York and an MA in Political Analysis and Management from the University of Belgrade. Dr. Simendić teaches History of Political Thought, and he is especially interested in early modern political thought.

Kersuze Simeon-Jones is currently an Associate Professor in the Department of Africana Studies and the Department of World Languages at the University of South Florida, Tampa. Her primary research and teaching interests include: Intellectual History, Political Movements of the Black Diaspora, Francophone Studies, Haitian History and Literature and Women's History within the Black Diaspora. Dr. Simeon-Jones is the author of *Literary and Sociopolitical Writings of the Black Diaspora in the Nineteenth and Twentieth Centuries* (Lexington Books). She has also published numerous articles, book chapters, and encyclopedic entries. Her works include: "The Négritude Philosophy and the Movement" in the *Blackwell Encyclopedia of Postcolonial Studies*; "Noiristes: Black Power and Black Pride" in the *Digital Library of the Caribbean*; "Démences, Psychoses et Liberté Psychique dans *Le Cri de l'oiseau rouge*" in *Ecrits d'Haïti: Perspectives sur la littérature haïtienne contemporaine* (Editions Karthala); "Masculinity in Hurston's Texts" in *The Inside Light: New Critical Essays on Zora Neale Hurston* (Praeger Books); "Haiti's

228   Contributors

Politico-Cultural Transcript: Moving toward National Rehabilitation" in *Negritud: Afro-Latin American Studies* and "Free Poetics, Nation Language in Caribbean Literature" in the *Journal of Caribbean Studies*. Dr. Simeon-Jones holds an Interdisciplinary Doctoral degree in the History and Literature of the Black Diaspora from the University of Miami, Florida. She completed a Master's Degree in Francophone Studies at Rutgers University. She received her Bachelor's Degree in French Literature and Spanish Language and Literature, also from Rutgers.

Index

African condition 212, 213, 215
African philosophy 7, 190, 192, 204, 209, 215, 218, 220, 222
ahimsa 9, 135–9, 141, 142, 144–7
Al-Sheikh *see* El-Sheikh, Hanan
anarchism 8, 63–5, 72, 76
associative democracy 8, 9, 97, 98, 102–10
autonomy 2, 8–11, 29, 35–41, 54, 67, 69, 72, 81, 82, 92, 94, 102, 106–9, 160, 163–5, 194, 211

Bader, Veit 102, 103
Black Studies 209, 210, 218, 221, 223
Bookchin, Murray 65, 68

China 2, 3, 7, 10, 116, 133, 141, 153, 154, 156, 158–68
Chinese Muslims 159–61, 165
citizenship 4, 45, 84, 91, 189–91, 200–6, 217
colonialism 23, 57, 63, 66, 73, 75, 91, 93, 176, 182, 196, 197, 205, 209, 223
commonwealth *see* state
community meals 135, 142, 145–8
customary law 10, 190, 192, 197, 200, 201, 205, 206

dairy 135, 141–8
Daoism 9, 140, 141, 146, 153, 154, 158, 162, 163, 166, 167, 168
decolonial 6, 9, 63, 64, 72–6
decolonization 73, 80, 81, 85, 90, 92, 94, 216
Déjacque, Joseph 66, 68
deliberative democracy 104, 105, 107, 190

democracy 7–10, 15–20, 22–7, 29, 36, 37, 40, 43–6, 49, 69, 94, 97, 98, 102–10, 115, 164, 189–91, 195, 196, 199–204, 206
diet 9, 121, 134, 135, 137, 139, 140–2, 144–8
diversity 1–5, 7–11, 15–17, 19, 20, 26, 27, 29, 30, 32–5, 37, 38–41, 43, 51–3, 56, 57, 64–6, 68, 70, 72–5, 80–2, 84, 93, 94, 115, 116, 120, 121, 124, 127, 133, 147, 190, 200, 213, 216, 218, 219
dynamic pluralism 44, 54, 56, 58

El-Sheikh, Hanan 10, 170, 171, 175, 178, 183, 184
equality 5, 9, 15, 16, 18–20, 25, 27, 71, 72, 81, 98, 101, 134, 153, 154, 156–8, 160, 165, 196, 200
erotic 172, 175–81, 183, 185
ethic 9, 48, 49, 57, 63, 72–4, 82, 115, 121, 135, 140–2, 145, 146, 193–6, 203, 212

factory farming 142, 144
food sharing 134, 147
freedom 4, 5, 7, 8, 10, 15, 16, 18, 19, 21, 22, 24–7, 29, 30, 32, 34, 40, 44–6, 53, 55, 58, 89, 97–101, 103–8, 160, 179, 182, 184, 190, 195, 200, 203, 213–15, 217, 218, 221

Garvey, Marcus 10, 211, 214, 215, 218, 222, 223
Grave, Jean 66–8
Green, TH 204
Gyekye, Kwame 10, 193–5, 204–6

230 *Index*

Han 159–67
heterosexism 97, 101, 102, 105, 106, 110
Hindu 101, 135–9, 142, 144–8
Hirst, Paul 102, 103
Hobbes, Thomas 7, 8, 29–41
homophobia 43, 106, 109, 110
Hui *see* Chinese Muslims
humanity 65, 68, 92, 140–2, 146, 173, 181, 186, 198, 209, 218, 219, 222
human rights 26, 82, 93, 128, 191, 192, 200, 205

identity 1, 2, 3, 4, 7, 8, 10, 20, 30, 37, 38, 43, 44, 52, 54–8, 63, 65, 68, 70, 72–4, 76, 80–5, 90, 91, 93, 94, 101, 102, 105, 109, 119, 121, 122, 126, 128, 165, 186, 194, 195, 199–203, 205, 206, 211, 222
imperialism 43, 63, 68, 72, 75, 81, 86, 87, 126, 185, 186, 197, 202, 203, 205, 206, 216
Indian philosophy 9, 133, 135, 137–9, 142, 146–8
intercultural 190
intersectionalism 63, 72, 75, 76
Islam 9, 10, 26, 72, 92, 101, 102, 104, 121, 140–2, 170–81, 183–6, 223

justice 3, 4, 10, 43, 44, 47, 49, 52, 54, 56–8, 76, 82, 97, 103, 106, 108, 119, 137, 190, 192, 196, 200, 201, 218

Karenga, Maulana 210, 218, 221, 223
karma 135, 137–9, 141, 142, 144–6
Kropotkin, Pyotr 64, 66, 67
kuffar 170–2, 178, 184, 185

lactose intolerance 145–7
Landauer, Gustav 65
Laozi 153–5, 157, 164, 168
liberalism 1, 3–11, 18, 21, 24, 25, 29, 37, 43–6, 48, 49, 52, 55, 58, 66, 69, 70, 72, 75, 80–5, 116, 118, 119, 121–3, 125, 126, 166, 167, 174, 189, 196, 203, 205
liberalism, critique of 45, 48, 49, 58, 82, 85
liberty *see* freedom
love 10, 140–2, 145, 172, 173, 178–80, 183–5, 209, 218, 222
love-making 179, 183–5

Malcolm X 211
Man *see* Manchu
Manchu 159–62, 165, 167, 168
Meng *see* Mongolians
Mignolo, Walter 73
milk *see* dairy
Mill, John Stuart 8, 23, 24, 115, 117, 121, 127, 128
mixed identity 8, 43, 52, 55–8
Mongolians 159–61, 165, 167
multicultural education 209, 210, 222
multiculturalism 1, 3, 4, 6–11, 15, 20, 24, 26, 27, 29, 30, 37, 41, 43, 44, 52, 54, 57, 58, 63, 64, 68–72, 76, 80, 82–5, 87, 88, 90, 93, 94, 97, 110, 115, 116, 118, 119, 121–8, 133–5, 142, 145–7, 153, 158, 166–8, 170–2, 174–6, 179, 181–5, 209–12, 216–19, 223
Muslim 1, 3, 22, 71, 72, 100, 102, 103, 109, 120, 123, 140, 141, 145, 146, 166, 170–8, 181–5

nationalism 64–8, 72, 76, 84, 86, 87, 89–91, 153, 158–60, 162, 166, 168, 179, 201–3, 205, 206
national liberation 67, 81, 88
Nietzsche, Friedrich 7, 8, 43–58

oppression 6, 9, 43–5, 47, 50, 57, 58, 72, 80, 81, 83, 86–90, 93, 94

patronage 167, 191, 192, 197, 201, 202
perspectivism 44, 50, 51, 54, 58
pluralism 8, 40, 41, 43, 44, 49, 51, 52, 54–6, 58, 72, 80, 102, 103, 115, 172, 199
politics of recognition 20, 54
post-modern 68, 178
power 2, 5, 9, 16, 17, 19, 20, 22, 23, 25, 27, 33, 34, 36–9, 44, 46–8, 50, 55, 58, 67–9, 70, 73, 75, 87, 97, 99, 102, 103, 105, 106, 108–10, 134, 135, 154, 163, 164, 168, 176, 177, 182, 184, 190–2, 197–9, 204, 206, 210, 211, 216, 221, 223

Quran 140, 170–6, 181, 183, 184, 186

racism 6, 9, 27, 43, 57, 63, 66, 69, 70–2, 75, 76, 84, 87–9, 90, 91, 93, 135, 145, 146, 168, 211, 214

Index   231

Ramnath, Maia 65, 73
recognition 4, 10, 11, 20, 21, 34, 35, 54, 55, 68, 70, 74, 76, 80–4, 87, 93, 94, 106, 119, 189, 191, 192, 202–6, 211
Red Action 70, 71
re-education 211
reification 80, 84, 203, 205, 206
reincarnation 135, 137–9, 142, 144–6
Rocker, Rudolph 64, 65

Saleh, Tayeb 10, 170, 171, 174–7, 180–2, 185, 186
self 8, 52, 54, 56, 58, 154–6, 177, 183, 184, 192
self-determination 9, 72, 74, 85–9, 94, 160, 194
sex *see* love-making
social transformation 69, 72, 212, 213, 220
South Africa 7, 65, 100, 134, 189–93, 195, 200–5
state 4, 5, 7–10, 17, 19, 20, 25, 29–41, 43, 63–5, 67, 69, 70–2, 75, 76, 80, 84, 86, 89, 98, 102, 103, 105–10,

126, 134, 154, 157, 158, 160–8, 189–93, 195–200, 202–6, 212, 216, 217
subjectivity 44, 52–4, 56, 58

Tibetans 159–61, 165, 167
Tocqueville, Alexis de 7, 8, 15–27

Ubuntu 190, 191, 195, 196, 201, 202, 206
unity 7, 10, 26, 29–33, 39, 40, 54, 65, 69, 81, 85, 118, 202, 212, 213, 216–19
universalism 8, 24, 27, 51, 63, 68, 73–6, 83, 110, 140, 185, 198
utilitarianism 8, 115–28

vegan 9, 134, 140, 141, 144–8

Walia, Harsha 73

Zang *see* Tibetans
Zhang Taiyan 9, 10, 153–68
Zhuangzi 153–5, 157, 158, 165, 166, 168